Language and Linguistics

Language and Linguistics
A Scientific Approach to Language

Dr. Niladri Sekhar Dash

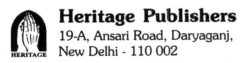

Heritage Publishers
19-A, Ansari Road, Daryaganj,
New Delhi - 110 002

First Published in 2011
by HERITAGE PUBLISHERS
19-A, Ansari Road, Daryaganj,
New Delhi - 110 002
INDIA

© Dr. Niladri Sekhar Dash
Assistant Professor
Linguistic Research Unit
Indian Statistical Institute
203, Barrackpore Trunk Road,
Kolkata-700108, West Bengal (India)

Typeset in Book Antiqua.

ISBN 10: 8170262704
ISBN 13: 978-81-7026-270-1

Printed at : Swan Press, New Delhi

Contents

To
Shrotriya and *Somaditya*
(Two wings of my life)

Preface

The relevance of the book lies in its presentation of information and data for general academic and referential purposes. The book is the first of its kind that tries to furnish new information and findings hardly presented before the students and scholars willing to know more about the general aspects of language and linguistics. This introductory book covers almost all the major areas, issues, and aspects of general descriptive linguistics in a very lucid and simplified manner so that anyone interested in language and linguistics can easily gather some general ideas about the field. Since the level of the book is a general one, it does not include the findings of research and investigation, which are more complex in nature and which ask for specialized knowledge of the discipline as traced among the scholars baptized in linguistics. Rather, the book includes simple descriptions and analyses of some notable findings and studies on the general areas of linguistics which can easily fall within the likings of the learners and general people.

In the present Indian scenario, there is hardly any book on general and descriptive linguistics which can be useful for the students of English and Linguistics who study in different Indian universities and colleges. This book is written to address the need of the learners. Thus, the target readers of this book are the students of both undergraduate (BA) and postgraduate (MA) levels of Linguistics of the Indian universities. Besides the book shall also be highly useful for the students of MA in English of the Indian universities, as it has become mandatory to include one paper of Linguistics in MA English level with a focus of general linguistics. Moreover, the book can be used by general readers interested in language and linguistics, as well as by the scholars and researchers working in various fields of general linguistics (e.g., *descriptive linguistics, features of language, origin of language, branches of linguistics, functions of language, human and non-human communication*, etc.). I take liberty to consider this book a reference-cum-text book, which students and teachers of Linguistics and English can use in classroom teaching.

3rd January 2011

Niladri Sekhar Dash
Linguistic Research Unit
Indian Statistical Institute
Kolkata, West Bengal, India

Foreword

Language and Linguistics, is a very scientific and well written book on the subject. Dr. Niladri Sekhar Dash, has been extremely methodical and systematic in covering all key aspects of Language.

The first part of the book carefully defines Language, its features and means of communication. It goes on to cover Design features and Origin of Language explaining various theories which have led to evolution of Language over the years. The book goes on to define Linguistics carefully covering its various levels including Phonetics and Phonology, Morphology, Syntax, Semantics and Discourse. Dimensions of Linguistics and its Branches have been duly covered to enable the student to understand the subject using a very structured approach.

Dr. Dash goes on to elaborate on New Branches of Linguistics and Functions of Language. He has covered the subject in great depth, starting from John Locke and covering major writers who have transformed literature over centuries and left indelible mark by contributing to its present form. These include linguists and writers like Noam Chomsky, Rabindranath Tagore and Ludwig Wittgenstein.

The book is unique in its approach, as is written in easy to understand language, and can be of immense use to students, professors and researchers alike. The presentation of the book, its meticulous coverage of subject and Dr. Dash's scientific approach surely deserve an applause. I congratulate Dr. Dash on such a splendid piece of work and am sure that students and teachers will benefit from the book. I thank Mr. Prashant of Dastavej Prakashan for his valuable input, our pre-press team and editors in bringing out the book in time.

Himanshu Chawla
New Delhi
15 January 2011

Acknowledgements

Let me state very clearly and humbly that the data, the examples, and the information presented in this book is not the output of my own research and investigation. Keeping the goal of the target users in mind, I have tried my level's best to gather information and data from various sources such as the websites, homepages, newspapers, emails, e-journals, journals, periodicals, books, monographs, blogs, and other printed and electronic sources as far as it has been possible for me. Moreover, I have tried to represent the data and information in the book in a very systematic manner without making much change in the original content of the materials for easy reference and access by the target users. To dissolve all possible ambiguities in understanding the content of the book, I have meticulously referred to and furnished the sources of information in the bibliography, so that a reader, if interested, can directly refer to the source for further information. Therefore, I honestly decline to claim credit of any kind for this book — the credit should better go to those scholars who have made their works available in different ways for general access and reference. However, I humbly express my willingness to take the whole responsibility for any mistake or error in presentation of information and data in the book.

The entire credit for bringing out my presentation in the form of a book should invariably go to *Himanshu Chawla*, of *Heritage Publishers*, New Delhi. He has happily taken the initiative and utmost care to produce this book for the benefit of students and common readers. I am happy to thank him with my open arms for this. I take this opportunity to thank *Subhradeep Jashu, Payel Dutta Chowdhury, Arpita Roy,* and *Anirban Sarkar,* who have gone through the early drafts of some chapters and expressed formative criticisms for better presentation of information in the book. Finally, I like to express my gratitude and thanks to my wife *Soma,* daughter *Shrotriya,* and son *Somaditya* for their fathomless patience and encouragement without which this project would not have been materialized. I shall consider my efforts are amply rewarded if the university students, teachers as well as common readers find this book useful for their academic and non-academic endeavours.

3rd January 2011

Niladri Sekhar Dash
Linguistic Research Unit
Indian Statistical Institute
Kolkata, West Bengal, India

Introduction

In this new millennium the discipline *linguistics* is no more confined within the traditional panorama of language description. To face the new challenges of life and society, it has been passing through a kind of metamorphosis to acquire several new dimensions, which are being incorporated regularly to this discipline to address not only the new linguistic problems people face in the society but also to develop and design new linguistic resources and strategies for the betterment of life and living of people, at large.

In the new era of information explosion, concept sharing, joint venture and collective enterprise, language is no more used as a mono-dimensional entity, but as a multi-dimensional enterprise, which dares to spread up its wings in every sphere of human existence. Now whenever we say "your language is your identity", it does not mean only the identity of a particular language one uses for expressing his mind and communicating information to others, it means many more things — his linguistic skill, communication capability, ways of expression, style of representation, intention behind his expression, socio-cultural affiliation, geographical background, strategies adopted in communication, registers, state of mentality, attitude, approach towards others, goals in mind, socio-national identity, relation with the interactants he tries to communicate with—and many more things, which are implicitly/explicitly embedded with the language he uses for expression and communication.

Therefore, when linguistics—as the prime discipline entrusted with the task of language study—tries to explore all these aspects involved in various events of linguistic communication, it cannot be mono-dimensional—as our earlier thinkers liked to envisage—but has to be multidirectional in goal, multidimensional in nature and multifunctional in application. The present goals of linguistics are, indeed, propelled in these directions.

During the last few decades linguistics has evolved as a discipline, which is much more concerned with application of linguistic data, information and observations in various domains of human enterprise. This has been possible due to change in attitude of people engaged in the discipline as well as due to the emergence of several new fields of linguistics, such as, *sociolinguistics, computational linguistics, corpus linguistics, ecolinguistics, cognitive linguistics, language teaching, dictionary compilation, translation, biolinguistics* and others, the existence of which is related to direct utilization of linguistic examples, data and information.

The mind-boggling multidirectional and multifunctional activities related to language and linguistics in the present century may be—within a broader scheme—classified into several dimensions. The first dimension relates to the approach which argues for the usage-based description of language. The present research and analysis activities in the area of *corpus linguistics* have succeeded to establish the truth that description of a language should always be based on data, examples and information obtained from the evidences of actual language use. Without reference and presentation of evidence of actual language use any description of language is bound to be skewed, deceptive and non-reliable. The future of this approach appears to be highly promising as old and new branches of linguistics are gradually accepting this argument as a maxim to redesign their research methodologies accordingly.

On the other hand, *generative linguistics* wants to go beyond the realms of simple language description to understand the devices and mechanisms deployed in linguistic generativity by human beings, in general. It is not concerned with what people say; it is concerned with how human beings are empowered to generate infinite number of valid linguistic constructions by way of using finite number of rules operational at various levels in linguistic expressions. This has been a dominating question for the entire second half of the last century and it still haunts a number of linguists even today, as it is not yet understood how people are so productive in linguistic formation even if they are not properly trained or cultivated. In my view this problem will haunt for many more years until and unless we find a satisfactory answer to this question.

The utilization of language data and information in both first and second *language education* has become another crucial area of serious concern for the linguists. In the new millennium, in a country like India, when collective attention is carefully directed towards mass education, mass literacy and adult literacy, development of necessary text-books, reference materials and study materials become indispensable; and in these activities, language and linguistics become the basement on which the palace of Indian education system can stand on. The issue of language education also becomes a crucial domain of *language planning*, where the promotion, the documentation and the standardization of a language or a variety is interwoven with the growth and development of a speech community or the other. These issues will invariably draw attention of the concerned people and the policy makers in years to come.

Another important issue of modern linguistics has been the problems for understanding the interface that underlies between *language and society*. It is observed that language often changes its form and function when it is used by people belonging to different walks of life. In fact, several socio-cultural issues and register variables such as, ethnicity, culture, education, gender, economic status, race, occupation and religion, etc. of people become quite vibrant in final formulation

3

and exchange of linguistic messages with others. Also, geographical location, regional uniqueness and localised individuality are intermingled with the language people use in their daily interactions. Thus, linguistics becomes a mirror of a society that reflects on many hidden aspects of life and living hardly perceived through any other methods of representation. Modern linguistics is determined to probe into this sphere to gather a better insight about the society and the language people use.

Repairing linguistic disorders of the linguistically challenged people has been another challenging area of modern linguistics. This has given birth to some new branches of linguistics such as *psycholinguistics, neurolinguistics,* etc. which are interested not only to explore and understand the patterns and the nature of linguistic disorders people suffer from, but also are interested to provide necessary remedies and solutions to these problems —as a part of its collective social responsibility and obligation. Remarkable advancement made in the area of medical science, neurology and technology has provided strong impetus to the investigators to analyse linguistic disorders, define the nature of impairment and to provide applicable solutions. Let us assume, this domain of linguistics will also expand more and more with its clear social and applicational relevance with the procreation of new generations of language users.

The recent interface between language and computer has opened up a new range of benefits for the people of most societies. It is understood that a happy marriage between language and computer will bring unprecedented changes in various spheres of life not only to supply solutions to several language-related problems but also to provide amicable platforms for on-line education, e-governance, customised education and solutions for mass literacy and adult education. We can visualize that in near future classroom education in Indian schools and colleges will invariably incline towards computer-assisted teaching, where learner-based interfaces will be required for addressing both linguistic and non-linguistic needs of the students and teachers. In this sphere *computational linguistics* will have a vital role to play for developing academic resources and materials as well as for designing hassle-free need-based systems for the end users.

Understanding the complexities and dimensions of *language cognition* by human beings and the role of human brain and mind in this work have been other intriguing areas of modern linguistic research. There have been efforts for knowing how human brain is stimulated at the time transmitting and receiving linguistic signals; how different parts and portions of human brain are activated in the act of language cognition; and how various non-linguistic factors and issues become responsible for triggering a human brain in the act of language understanding. In years to come, all these problems will inspire a galaxy of experts from various fields to dissolve the enigma of language cognition, the understanding of which will definitely give birth of a new line of hope for dissolving several problems of *cognitive linguistics*.

Finally, the questions of what is universal to language, how language can vary and how human beings come to know languages will arise. All human beings are endowed with a celestial gift for achieving linguistic competence in whatever language is spoken around them when they grow up, with apparently little need for explicit and conscious instruction. The puzzle is still there that while non-human animals may acquire their own communication systems, they do not acquire human language in this way, although many non-human animals can learn to respond to human language, or even can be trained to use it to a certain level. Therefore, linguists are led to assume that the ability to acquire and use human language is an innate, a biologically predetermined potential of human beings, similar to their ability for walking. However, there is no consensus as to the extent of this innate potential, or its domain-specificity (the degree to which such innate abilities are specific to language). While some scholars claim that there is a very large set of highly abstract and specific binary settings coded into the human brain, others claim that the ability to learn language is a product of general human cognition. It is, however, generally agreed that there are no *genetic* differences underlying the differences between languages and due to this factor, an individual will acquire whatever language(s) he or she is exposed to as a child, regardless of parental or ethnic origin. This domain of linguistic research is also destined to go a long way before it succeeds to dispel the long-standing enigma of language inheritance and linguistic innateness in language acquisition.

The term *language* has several shades, as it denotes different concepts and ideas in different situations of its use. In **Chapter 1,** I have made an attempt to capture these shades of the term as reflected in various domains of human knowledge. In different sections of the chapter, I have tried to reflect on the term from different perspectives to show how the scholars across space and time have tried to formulate an all-purpose definition of *language* and what the main limitations of these definitions are. Also this chapter discusses the characteristic features of language with special reference to those differences normally observed in case of the *Animal Communication System* (ANICOM). In subsequent sections of the chapter, attention is directed towards the rules of language, which are invariably used to shape the ways a language is written, spoken, communicated and interpreted with in various spheres of human linguistic activities.

Human being, according to scholars, is the only animal in this world who can communicate by means of abstract symbolic system known as *language*. Moreover, intimate investigations into the forms and functions of the human language have succeeded to identify a set of features, which are found to be unique to a large extent to all human languages. Several investigations as well as the frames of reference have claimed that if all the human languages are compared to each other, these will exhibit some identical features, which are not attested in the ANICOM—not even in case of the communication systems of hominoids like gibbons and great apes, who are considered to be the closest living relatives of the humans. These features are, in general, are identified as the *Design Features*, since these are the basic features of the human languages and are rarely observed in the ANICOM or machines. In **Chapter 2**, these design features are discussed in some details following the lines of argument defined by noted scholars like Charles F. Hockett, Joseph Greenberg, John Lyons and others. Also, attempt is made to show how the ANICOM, in general, lacks in some of these features.

Perhaps, one of the biggest debates among linguists and other scholars across generations has been about the origin of language. Also there have been debates on the line whether one can account for a language by using only the basic mechanisms of learning or whether one needs to postulate some special built-in language devices for this. Although it has been taken for granted that speech has developed much before the advent of writing, no one knows for certain how human language has actually originated or evolved. There are, however, some speculations and theories, which have tried to give some explanations about the origin of human languages. Some of these speculations and theories are reported in brief in **Chapter 3**. After referring to the general history about the assumptions fabricated over the centuries for tracing the origin of language, in this chapter, I have attempted to discuss in brief the *Divine Theory*, the *Bow-Wow Theory*, the *Pooh-Pooh Theory*, the *Ding-Dong Theory*, the *Yo-He-Ho Theory*, the *Sing-Song Theory*, the *Oral-Gesture Theory*, the *Natural Selection Theory*, the *FOXP2 Speech Gene* and some other short theories related to this assumption.

The question *what is linguistics* has been directly linked with the question *what is language*. In **Chapter 4**, attempt is made to define the term *linguistics* in a holistic sense, which is wider in scope as it takes almost all the basic aspects of language and its speakers into its area of investigation. In a step-by-step manner this chapter discusses the significance and implication of the term *linguistics* at different points in time; discusses in details if *linguistics* can be identified as a *science*; refers to various levels of linguistic analysis; and shows how each level of language is interfaced with the other to give *linguistics* a complete form. While studying a natural language it becomes necessary to sub-divide its domains and study these domains in minute details in order to study the language in analytical and systematic manner. In addition to these levels of linguistic representation, language has also some equally important levels (e.g., *graphology, lexicography, pragmatics,* etc), which are also discussed in this chapter. Finally this chapter refers to the core areas of linguistics, addressed in traditional frame of linguistics and grammar.

The recent birth of many new fields of linguistics has made it possible to look at the languages from different perspectives. Due to this reason, it has been possible to present new accounts about the languages as well as to trace the differences existing in context-bound use of languages. The new interface has also evoked a conflict between the traditional and the modern linguistics, which continues to haunt scholars for generations. Although the modern linguistics has been largely different from traditional linguistics in approach, attitude, methods, orientation, subject matters and focus, it has not yet succeeded to ignore the basic dimensions of traditional linguistics, without which linguistic study of any kind is bound to be skewed, incomplete and insignificant. These basic dimensions (*descriptive* vs *prescriptive, theoretical* vs *applied, micro* vs. *macro* and *synchronic* vs *diachronic*) are discussed in some details in different sections of the **Chapter 5**. The understanding of these dimensions provides us the required knowledgebase to comprehend various factors, features, issues and events directly or indirectly related to both the traditional and the modern linguistics.

The change in approach or strategy in language study has become highly beneficial to the discipline *linguistics* as well for the whole mankind. We are now in a better position to realize that language is not only a useful means of communication, but also a highly reliable resource for understanding human mind, human societies, human behaviour and human cognition. Moreover, understanding the form and texture of language data in new perspectives has become valuable input for information exchange, mass literacy and language education. For instance, analysis and interpretation of newly accumulated data and information of language use has made a sea change in the approach and strategies used in language teaching and planning—two important areas of applied linguistics, which are considered indispensable in the back drop of mass literacy and progress of societies. It may appear to some that the new fields of linguistics are separate from each other completely and there exists hardly any link between these fields. In reality, however, these fields are not at all isolated from each other. Rather, these are closely interrelated as their common resource is nothing but language. Even then, independent status of each field cannot be ignored, as each field has its own core concepts to foster significant scholarly inquiry and research. In **Chapter 6,** an attempt is made to focus on a few new branches of linguistics (e.g., *anthropological linguistics, cognitive linguistics, computational lexicography, computational linguistics, corpus linguistics, discourse analysis, ecolinguistics, ethnolinguistics, forensic linguistics, neurolinguistics and pragmatics*) without discussing those traditional branches, which are often discussed in any general book on descriptive linguistics.

Human languages are used in various manners in different purposes and hence, it has different functions. In **Chapter 7,** an attempt is made to describe the observations and arguments made by scholars regarding the functions of language in general as well as the functions of specific components and properties of language in overall understanding the roles of language both as a mean of communication and as a symbol of manifestation of social identity of the language users. This chapter records observations of the early thinkers of the

Medieval Europe with a short reference to the traditional assumptions and the views expressed by Karl Bühler. It also refers to the views expressed by the thinkers such as Ludwig Wittgenstein, Roman Jakobson, Dell Hymes, M.A.K. Halliday and others. It also compares the interfaces existing between the observations of Halliday and the observations made by other thinkers of the last century; and refers to the observations made by some Indian scholars. Finally, it discusses the arguments and explanations presented by recent scholars who argue to consider functions of language from the perspectives of Darwinian principle of natural selection.

Non-verbal communication, like that of verbal communication, is one of the intriguing areas of human communication system. In general, it refers to the exchange of message primarily through those non-linguistic means that includes *paralanguage, body movement, kinesics, facial expression, eye contact, tactile communication, personal space and territory, environment, smell, silence* and *time*. Within the broader frame of discussion, all non-linguistics symbols as well as the *sign language* are included within the domain of non-verbal communication. Several experiments have been carried out for estimating the functional and communicative relevance of non-verbal communication over the years and most of the studies show that human beings can communicate directly by non-verbal means without using speech or texts quite effectively. In **Chapter 8**, an attempt is initiated to discuss the features of non-verbal communication; the interface between verbal and non-verbal communication and setting; and means and strategies adopted in non-verbal communication by human beings. It also describes all the major strategies of the non-verbal communication in a situation where person-to-person communication is the central theme for information exchange and emotion sharing.

The ANICOM refers to the methods and systems used by the animals to communicate with other animals belonging to the same species or to transmit signals to animals belonging to other species or to humans. It is known that animals, like human beings, also use a communication system of their own for their basic biological needs, which is different from the human language. The ANICOM is a kind of behaviour of the animals that has an effect on the current or future behaviours of animals. Intimate analysis of ANICOM plays an important role in *Ethology, Eociobiology, Semiotics* and *Linguistics* and in the area of animal cognition. Understanding the animal world as well as their communication systems in general are intriguing fields, which have been directly related to diverse fields such as linguistics, use of personal symbolic names, animal emotions, animal culture and learning and even the sexual behaviour of animals, etc. In **Chapter 9**, an attempt is made to identify the basic nature of ANICOM; to differentiate among the forms of ANICOM; to trace history of evolution of ANICOM; to interpret the message embedded in ANICOM; to define the nature and patterns of interspecies communication; to explore the interface between human and ANICOM; and to differentiate between human language and ANICOM.

15th October 2010

Niladri Sekhar Dash
Linguistic Research Unit
Indian Statistical Institute
Kolkata, West Bengal, India

Chapter 1
What Is Language?

1.1 Introduction

The everyday use of the term *language* is made of several different shades, which a baptised linguist can distinguish if he carefully takes into account finer sense variations of the term. In general, the term refers to the concrete act of speaking in a given situation to denote the notion of *performance* of the speakers involved in a spoken interaction. This particular linguistic system underlies the usage of *language* of an individual at a given point in time and place, which is identified in sociolinguistics as **idiolect**[1].

A particular variety of speech or writing of members of a particular group is also referred to as *language* such as *scientific language, corporate language, commercial language, adult language,* etc.—which becomes directly related to sociolinguistic or stylistic restrictiveness of language use in specific contexts. In applied linguistics, on the other hand, phrases like the *first language,* the *second language,* the *third language,* etc. often refer to the abstract system that underlies the collective totality of speech and writing behaviours of a speech community and the knowledgebase of this system of an individual.

The term *language* is also used in synchronic sense such as the *Modern English Language,* as well as in diachronic sense such as *English language since Chaucer, English of the Medieval Period* etc. Furthermore, the term *language* is also used to refer to the higher order of grouping of different speech varieties as observed in the notions such as the *Romance languages,* the *Creole languages,* etc. All these examples invariably fall under the heading natural language—a generic term, which is often contrasted with those artificially constructed systems used to expound one or more conceptual areas such as *computer language, formal language,*

13

logical language, etc., or to facilitate the language like *Esperanto,* which is artificially devised for communication among the people across the world.

In contrast with the instances of *individual languages, idiolects,* etc., there is also an abstract sense of the term *language,* which refers to *biological faculty* of an individual, by which a human being is enabled to learn and use language. This is implicit in the notion called **Language Acquisition Device** (LAD) in psycholinguistics. On the other hand, at a comparatively abstract level, the term *language* is postulated as a defining feature of human behaviour—the universal properties of all the speeches and writing systems, especially as it is characterised in terms of the **Design Features** such as *productivity, duality of petterning, learnability,* etc., as proposed by Hockett (1960), Greenberg (1963) and other linguists.

1.2 Understanding the Spectrum

We can know about the language used by a community by studying the varieties or dialects and developing a realistic policy concerning the selection and the use of different varieties at different geographical locations. The term *language,* however, enters into technical intricacies when we talk about the issues such as *language teaching* or language *learning.* We require minimum knowledge to understand the *first language* (i.e., the mother tongue), which is distinguishable from the *second language* (i.e., the language other than one's mother tongue) used for several practical purposes such as *government works, education, migration, tours and travels and commercial activities,* etc.

Many languages use two different words to translate the English word *language.* For instance, French uses forms like *Langage* and *Langue;* Italian uses *Linguaggio* and *Lingua;* and Spanish uses *Lenguaje* and *Lengua,* etc. In each of the languages, the difference between the two words correlates with the difference in two senses of the English word *language.* For example, in French, the word *langage* is actually used to refer to the language in general while the word *langue* is often used to refer to particular languages. It so happens because English assumes that a person not only possesses a *language* (e.g., *English, Chinese, Bengali, Hindi,* etc.) but also has *the language* (i.e., the language faculty). Although philosophers, psychologists and linguists argue that it is the possession of this *language faculty* that clearly distinguishes a man from other animals, the important fact is that one cannot posses (or use) a natural language without possessing (or using) some particular language.

The term *language* is applied not only to human languages like *English, Chinese, Bengali, German*, etc., but to a variety of other systems of notation, communication or calculation, about which there is enough room for dispute. For example, mathematicians, logicians and computer scientists frequently use the term *language* to describe the notational systems, which are artificially designed rather than naturally evolved. So does the *Esperanto*, which was invented in late 19th century for the purpose of international communication. It is, in essence, an artificially made language, although it is developed with resources of pre-existing natural languages.

Furthermore, there are other systems of communication—both human and non-human—which are definitely natural but which do not seem to be the *languages* in the strict sense of the term, even though the term *language* is often used to refer to them. For instance, let us consider phrases such as *sign language, body language* or *language of the bees* in this connection. People will agree that the term *language* is used here in a metaphorical or figurative sense. Interestingly, it is the *langage* rather than the *langue* that will naturally be used in translating such phrases into French[2].

The discussion given above shows that the question 'what is language?' carries with it an important presupposition that each of the several thousand distinct natural languages spoken throughout the world is a specific instance of something more general. Since linguists are concerned primarily with these natural languages, what they want to know is whether all the natural languages have something in common, which are not usually shared by other systems of communication— either human or non-human—such that it is right to apply to each of them the word *language* or deny the application of the term to the other systems of communication. Perhaps, we need to assign the characteristic features of natural languages to the other systems of communication before we can call them *language*.

1.3 Some Definitions of Language

Definitions of *language* are not difficult to find out in the score of literature related to language and linguistics. These come not only from the classic works of well-known linguists, but also from amateurish attempts made by the novices. Taken together, these can serve as preliminary indications about the properties that linguists tend to think of being essential to the languages. Some definitions of language presented by scholars are critically estimated in the following paragraphs.

Sapir in his *Language* (1921) stated, "Language is a purely human and non-instinctive method of communicating ideas, emotions and desires by means of a system of voluntarily produced symbols". This definition suffers from several defects. However broadly we define the terms *idea, emotion* and *desire*, it is clear that there is much that is communicated by language, which is not covered by any of them and the term *idea*, in particular, is inherently imprecise. On the other hand, there are, indeed, many systems of voluntarily produced symbols that we only count as languages in what we feel to be an extended or metaphorical sense of the word *language*. For example, the popularly referred expression *body language* such as *gestures, postures, eye gazes, winks*, etc., seems to satisfy this point of Sapir's definition. Whether it is purely human and non-instinctive is open to doubt and question. Moreover, there is the question whether languages properly so-called are both purely human and non-instinctive.

In *Outline of Linguistic Analysis* (1942) Bloch and Trager informed, "A language is a system of arbitrary vocal symbols, by means of which a social group cooperates". This definition also makes no appeal, except indirectly and by implication, to the communicative function of language. Instead, it puts all the emphasis upon its social function and in doing so, it takes a rather narrow view of the role of language in society. The definition brings in the property of *arbitrariness* and explicitly restricts language to the spoken form only by which it makes *written language* contradictory in sense. The term *arbitrariness* is here used in a rather special sense. The question of relation that holds between language and speech becomes very important here. As far as natural languages are concerned, there is indeed a connection between language and speech. Logically, the later purposes the former. One cannot speak without a language (i.e., without speaking in a particular language), but one can use language without speaking. However logically agreed that language is independent of speech, it is known that in all natural languages speech is historically and perhaps biologically, prior to writing. And this view is universally proved correct and globally acknowledged.

In *An Essay on Language* (1968) Hall stated, "Language is the institution whereby humans communicate and interact with each other by means of habitually used oral-auditory arbitrary symbols". First of all, the terms like *communicate* and *interact* are introduced into this definition (interaction being broader and better than co-operation) and secondly, the term *oral auditory* can be equivalent to vocal. The term *vocal* differs only in that *oral auditory* denotes to the receiver as well as the sender of the vocal signals that we identify as language utterances. Hall treated language as a purely human institution and the term *institution* has made explicit the view that the language, which is used by a particular society, is the part of that society's culture.

The use of the phrase *habitually used* is historically important in the sense that both *linguistics* and *psychology of language* were influenced by stimulus-response theories of the behaviourists and within the theoretical framework of behaviourism the term *habit* acquired a special sense. It was used with reference to the queues of behaviour that were identifiable as statistically predictable responses to particular stimuli. Also, much of our thinking was considered as a matter of habit and was brought within the scope of behaviourists' version of stimulus-response theory of *language use* and *language acquisition*. It is now generally accepted that this theory has a very restricted application in linguistics as well as in psychology of language.

The term *symbols* refers to vocal signals which are transmitted from the sender to the receiver in the process of communication and bidirectional interaction. However, it is not clear how these symbols can be *habitual*. If *symbol* is being used to refer, not the language-utterance, but to the words or phrases of which they are composed, it would be wrong to imply that a particular speaker used such and such a word, as a matter of habit, on such and such occasions. One of the most important facts about natural language is that there is no connection between words and the situations in which they are used such that occurrence of particular words is predictable. For instance, we do not habitually form an utterance containing the word *bird* whenever we see a *bird*; indeed we are no more likely to use the word *bird* in such situations than we are in all sorts of other situations. Language, as we all know, is not triggered by stimulus; it is usually free from stimuli.

In *General Linguistics: An Introductory Survey* (1964) Robins has stated, "Language is a symbol system... almost wholly based on pure or arbitrary convention ... infinitely extendible and modifiable according to the changing needs and conditions of the speakers". Robins has paid maximum emphasis on the flexibility and adaptability of natural languages. There is, however, no logical compatibility between the view that languages are systems of habit (as *habit* being constructed in a

17

particular sense) and the view is expressed by Robins. It is after all, conceivable, that a habit-system should itself change over time, in response to the changing needs of its users. But the term *habit* is not one that we usually associate with adaptable behaviour. The notion of *infinite extensibility* also needs close investigation. Distinction must be drawn between *the extensibility and modifiability of a system* and *the extensibility or modifiability of the products* of that system. It is also important to recognise that some kinds of extension and modification are theoretically more interesting than others. For example, the fact that the new words can enter the vocabulary of a language at any time is of far less theoretical interest than is the fact that new grammatical construction can arise in the course of time. One of the central issues in linguistics is whether there are many limits of this latter kind of modifiability and, if so, what the limits are.

In *A Description of English* (1967) Derbyshire has argued, "Language is undoubtedly a kind of means of communication among human beings. It consists primarily of vocal sounds. It is articulatory, systematic, symbolic and arbitrary". Derbyshire has clearly emphasised on the aspect that language is the sole property of human beings and that it is primarily speech, which has been used from the beginning of human civilisation as an indispensable tool or means of communication among humans. Before the start of civilisation, they might have used language in the form of sign like other animals, but it must have had a very limited scope to address the varieties of need of human communication. With the advancement of human civilisation, language has gradually evolved to develop into a full-fledged means of communication, which civilised human beings have been using today for conveying and receiving millions of messages across the world. Language with some of its unique features of *systematicity*, *symbolism* and *arbitrariness*, has changed the entire scenario of human communication and has made it possible for human beings to grow into a separate living entity in the world.

The last definition quoted below strikes altogether a different note. Chomsky in *Syntactic Structures* (1957) has mentioned, "From now on I will consider a language to be a set of (finite or infinite) sentences, each finite in length and constructed out of a finite set of elements". This definition intends to cover much else besides natural languages. According to Chomsky, all natural languages, either in spoken or in written form, are languages in the sense: since (a) each natural language has a finite number of sounds in it (and a finite number of letters in its alphabet); and (b) although there may be infinitely many distinct sentences in the language, each sentence can be represented as a finite sequence of these sounds (or letters). It is the primary task of linguists to describe some particular natural languages to determine which of the finite sequences of elements in that languages are sentences and which are non-sentences. Also, it is the task of the linguists to discover the structural properties, if there are any, whereby natural languages differ from the non-natural languages.

Chomsky has stressed increasingly in his subsequent works that not only there are indeed such structural properties, but that they are so abstract, so complex and so highly specific to their purpose that they could not possibly be learned from scratch by an infant grappling with the problem of acquiring his native language. They must be known to the child, in some sense, prior to and independently of his experience of any natural language and used by him in the process of language acquisition[3].

Chomsky's definition of *language* is stated above to show the contrast it provides with the others—both in style and in content. It says nothing about the communicative aspect of a language—either natural or non-natural. Also, it says nothing about the symbolic nature of elements of sequences of them. Rather, it purposes to focus on the purely structural properties of languages and argues that these properties can be rationally investigated from the mathematical point of view. Perhaps, this is one of the Chomsky's major contributions to the discipline named *Linguistics* where he has given special emphasis on *structure dependence of processes* in which sentences are actually constructed in a natural language; and formulates a general theory of grammar based upon the particular definition of this property.

In the following section some more notable definitions of language are presented without elucidation:

- Speech is the representation of the experience of the mind. (Aristotle)
- Language may be defined as the expression of thoughts by means of speech sounds combined into words. (Sweet 1900)
- The totality of the utterances that can be made in a speech community is the language of that speech community. (Bloomfield 1933)
- Language is human ... a verbal systematic symbolism ... a means of transmitting information... a form of social behaviour...[with a] high degree of convention. (Whatmough 1957)

- Human languages are unlimited...an unlimited set of discrete signals...have great structural complexity... structure on at least two levels...are open-ended...allow for transmission of information. (Langacker 1967)
- A language is a system of arbitrary vocal symbols by which members of a social group co-operate and interact. (Sturtevant 1947)
- When we study human language, we are approaching what some might call 'human essence', the distinctive qualities of mind that are, so far as we know, unique to man. (Chomsky 1968)
- Languages are the principal systems of communication used by particular groups of human beings within the particular society (linguistic community) of which they are members. (Lyons 1970)
- Language, in its widest sense, means the sum-total of such signs of our thoughts and feelings as are capable of external perception and as could be produced and repeated at will. (Gardiner 1932)
- Language is the most valuable single possession of the human race. (Hockett 1958)
- Man is man through the use of language alone. (Humboldt 1988)
- Language is a system by which sounds and meanings are related. (Fromkin and Rodman 1993)
- Language is the most sophisticated and versatile means available to human beings for the communication of meaning. (Brown 1984)
- A language is a system of arbitrary vowel symbols by means of which the members of a society interact in terms of their total culture. (Bloch and Trager 1942).
- Language is a patterned system of arbitrary sound signals, characterised by structure dependence, creativity, displacement, duality and cultural transmission. (Aitchison 1978)
- Language is a system of sounds, words, patterns, etc., used by humans to communicate thoughts and feelings. (*Oxford Advanced Learner's Dictionary* 1989)
- Language is a system of conventional spoken or written symbols by means of which human beings, as members of a social group can participate in its culture, communicate. (*Encyclopaedia Britannica* 1996)
- Language is a system of communication by sound, i.e., through the organs of speech and hearing among human beings of a certain

group or community, using vocal symbols possessing arbitrary conventional meanings. *(The Dictionary of Linguistics* 1997)

- It is the words, their pronunciation and the methods of combining them to be used and understood by a speech community... audible, articulate, meaningful sound as produced by action of vocal organs ...a systematic means of communicating ideas or feelings by the use of conventionalized signs, sounds, gestures, or marks having understood meanings...the suggestion by objects, actions, or conditions of associated ideas or feelings...the means by which animals communicate. *(Merriam-Webster Online Dictionary* 2003)

From the definitions given above it appears that none of these can define completely what a 'language' is, although each one has focused on a few or some of the salient aspects of a natural language[4]. However, these can serve to introduce some properties considered indispensable for comprehending a language. For most of the linguists, languages are the systems of signs and symbols designed for the purpose of communication. And this is how we try to look at the languages[5]. Some of the properties of language stated in these definitions include *arbitrariness, flexibility, freedom from stimulus-control frame, modifiability* and *structure-dependence,* etc. Other features are discussed as the **Design Features** of language in Chapter 2.

1.4 Characteristic Features of Language

It is believed that in this world human beings are the sole species, who can use 'language' because of their sharp intelligence and appropriate structure of their vocal tract. It is, however, learnt that animals are also highly capable of communicating among themselves in their own ways, as bees can do it by tail-wagging or whales can do it by way of 'singing', etc. (Heart 1996). Even then, there are certain apparent differences between human and animal ways of communicating messages based on characteristic features unique to the human language and the **Animal Communication Systems (ANICOMS).** Although some characteristic features are proposed to be common to all the human languages, linguists are interested in ascribing certain properties only to human languages[6]. The characteristic features generally attributed to all human languages include the followings: (a) language is a means of self-expression and communication; (b) language is arbitrary, (c) language is symbolic, (d) language is non-instinctive, (e) language is conventional, (f) language is systematic, (g) language is verbal and vocal, (h) language is a form of social behaviour, (i) language is human, (j) language is open-ended, (k) language is creative, extendable and modifiable, (l) language is complex structurally and (m) language is culturally transmitted. In the following sub-sections all these characteristic features are discussed in some details.

1.4.1 Language is a Means of Communication and Self-Expression

Language is considered to be the most powerful, convenient and permanent means of communication. Though non-linguistic symbols such as *expressive gestures, signals of various kinds, traffic lights, road-signs, flags, emblems* and many more such things as well as shorthand and other codes, deaf and dumb signs and *Braille* alphabets, symbols of mathematics and logic, etc. are also treated as means of communication, these are not so much perfect, flexible, comprehensive and extensive as a natural language is.

Language is also considered as the best means of self-expression. It is through language that human beings can express their thoughts, desires, emotions and feelings; and it is through this medium that human beings can store knowledge and transmit messages from one person to another as well as can share their experiences with others across space and time. Most of these activities in the world are carried on through or by language. Also, it is through the language that human beings can interact in one-to-one or one-to-many situations. It is the language again that can combine present, past and future together with all their tensual varieties.

Language is an abstract set of psychological principles and sociological considerations that constitute a person's **competence** as a speaker in a given situation. These psychological principles make available to him an unlimited number of sentences he can draw upon in concrete situations and provide him with the ability to understand and create entirely new sentences. Hence, language is not just a verbal behaviour; it is a complex system of rules that establish correlations between meanings and sound sequences. It is a set of principles that a speaker masters; it is not anything that he does. In essence, language is a code which is different from the act of encoding; it is speaker's linguistic competence rather than their linguistic performance.

Mere linguistic competence is not enough for making a communication successful. It also needs to be coupled with

communicative competence. This is the view of the sociolinguists (Hymes 1962), who emphasise on the use of language according to the occasions and contexts, speakers and listeners, gender and age, professions and social statuses of the people concerned. That language is the result of social interaction is an established truth.

1.4.2 Language is Arbitrary

By the term *arbitrary* we mean that there is no inherent or iconic relation between any given element of a language and its meaning. The relationship is entirely arbitrary as there exits no direct and necessary connection between the nature of things or ideas and the linguistic units a language deals with. Linguistic units are arbitrary symbols by which these things or ideas are expressed. There is no reason why the four-legged domestic animal should be called *dog* in English, *kutta* in Hindi, *sarameya* in Sanskrit, *kukur* in Bengali, *kukura* in Oriya, *nai* in Kannada, *kukka* in Telugu, *chien* in French, *hund* in German, *kutra* in Marathi, *kutro* in Gujarati, *kalb* in Arabic and so on. That those particular words rather than any other forms are used in these different languages is merely an accidental feature of linguistic history. There is no natural connection between the word or sound and the thing it denotes. This means we cannot tell what can be the meaning of a word simply by looking at it. Nothing in the German word *handyspiele* tells us that it means the same as the English word *handball*.

Although this rule applies to the most of human languages there are certain exceptions. In order to understand the *arbitrariness* one has to know a specific language, although there are a number of *iconic* symbols in every language that can be understood without knowing the language system in full details. The **onomatopoeic words** which imitate sounds (e.g., *buzz, hiss, hum, bang, kalkal, gungun, pinpin*, etc.) fall in this category and these words are present in the majority of languages. **Onomatopoeia,** which refers to the use of words that imitate the sounds of their referents, may seem to invalidate this statement, but such words are comparatively very few in different languages and the accuracy of the imitation depends on the sounds available in the language. Furthermore, these are at variation in different languages of the world and have no uniformity in form and sense denotation.

1.4.3 Language is Non-instinctive or Conventional

No language in the world (except for some artificially developed languages such as *Esperanto, Volapuk, Ido, Klingon,* etc.) was created in a day or two out of a mutually agreed upon formula by a group of humans. This implies that a natural language is the outcome of evolution and convention carried out over numerous human generations. Each generation transmits this convention on to the next generation. Like all human institutions, every human language changes, grows, expands and dies. Every language is, then, a convention in a community. It is non-instinctive because it is acquired by human beings. Nobody gets a language from his ancestors through his heritage. One has to acquire it and for this every normal human being is provided with an innate ability. Animals may inherit their system of communication by heredity, but humans do not.

1.4.4 Language is a System of Symbols

The idea that a language is a *system of symbols* is actually a consequence of the feature of arbitrariness discussed above. In general, a symbol is an object or idea that stands for something else; it is something that serves as a substitute for an idea or object. All human languages are viewed from this perspective as language is a system of vocal symbols, which are arbitrarily used to denote objects and ideas. Every language has several sounds and words which one can use as symbols for concepts, things, ideas, objects, etc. available within a language community. Speakers use words essentially as symbols and not as signs (as it is observed in case of Mathematics or pictorial presentations of ideas) to represent concepts, ideas and objects. That language is a system of signs is best represented in the proposition of *signifier, signifie* and *signified* made by Ferdinand de Saussure (1966: 27). His clarification of the three ideas is made clear from the following diagram (Ogden and Richards 1952: 10-11):

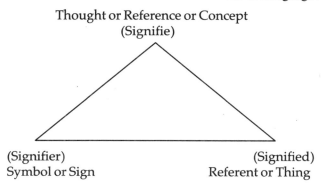

Fig. 1.1: Conceptual interface between *signifie, signifier* and *signified*

Ogden and Richards (1952: 10-11) commented, "...between a thought and a symbol a causal relation holds, between the thought and referent there is also a relation more or less direct, between the symbol and the referent there is no relevant relation other than the indirect one (imputed relation)". According to this model the relation between the sound and referent is not direct at all. It is imputed and is mediated by concept or designation. A person observes different objects of the external world and marks different occurrences of the referent. He compares similar and contrasting features of this referent with those of the other referents. This enables him to make abstractions and form a general idea or concept of the thing in his mind.

1.4.5 Language is Systematic

Language is symbolic and the symbols are arranged in a particular system or order. All the languages have their own systems of arrangement. Although symbols in each language are finite, they can be arranged infinitely; that is to say, we can produce infinite sets of sentences by a finite set of symbols.

Every language is a system of systems. All languages have phonological and grammatical systems and within these systems, there are several other sub-systems. For example, within a grammatical system a language preserves morphological and syntactic systems and within these two sub-systems a language has several other rule-based sub-systems such as those of plurals, of mood, of tense, of aspect, etc.

When we say a language is *systematic*, we mean the following: speakers of a language use only certain combinations. For instance, although the sounds *b* and *z* occur in English, there is no word in English which begins with *bz*. Similarly, we can say that *"A beautiful girl chased the brown dog"* is a sentence in English, but cannot say this to *"the ed fullbeauti chase girl brown dog the"*. Thus, all languages, although linear in their visual manifestation, have a dual system of sound and meaning. In other words, language is the systematic composition or arrangement of linguistic units which correlate word and meaning. Each language, therefore, can be described as a special system, suitable for conveying messages within its own framework of structure and meaning. It has very little direct physical relation to the meanings or the acts which it involves.

1.4.6 Language is Verbal or Vocal

Language is an organisation of vocal sounds—sounds which are produced in mouth with the help of various organs of speech to convey some meaningful messages. It also means that speech is primary to writing. There are several languages in the world which have no writing system, yet these are languages because these are spoken. Music and singing also employ vocal sounds, but these are not languages because these lack in many features inherent in language. Language is the manifestation of a systematic verbal symbolism; it makes use of verbal elements such as sounds, words and phrases, which are arranged in certain ways to make sentences. Language is vocal in as much as it is made up of sounds, which can be produced by the organs of speech.

1.4.7 Language is a Form of Social Behaviour

Language is a set of conventional communicative signals used by humans for communication within a speech community. Language, in this sense, is a possession of a social group, comprising an indispensable set of rules which permits its members to relate to each other, to interact with each other, to co-operate with each other.

Language is a social institution. It exists within a society. It is a means of nourishing and developing culture and establishing human relations. It is as a member of society that a human being acquires a language. We are not born with an instinct to learn a particular language such as *English, Hindi, Russian, Chinese, Bengali, Tamil* or *French*. We learn a language as members of the society using that language, or because we want to understand that society, or to be understood by that speech-community.

If a language is not used in any society, it dies. Language is thus a social event. It can be fully described only if we know all about the people who are involved in it, their personalities, their beliefs, attitudes, knowledge of the world, relationship to each other, their social status, what activity they are engaged in, what they are talking about, what has gone before linguistically and non-linguistically, what happens after, what they are and a host of other facts about them and the situation they are placed in.

1.4.8 Language is Human

No species other than humans has been endowed with language. Animals cannot acquire human language because of their own physical inadequacies and for the complex structures of human language. Animals do not have the type of brain which the human beings possess. Moreover, their articulatory organs are very much different from those of human beings. Furthermore, the animal communication system (ANICOMS) does not make use of the feature *duality of patterning*—the concurrent systems of sound and meaning.

1.4.9 Language is Unique

Language is a unique phenomenon of this Earth. Other planets do not seem to have any language. This fact may however be invalidated if we, by chance, happen to discover an extra-terrestrial species on any other planet, which has a language system like us or a more sophisticated one. But so far there is no evidence of the presence of language on any other planet except the Earth.

Each language is unique in its own form and texture. By this way we do not mean that languages do not have any similarities or universal features. What we mean, despite their common features and universal similarities each language has its own peculiarities and distinct features by which a language can easily be distinguished from its nearest peer.

1.4.10 Language is Creative, Extendable and Modifiable

Every human language has the property of creativity and productivity. The structural elements of human language can be combined in various ways to produce new morphemes, words, sentences and phrases, which neither the speaker nor the hearers may have ever made or heard before, yet which both sides can understand without difficulty.

Language changes according to the needs of the society. The Old English, for example, is different from the Modern English; so is the Old Hindi different from the Modern Hindi. Laukik Sanskrit, Pali and Prakrit are the various forms of Sanskrit that evolved due to number of changes. In sum, human language is open-ended, extendable and modifiable with time for addressing the needs of a speech community which uses it as a mark of their unique identity.

1.4.11 Language is Structurally Complex

Human language is understandably a far more structurally complex system than the system of communication of animals and it is because of this feature that human language belongs to a class of its own. For instance, English has 44 sounds that can be joined in different groups and patterns to form millions of distinct words. These words can be arranged into millions of sets to frame different sentences. Each sentence has its own internal structure, which is not only complex but also different from other sentences. Indeed, there are so many complexities involved even in a simple sentence that we need enough mastery over the finite sets of grammatical and semantic rules to decipher its hidden information. Such structural complexities are never found in animal communication systems, such as the beatings of lambs, chirpings of birds, or cries of monkeys.

1.4.12 Language is Culturally Transmitted

Although human beings are born with certain fixed biological predisposition for language acquisition and use (e.g., shape of the vocal tract), it does not predetermine the language which a human being is actually going to use as his or her mother tongue. A Bengali baby brought up in English speaking society and raised by an English speaking family is going to speak English and not Bengali, although it will still look like a Bengali.

The above mentioned characteristic features of language do not constitute the complete set that all the linguists do unanimously accept. There are many more arguments concerning the characteristic features of language, but owing to their minor importance and not very frequent occurrence in literature these have been omitted in this discussion. In sum, every language has a grammar; phoneme, morpheme, syntax and semantics. Also all the human languages are oral, social, symbolic, arbitrary, changeable, systematic and describable, unique and diverse, learnable, dynamic, intellectual, non-instinctive and conventional.

1.5 Rules of Language

All human languages are typically said to be governed by a set of unspoken rules that include phonological rules, prosodic rules, semantic rules, syntactic rules, pragmatic rules and communicative rules. These rules are invariably used to shape the ways a language is written, spoken, communicated and interpreted. How these rules actually operate is discussed below.

(a) Phonological Rules: These describe the systematic relationship between the sounds. They are responsible for determining what a symbol, or letter of the alphabet, sounds like. For example, the *gh* in the word *cough* creates an *f* sound in that particular word, whereas the same two letters remain silent in the word *although*.

(b) Prosodic Rules: These rules of communication inform us what kind of intonation, rhythm, volume, pitch, tempo and stress is to be used during a conversation. It relates to the paralanguage[7] of communication, which is the non-verbal component of verbal communication. By shaping these qualities, a speaker reflects his or her emotional state and can add more meaning or feeling to a message. When a speaker is speaking at a slow pace, low pitch and soft volume, he or she most likely is in a calm and relaxed state. On the contrary, by speaking at a fast pace, high volume and pitch and with extreme stress on words, a speaker is probably expressing anger or excitement to the recipient of the message.

(c) Semantics Rules: These refer to the relationship between the symbols and the things they refer to. These are definitions of words agreed-upon by the members of a particular speech community. These rules are specific to each language and to each group of symbols used in the language.

(d) Syntactic Rules: These rules refer to those rules that are used in formation of grammatically valid sentences in a language. Also syntactic rules are used in communication to describe how things are organized or arranged. The order of words is very important here because without the rules to govern how sentences are structured there would be no communication. In other words, there would be no understanding because there would be no common and basic forms for everyone to rely on.

(e) Pragmatic Rules: These rules are used in social communication. These depend on the context of the situations. Pragmatic rules include the use of languages for different purposes, changing language so that everyone within a group can understand following social rules. Pragmatic rules are important because they contain and control the key cultural and social factors that are used to govern social relationships. Along this line, these rules are also considered for maintaining relationships already formed between people, as well as the type of language used in such situations.

(f) Idiosyncratic Rules: These rules tell us what type of words and language are to be used when speaking with people. Different word choice is adjusted due to the relationships between the communicators, the context of the conversation, the content of the conversation and the cultural differences between communicators. For instance, **jargon** is a specialized language between certain people or professionals and it is one of those examples that can show how different words and language are to be used between people belonging to different professions and social groups. For example, doctors and lawyers use jargon relating to their professions when they communicate with each other, but adjust their word choices when they speak with patients or clients so that they do not confuse or create misunderstandings.

1.6 Concluding Remarks

Language is an enigma. It is the identity of a person. The impact of language (either spoken or written) depends on various things. Since meaning(s) of an utterance (e.g., *sentences, clauses, phrases, words,* etc.) does not depend entirely on its form, it depends heavily on its function in particular settings. That means, the meaning of what is said depends on various factors such as who says it to whom, when, where, in what purpose and with what effect. In other words, the context of situation, in which an utterance is made, becomes very important in deciding its overall meaning.

There are several factors that operate behind understanding meaning(s) of an utterance. The factors include **societal identity of participants** (i.e., relationship between speakers and hearers, their occupation, sex, age, socio-cultural status, ethnicity, etc.); **relationship of participants** (e.g., teacher-student, father-son, husband-wife, manager-labour, brother-sister, seller-buyer, doctor-patient, etc.); **nature of participation** (e.g., face-to-face, over telephone, conversation, in large group, in small group, in classroom, at public meeting, in gossip, in debates, in quarrels, etc.); **functions of speech events** (e.g., command, order, request, persuasion, mediation, appeasement, negotiation, etc.); **modes or mediums** (e.g., speech, writing, reading from written texts, scripts, gestures, etc.); **kinds of discourse** (e.g., epic poems, conversation, dialogues, political speech, religious sermons, reporting, dirty jokes, etc.); **topics of discourse** (e.g., science, art, economics, sports, politics, market, marriage, recent accident, illness, sex, art, cinema, etc.); **physical settings** (e.g., public place, private place, noisy place, quiet place, bus stand, classroom, seminar room, market place, etc.); **socio-cultural background** (e.g., Bengali to Bengali, English to English, English to Indian, Indian to Indian, Bengali to Tamil, etc.); **real-world knowledge** (e.g., everything under the sun which include common faith and beliefs of speakers and listeners who may come from same family, social, institutional, religious groups, etc.); and **speaker's intension** (e.g., narrative, descriptive, informative, reflective, provocative, influential, terrorising, etc.).

Notes and Comments

[1]   The term **idiolect** may be extended to synchronic level of analysis of the entire body of language a person has used such as *Shakespeare's language, Milton's language, Homer's language, Tagore's language,* etc.

[2]   French word *langage* (Italian *linguaggio* and Spanish *lenguaje*) is more general than other member of the pair, not only in that it is

used to refer to language in general, but also in that it is normally applied to the systems of communication, whether they are natural or artificial, human or non-human, for which English word *language* is generally employed.

[3] Because of this view Chomsky describes himself as a *rationalist*, rather than an *empiricist*.

[4] Since it is not possible to find out a single definition that can encompass all the features and properties of a natural language, it is, therefore, sensible to refer to the most well-known definitions given by scholars. Taken together, they can present a better picture of *language* than a single definition can aspire for.

[5] Within the purview of definition, *semiotics* becomes a co-discipline of study which is devoted to investigation of symbolic and communicative behaviour. The question that can concern us whether there is any single property or set of properties that distinguish natural languages from other semiotic systems.

[6] In some cases, however, it appears that the animal communication systems (i.e., ANICOMS) possess some partially developed characteristic features, which appear to be unique to human languages.

[7] Paralanguage refers to non-verbal elements of communication used to modify meaning and convey emotion. Paralanguage may be expressed consciously or unconsciously and it includes pitch, volume and in some cases, intonation of speech. Sometimes the definition is restricted to vocally-produced sounds. The study of paralanguage is known as **Paralinguistics**. The term is sometimes used as a cover term for body language, which is not necessarily tied to speech and paralinguistic phenomena in speech. The latter are phenomena observed in speech (Saussure's *parole*) but that do not belong to the arbitrary conventional code of language (Saussure's *langue*). The paralinguistic properties of speech play important role in human speech communication. There are no utterances or speech signals that lack paralinguistic properties, since speech requires the presence of a voice that can be modulated. Voice must have *some* properties and all the properties of a voice as such are paralinguistic. However, distinction between linguistic vs. paralinguistic applies not only to speech but to writing and sign language as well and it is not bound to any sensory modality.

Chapter 2
Design Features of Language

2.1 Introduction

Human being, according to Hockett (1960), is the only animal in this world who can communicate by means of abstract symbols. This unique ability, shares some features with the animal communication systems (ANICOMS) and due to this fact, it has been assumed that the human language might have arisen from the communication systems of the animals. Although various comparative methods of investigation have not yet been successful to trace the origin of languages; intimate investigations into the forms and functions of the human languages have succeeded to throw light on a set of features, which are found to be unique to a large extent in human languages.

There are solid empirical justifications behind the belief that all human languages of the world share certain common attributes—either explicitly or implicitly and which can be observed if the nature, function and form of the languages are analysed in close comparison. At the first sight some of the similarities appear so trivial that one will not try to look at them and consider them relevant. But these will become worthy of mention only when it is realized that some of the ANICOMS and certain human systems, other than language, lack them.

If we attempt to account for the origin of human language by considering that it has evolved from one of the kinds of communication systems used by animals, we must explain exactly how the feature of *duality of pattering* has arisen. The fact is that animals, in spite of very deliberate instructions, cannot learn human languages, which suggests that the difficulty is genetic due to which animals lack the very capacity of a language. Not even the 'brightest' animal has the 'intelligence' to master a human language, whereas all human beings, unless

33

pathologically afflicted, can learn to use a natural language and most of them can accomplish this learning in the first three to four years of their lives, to all intents and purposes. This implies that no animal is even as 'bright' as a four-year-old human child in linguistic matters.

The question that arises is one of explaining the genetic changes that have occurred in human beings. However, we need to decide exactly which of the characteristics of language are genetic and therefore *universal* and which are not genetic and therefore have to be learnt as individual languages are learned. Once again we understand how important it is in linguistic work to be concerned with the theoretical issues having to do with the nature of human languages.

The investigations as well as the frame of reference have claimed that if all natural languages are compared with each other, they can exhibit certain identical features, which are not attested in the ANICOMS—not even in case of the hominoids like gibbons and great apes, who are considered to be man's closest living relatives. These features are, in general, identified as **design features**[1], since these are the basic features of the human languages and are rarely observed in the ANICOMS or machines.

The design features listed in this chapter are found to be present in every human language on which we have reliable information. Interestingly, it has been noted that the ANICOMS may possess one or two of the features found in human languages, but there is no communication system in any animal, which is endowed with all the features present in human languages. In the following sections of this chapter we have discussed all the sixteen design features of human language in the light of Hockett (1960), Greenberg (1963), Lyons (1968) and Wardhaugh (1977) and others and have tried to show how ANICOMS lack in some of these features.

2.2 Vocal-Auditory Channel

This signifies that a human language is a systematic organisation of sounds and vocal symbols, which are produced by a system known as the **speech production mechanism** and perceived through another system known as the **auditory system**. The transfer of vocal sounds produced through the speech production mechanism and received through the auditory system requires an unbroken channel through which sounds can reach to the auditory system for reception. The sounds produced from a human mouth with the assistance of various organs-of-speech also require a unique coordination of some of the organs-of-speech in production of speech sounds, as well as ask for a medium through which they can reach to the ear of a listener for conveying some meaningful messages. Since human language is primarily vocal in nature, it is made up of some discrete sounds, which can be produced by the organs-of-speech a normal human being possesses.

The vocal auditory channel is perhaps the most obvious and distinctive feature of human language, as the basic linguistic communication of humans is vocal-auditory. In case of ANICOMS, we can come across the systems of communication that use channels such as *gestures, smells, body movements*, etc. It has been also observed that some animals have a communication system, which is auditory but not vocal in the true sense, as it happens in case of crickets; while some other animals use the *kinetic-tactile channel* as it happens in case of *bee-dance*. According to Hockett (1960) the vocal-auditory channel has certain advantages for the human beings as it can leave much of their body free for other activities that can be simultaneously carried on at the time of speaking[2].

2.3 Broadcast Transmission and Directional Reception

This refers to the feature that all linguistic signals produced vocally is open to be transmitted, broadcast and received from all directions. These properties are the immediate consequences of the nature of sound of our binaural hearing system and of the mobility of sound, which are linked to vocal- auditory channel. In fact, directional reception is the general rule of sound except some occasional masking where the sender may try to obstruct the spread of sound in certain directions.

In ANICOMS, this is also observed in some species, where the barking of dog or the howling of jackals are also received by other dogs and jackals and are responded in equal manner. However, for certain species, it is mostly one directional. A fine example of the kind is found in a field full of crickets, where locating a particular cricket from its call is difficult, even for another cricket.

Broadcast transmission and directional reception carry some advantages as well as some disadvantages. A warning cry of a monkey may tell all the members of its group about the location and direction of a predator; at the same time, it may warn the predator as well as can inform the predator where the prey is[3].

2.4 Rapid Fading

All linguistic symbols produced orally are evanescent (i.e., the moment these are produced they fade). To hear what some one says we must be within earshot at the right time and place with proper attention. Although normal speeches and utterances fade very quickly, spoors and trails take more time to fade as these fade usually slowly.

The feature of *rapid fading* is treated as a consequence of vocal-auditory channel. It implies that the messages which are already transmitted do not clutter up the channel as well as do not impede the transmission of new ones (as it happens, sometimes, when several people start talking together at the same place in same speed and volume). Thus emergent speech signals can easily get through the ears of the listeners. On the other hand, it implies that the import of a vocal message has to be stored only internally by the receiver, if at all it is to be stored anywhere. It takes considerable amount of 'attention span' or 'attention time' on the part of human hearers to take in a long and involved sentence, when measured on the general scale used in ANICOMS. The evolution of the capacity for such an attention span has been naturally conditioned by the feature of *rapid fading* of vocal-auditory communication system and it has been related to the development of *displacement* as well as to mono-linguistic matters such as *tool carrying* and *tool making*. In case of the ANICOMS, animal tracks and spoors often persist for a while for its proper reception and recognition.

Rapid fading is not an 'incidental' property of human language, because it registers a long and lasting consequence in the growth of human life and civilisation. When it became necessary to preserve the speeches produced by speakers, it indirectly led to the invention and development of writing system, which was, to a large extent, successful in restoring the content or the message embedded within speech. Thus, the invention of writing system as a reliable and comparatively permanent means of speech representation has brought in a great revolution in the history of mankind.

2.5 Interchangeability

The feature signifies that a human being who uses a language for the purpose of communication can both send and receive any permissible message within that communication system. It means an individual can both be a producer and a receiver of the same linguistic message.

There is no distinction about the use of language based on the social or demographic variables such as *sex, age, ethnicity, education* or *race*. A human not only produces a speech signal, but also receives it at the time of production of the same. Even if a hearer is not present within the immediate context of production of a speech sound, the man who produces it can also hear it.

This feature is not always present in all ANICOMS. For instance, among some species of crickets, only the male crickets can chirp and both the male and female crickets can respond to the chirping. Gibbons and bees can produce and receive signals, but in case of some birds, only the male birds can produce calls while their female counterparts cannot. Also some fish have unique sex-related types of communication, which are highly specific either to the male members or to the female members. In these cases, the calls and patterns of communication are not interchangeable between the sexes.

2.6 Complete Feedback

A human transmitter produces and receives linguistic signals. At the same time he can perceive what he transmits and can make necessary corrections if he makes error. Although an individual speaker of a language can produce any linguistic message he can understand, in case of communication between a human mother and her infant, neither of them is very much apt to transmit the characteristic signals or to manifest the typical responses of the other. Even then, the speaker of a language hears, by total feedback, everything of linguistic relevance in what he himself says. Complete feedback becomes important in the context when it makes possible the so-called internalisation of communicative behaviour that constitutes at least a major portion of the process of 'human thinking'.

In case of ANICOMS, due to some pathological reasons, in some varieties of *kinetic-visual communication*, as it is noted in courtship dance of *sticklebacks*, the sender of the message cannot always perceive some of the crucial features of the signal being emitted. Since the characteristic courtship motions of the male and female *sticklebacks* are different, neither can act out these actions appropriate to the other member. Female *stickleback* produces a red glow in her eyes and abdomen when she is ready for mating. Although the male member receives this signal and can respond accordingly, the female member is not aware about this change triggered biologically. That means the female *stickleback* does not see the colour of her own eye and abdomen that are crucial in stimulating the male.

2.7 Specialisation

This feature implies that in linguistic communication an individual does not need to have total physical involvement in the act of communication. He does not need to stop what he is doing to make a vocal response, nor does the response need to be totally determined by stimulus. An individual can talk while engaged in activities totally unrelated to the subject under discussion. He can talk about difficult actions he has to do to accomplish his goal while doing things that are not related to the topic. For instance, a man can talk about his school days while repairing a machine he uses.

In ANICOMS, a communicator is completely involved physically in the act of communication process itself. For instance, when a bee communicates through dance, it is totally involved in the act of dancing. Similarly, a male *stickleback* will not court a female unless her abdomen is distended with roe. Distension here becomes an essential part of her signal to the male. However, deviations of this feature are observed in case of wild animals. For instance, Washoe, the chimpanzee, could 'speak' and play at the same time, but Sarah, another chimpanzee, was more wholly involved in communication when she was communicating, mainly because she was a laboratory animal whereas Washoe was brought up in a much more homelike environment[4].

2.8 Semanticity

It indicates that language is used to mean something. It is not just 'sound and fury', but has content embedded in it. The linguistic signals produced by humans function to correlate and organise the life of a speech community because there are inherent associative links between the signal elements and the features observed in the external world. While some linguistic forms have denotative and referential functions, other linguistic forms have connotative functions. The whole world of **symbols** (i.e., language) is used regularly to convey ideas and information in human societies. People, by their own efforts and talents, have developed this world of symbols by which they exchange ideas and information about the material world around them in spite of detaching themselves from it completely. One can think of *fire* or *water* by these words without having the materials present physically before him[5].

In a semantically appropriate communicative system, the links between the message elements and their meanings can be arbitrary or non-arbitrary. In case of human languages, links are mostly arbitrary. For example, the word *salt* is not salty or granular; *dog* is not 'canine'; *whale* is a small word for a large object; *micro-organism*, on the contrary, is a large word for a tiny particle. Since meaningful human language carries a message, it triggers a particular result. It does so because there are relatively fixed associations between the elements in language (e.g., words) and the recurrent features or situations of the world around us. For example, the English word *salt* means salt, not sugar or pepper. A picture, on the other hand, looks like what it is a picture of.

Theoretically there is no relation between a word and its meaning, but the conventions of implication between the two continue for a certain period of time in each language. This convention or system changes with the change of time, context, or place. The signals at the crossing of roads have a 'meaning' for the movement of the vehicles and people. The signal of *red light* denotes 'stop' whereas that of *green light* denotes 'move'. But these meaning are not the natural meaning of the lights. The meaning is imposed on them by people to give some information to the passers by. It is totally conventional. If we decide from tomorrow that the implication of the lights will be quite contrary from the present one, there will be no difficulty once the people know the change of the system. So the *red light* has originally no meaning, so does the *green light*.

Some of the ANICOMS also possess *semanticity*. In case of *bee-dance*, a bee will dance faster if the source of nectar, it is reporting, is closer to the hive; or it will dance slower, if the source of nectar is located far away. The calls of the gibbons also possess certain amount of *semanticity*. They have a separate call for danger, although the hidden meaning of the call is broader and mostly vague than being specific and particular. The distension by roe of abdomen of the female *stickleback* is a part of an effective signal, but it does not 'stand for' something else. Similarly, the panting of dogs does not exhibit *semanticity*. It is not a signal meaning that the dog is hot; it is just a part of being hot.

2.9 Arbitrariness

This feature refers to the unpredictability of human language as there is no connection between a symbol and an object it refers. That means there is no permanent relation between a word we use and the item it denotes. Although it appears to be disadvantageous for language to be arbitrary, in practicality, it has many advantages as it opens a scope for communicating anything and everything by arbitrary use of language symbols. As there is no predictability in many of its characteristics, there is hardly any inherent connection between a symbol and an object. In fact, the relation between a linguistic symbol and its denotation in a language is independent of any physical or geometrical resemblance between the two and it is entirely based on norms and rules of a particular language community. So the relationship between a symbol and an object is destined to be 'arbitrary' rather than 'iconic'. The relation between a landscape painting and the landscape is iconic, whereas the relation between the word *landscape* and the landscape itself is arbitrary. There are, however, a few exceptions to this feature that include the traces of sound symbolism and onomatopoeic words.

Since arbitrariness is an important property of language, let us see how it works. The smallest units of words are called phones or phonemes. A word is formed by arranging these phonemes in certain patterns. The phonemes have no meaning of their own but a word has. In Bengali when we say $k\bar{a}k$ we can understand that this word denotes a bird which is the meaning of this word. But the word is formed by arranging the phonemes (k +ā+ k), which has no meaning at all. In Hindi, it is *kāuvā* or in English it is *crow*. That means the relation between the word $k\bar{a}k$ and the bird it denotes is not natural or iconic. It is completely arbitrary and conventional as decided by the speakers of the community. If there would have been any natural relationship between the two then there would have been a single word in all the languages to denote it. But we know that a single thing has different names in different languages. So words have no meaning of their own but the meaning is imposed on them by the people. Another example is *water*. It is *jal* in Bengali, *pāni* in Hindi, *water* in English, *tonnir* in Tamil, *wasser* in German and *udaka* in Sanskrit.

The ANICOMS, on the contrary, are mostly iconic. For instance, *bee-dance* is iconic because it directly represents the subject matter. A direct connection exists between the dance itself and the source of nectar, amount of nectar and the direction of the source. We consider most of the ANICOMS to be iconic, because these systems themselves are quite limited both in the number of calls available and the uses made of the calls. If we go to search for similar iconicity in human language, we cannot find it except in some mathematical or geometrical notations.

The number system of most of the human languages appears to be iconic: *one, two, three, four, five, six, seven.... ten...thousand* and so on, not *one, one-one, one-one-one, one-one-one-one...* and so on. *Four* is not four times as long as *one*.

2.10 Discreteness

Discreteness refers that human language makes use of discrete elements, e.g., phonemes and morphemes, not continuous waves. It is digital, not analogue, in nature. An utterance in a language must differ from other utterances of the same length by at least a whole phonological feature. Linguistic utterances can never be indefinitely similar to each other. Although human vocal organs can produce a huge variety of sounds, in a language, only a relatively small set of sounds is actually used and the differences between these sounds are functionally absolute. For example, the words *kill* and *gill* are different to our ear only at one point. If one produces a syllable that deviates from normal pronunciation of *kill* in the direction of that of *gill*, he is not producing still a third word, but just saying *kill* (or perhaps *gill*) in a noisy way. The hearer compensates it as far as he can on the basis of context, or otherwise, fails to understand. Thus the feature of *discreteness* is the elementary signalling unit of a language, which contrasts with the use of sound effects by way of vocal gesture. There is, however, a continuous scale of degrees to which one may raise voice in anger or lower it to signal confidentiality.

In ANICOMS, *bee-dance* is not a discrete, but a continuous process. In any way, it cannot be broken into separate discrete elements and thereby elements can be assigned separate meanings. Since a continuous semantic system is necessarily iconic, *bee-dance* is the repertory of possible dances constituting a two-fold continuum. This signifies that in ANICOMS, at least, the semantics in a continuous semantic system must be iconic rather than arbitrary.

2.11 Displacement

This design feature of language refers to the ability to speak not only about what is happening at the moment and place of talking, but also about other situations, past and future; real, unreal, or imagined matters. It can even be used to talk about the language itself. We can talk about the electronic parts catalogue while we are playing cards and without ever seeing one. Only human beings indulge in complicated sessions of questioning and answering, talk about talking and even, they can invent a **metalanguage** with which they can talk about a language. The utterances in a human language can be freely displaced or not. Due to this feature planning is not impossible and fictions, speculations, literature and science, are possible.

In contrast to other animals, humans have a sharp sense of the past and the future. A gorilla, for example, cannot tell his fellows about his parents, his adventures in the jungle, or his experience of the past, but a human can easily do. That means the use of language to talk about the things other than 'the here and now' is a characteristic of human languages. Displacement is thus the ability of human beings to convey a meaning that can easily transcend our immediately perceptible sphere of space and time.

In ANICOMS, the majority of animals cannot use their communication systems as humans can use their language, even though recent research has suggested that a bee can direct other bees to a food source. This implies that the communication system of bees also possesses this feature, although in a very limited fashion. Of course, bees communicate the fact they have found a source of nectar when they are not in the presence of that source, but they do this immediately on returning to the hive. They do not dance about the source of nectar they had discovered on previous occasions, nor do they speculate about their future discoveries. The food calls of a gibbon result from his direct contact with food and it is made in the presence of the food. A gibbon never makes a call about something he had eaten last year, or what he will eat after a week. However, Washoe, the chimpanzee, was able to a certain extent, to express many of her needs and desires for food and entertainment. To that extent the 'language' she used showed displacement.

Although some animals seem to possess abilities appropriating to those of displacement, they lack the freedom to apply these to the new contexts. The dance of the honey-bee indicates the locations of rich deposits of food to other bees. This ability of the honey-bee corresponds to *displacement* in human language, except for a lack of variation. The bee frequently repeats the same patterns in its dance, whereas humans are able to invent new contexts.

2.12 Productivity or Creativity or Openness

Another important design feature of language is *productivity*, which refers to the fact that language provides opportunities for sending messages that have never been sent before as well as for understanding novel messages. With this feature a human can have the capacity to say things that have never been said or heard before and yet to be understood by other speakers of the language. Human language is open or productive, in the sense that one can coin new utterances by putting together pieces familiar from old utterances, assembling them by the patterns of arrangement also familiar in old utterances.

To understand the nature of human language, we need to understand the multiple ways and means human beings use for information exchange. Each means has some traits of language, but still it is not the language. The *body movement, facial expression, gesture, signals, face movement, eye movement*, or other activities can convey information, but these are all highly specified and confined. Here is the difference between these means and a language. The red or green signal at the crossing of the street is also a 'language' but with bound function. It can inform a passer by to stop, to wait, or to move. It cannot convey anything more than these three specified actions. Human language, on the contrary, has *productivity* or *creativity* through which a man can produce innumerable number of sentences not used or heard before. The grammatical properties of language (e.g., *phonetic, morphemic, lexical,* etc.) are limited but the ability for formation of novel sentences is unlimited.

Then what is there behind this unlimited productivity of human language out of limited grammatical properties? Some say it is the **analogical creation** as *I eat* or *I drink* or *I sleep* can be created following the method of *I do*. When we learn a foreign language, we do not necessarily learn all the forms of that language, but we learn it by analogy. We say *I played* or *I worked* or *I cooked* or *I *singed* or *I go-ed* following *I walked*. But modern linguists have proved that language is not an analogical creation but a complex structure controlled by linguistic rules of various types. If a person can learn these linguistic rules, he or she can produce unlimited number of sentences using these rules.

In ANICOMS this feature is highly restricted and closed. The call system of gibbons lacks *productivity* as they draw their calls from a fixed repertoire, which is rapidly exhausted and which disallows any possibility of novelty. If a gibbon makes a vocal sound, it is one or another of a small finite repertory of familiar calls it has genetically inherited from its ancestors. The gibbon call system can be characterised as a closed system. Also, the communication system of most other forms of life is usually non-productive. The *bee-dance*, however, does have certain amount of *productivity* in that it can be used to communicate about the nectar sources within a few miles of the hive in any direction. But the messages about such sources are the only kind of message that can be communicated through the *bee-dance*. Bees cannot communicate about their feelings, people, animals, hopes, failures and so on. Washoe's system of communication was to certain extent productive as she could 'say' some kinds of things. Sarah's system was much less productive, since she was required only to respond to the experimenter, not to initiate exchanges.

2.13 Cultural Transmission

Cultural transmission refers to the fact that the details of a linguistic system have to be learnt anew by each and every individual speaker. Since the ability of using language is not biologically transmitted through generations, it has to be acquired through a rigorous process of language learning. The systems and conventions of a language are passed down through the generations by teaching and learning and not through any genetic mechanism (i.e., germ plasma). Genes have an important role in supplying the potentiality for learning a language and probably it is a generalised feature of humans, since no non-human can learn a human language in spite of their long exposure to a human society enriched with language. On the other hand, a human can hardly be prevented from acquiring a language if he or she is exposed to a particular language society.

Although humans have a genetic capacity for learning a language, which language an individual will learn definitely depends on a particular linguistic environment the individual is given an exposure. That means learning a language is a culturally controlled fact, not a genetically controlled feature. In essence, human genes carry the capacity to acquire a language and probably also a strong drive toward such acquisition but the detailed conventions of any one language are transmitted extra-genetically by learning and teaching with proper exposure to a particular linguistic environment.

While a human being has to learn these grammatical rules to learn a language, animals just simply acquire their linguistic ability by birth.

A child of Russian parents cannot learn Russian by birth. He has to learn it sincerely. If he is brought up in China he will learn the Chinese language, not Russian. So language, the greatest gift of human civilisation and the most powerful tool of the human society, has to be learned through rigorous practice and sincere effort. In the first few years of his life a child has to learn a language by rigorous practice and by the age of five or six, the child becomes quite efficient in comprehending and using his language. This quality of language is called **cultural tradition** or **cultural transmission**.

On the other hand, ANICOMS are genetically transmitted, since these are completely determined by the genetic structure of the animals. Even minor variations in ANICOMS result from small genetic differences rather than from their learning. The uniformity of sounds produced by a particular animal species, whatver the species it may be, is so great that genetics must be responsible for it. If a particular animal does not develop its characteristic communication system, the cause may be inevitably either pathologic or a lack of triggering, i.e., it is either a genetic or maturational deficiency.

All the animals have their own unique system of communication, which is identical to other animals belonging to the same species. Barking, howling, chirping, growling as well as *bee-dance* is genetic. All kinds of gibbon call are mutually intelligible to each and all gibbons no matter where they are born and reared. No chimpanzee has learnt its system of communication from another chimpanzee, it is derived genetically. No dog that lives in India barks in a different way from the dog that lives in America, Alaska, or Antarctica. It was of great interest for the researchers to see whether the chimpanzee Washoe could communicate with her offspring in *American Sign Language* she has learnt through training. It has been found that the system she has acquired is just something to be used with human beings and not to be used to communicate with her offspring or co-members.

2.14 Duality of Patterning

This design feature of human language refers to the fact that human language contains two sub-systems: sound and meaning. In other words, all human languages have two levels: (a) the minimal units—the phonemes for speech and alphabets for writing, which do not have meanings of their own, and (b) the level of morpheme or words where the meaning emerges as a result of combination of the units from the first level. It is attested that with a limited set of phonemes or letters in the alphabet one can produce unlimited number of meaningful words and expressions. This feature is perceived as a unique feature that can differentiate human languages from ANICOMS.

With the help of this particular feature all the human languages are able to achieve economy in expression, as a discrete number of functional units of sound can be grouped and regrouped into units of meaning and then these units of meaning can again be grouped and regrouped into infinite number of sentences. These permissible groupings are called **tactical arrangements: (a) phonotactic arrangements** when these refer to possible sequence of sounds in words and **(b) syntactic arrangements** when these refer to the possible sequence of words or constituents for eliciting meanings.

Every human language has a phonological as well as a grammatical sub-system. By virtue of these systems a large number of minimum meaningful functional units (i.e., morphemes) are produced by arranging a small number of minimum meaningless but message-differentiating units (i.e., phonemes). This enables one to use a language in a very *economic* way for a virtually infinite number of linguistic constructions.

All human languages have a small and limited set of speech sounds. The limitation is mainly caused due to restricted capacity of our vocal organs and apparatus. These speech sounds are traditionally referred to as *consonants* and *vowels*. We cannot use isolated phonemes for communication, because isolated phonemes are, by themselves, meaningless. But we can assemble and reassemble these phonemes into larger linguistic units like morphemes and words, which have meaning, for the purpose of communication. Although our capacity to produce new phonemes is mostly limited, we coin new words, as our capacity to produce words is unlimited. For instance, consider the English words *apt, pat* and *tap*. These are distinct words having distinct meanings and these words are composed with three meaningless phonemes in different permutations and combinations[6].

The ANICOMS lacks *duality of patterning*, because no animal, even if it appears to possess it, does have it. The calls of gibbon or the calls of a monkey are actually discrete unitary calls and the barking of dog, is actually, an un-analysable whole. The linguistic systems taught to Washoe and Sarah (two chimpanzees) did not have this feature as it is usually interpreted. They had it insofar as the meaning units, the signs used in *American Sign Language* and the plastic symbols which were used on magnetic board, were, by themselves, composed out of another 'level' of units.

2.15 Prevarication

Human linguistic messages can be full of falsehoods. Also, these can equally be meaningless in the sense of logic. We can, through our fancy, assert that it is just a day's journey from earth to moon or that we can return to earth after our death if we like. Since this feature is not independent, it depends on other features like *semanticity, displacement* and *openness*. Without *semanticity*, any message is not available for testing its meaningfulness and validity; without *displacement*, situation referred to by a message must be always an immediate context so that a lie is instantly given away; and finally, without the feature of *openness*, meaningless messages can hardly be generated, although false ones are possible.

Prevarication is almost impossible in ANICOMS. Animals can hardly lie. It is an extremely rare event in animal world. In fiction or in our imagination, we can think of a situation where a chimpanzee is emitting a food call even when there is no food at all, but in reality, it is never observed in the call of a chimpanzee. Perhaps, however, one can imagine of a system with these three underlying properties (i.e., *semanticity, displacement* and *openness*) used by a species that had never lied. It should be, however, noted that without these features, the formulation of any hypothesis will become virtually impossible in human thinking process.

2.16 Reflexiveness

This feature refers to **metalanguage**—the act of using language to talk about language. That means we use a language to describe, analyse, investigate and use a human language. In human language, we can communicate about the communication itself—a unique feature of human language. This property largely rests on the feature like *openness* or *creativity*, i.e., circumstances and context. A tempting alternative to this property is *universality*, which implies that in human language we can communicate about anything.

Although the feature *reflexiveness* follows from the feature *universality*, the difficulty it generates is an empirical one. If there are indeed things which we cannot communicate about, the fact that we cannot communicate about them prevents us from recognising that they actually exist. The mechanism of *reflexiveness* and *openness*, in some ways or other, guarantees that we can communicate via language about anything that we are capable of thinking and experiencing, including the language itself.

This feature is hardly noted in ANICOMS. No animal is so far found to signal about the signal itself it makes. Honey bees dance about the place and direction of the source of nectar, but they cannot dance about their dancing.

2.17 Learnability

In case of human language it is observed that a speaker of one language can learn another language with some effort exerted in this direction. The relative ease with which a man can learn another language usually depends on the design feature called *cultural transmission* discussed above. It means a person can learn another human language if he or she is given proper training in that language or if he or she is exposed to that particular linguistic environment either by birth or by migration. Even without these conditions one can learn a second language if there is a need for it or if the person has a love for learning another language.

In case of ANICOMS it is generally observed that animals of particular species cannot use calls of other animals, although they can imitate their calls for some biological needs. Since there is hardly any flexibility for adaptation of others' call systems among the animals, there is no justification for discrediting animals for lacking this particular feature altogether. Animals learn their own communication signals through genetic inheritance as clearly manifested in *bee dancing, stickleback courtship, dogs barking* and others[7].

2.18 Concluding Remarks

The brief survey presented above shows that no ANICOM has all the features of human languages. Particularly it lacks in features such as *duality of patterning, learnability, cultural transmission,* etc., which are so central to human language. Also ANICOMS lack in the feature of *productivity,* which allows a human to generate 'infinite forms out of finite means'. On the other hand, features like *arbitrariness* and *symbolism* of human language appear to be less important, as some amounts of *symbolism* as well as some degrees of *arbitrariness* are also involved in ANICOMS.

The history of research into ANICOMS shows that the effort for teaching human language to animals has so far been partially successful (discussed in Chapter 8). An almost unbridgeable gap seems to exist between humans and animals in the kinds of systems that they use in communication. Attempts to train animals to respond to human language and to use what language items they learn meaningfully have not been successful because in each case the animal has been unable to bridge the duality gap. It has learned nothing more than to respond to words as whole units and certain combinations of words also as whole units. In ANICOMS, there is minimal *productivity* and little or no *duality in patterning*, since animals appear to have neither the articulatory possibilities, which humans do possess; nor the cognitive abilities, which make human language and the use of symbols possible.

Notes and Comments

[1]   Design features were first proposed by Hockett (1959), who initially included seven features in the paper *Animal Languages and Human Language*. However, after revisions, he settled for thirteen features and it was published in *Scientific American* (1960) as *The Origin of Speech*. Greenberg had extended this concept by adding more new features to make it a set of sixteen features and published it in *Universals of Language* (1963). This set of features, as revised by Greenberg, has been accepted as benchmark for differentiating human languages from the communication system of animals (ANICOMS). These are elaborated in Lyons (1968), Wardhaugh (1977) and others.

[2]   The most notable thing is that the design feature, namely, the *Vocal-Auditory Channel* excludes the written languages from the category *human language* and considers the spoken form of language the primary one over the written form. Moreover, it excludes the *drum signals* used by many aboriginal African tribes for communication.

[3]   In the modern world features like *broadcast transmission* and *directional reception* do not appear to be much important. But in the conditions that were prevalent during the ancient period, these properties were of high functional relevance as no one could ignore their relevance in the context of safety of life. These are the

49

parts of our heritage from pre-human times, which have conditioned our own evolution and of language. These are still relevant for, although their functional potentialities are hidden under special technological circumstances.

[4]   Specialisation is a general property of communication system of humans and animals. Investigators are hesitant to use terms 'system' and 'communication' to types of behaviour from which it is absent. It refers to the fact that bodily effort and spreading sound waves of speech serve no function except as signals. A dog, panting with its tongue hanging out, is performing a biological activity, since this is how a dog cools it off and maintains body temperature. A panting dog incidentally produces sound and thereby, informs others as to where he is and how he feels. But this information is nothing but a side effect.

[5]   Let us imagine that a man has seen a tiger in the forest near the mountain. How he can convey this message to his friends? To convey this information he just cannot carry the mountain or jungle or the tiger with him. He has to use some words which can easily carry the symbols of the elements he has seen.

[6]   Some recent investigators strongly suspect that a human language involves not just two; but at least three, major sub-systems: (a) phonemic, (b) morphemic and (c) sememic. The basic contrast is between one or more than one sub-system. A language deprived of duality will be extremely cumbersome, since each unit will have to differ holistically from the other. It is hard to imagine any species being able to handle or, at least, to evolve such a system.

[7]   In science fictions however, a writer can create a non-terrestrial species that can have a communication system like the human language in all respects. In that case the members of this species will learn a new language, besides their own language, but only with great effort similar to a human being who spends for learning a second language.

Chapter 3
Theories about Origin of Language

3.1 Introduction

Perhaps the biggest debate among the linguists and others about the origin of language is whether we can account for a language by using only the basic mechanisms of learning or whether we need to postulate some special built-in language devices for this. Scholars like Skinner (1968), who believed that language was a *learning-only mechanism*, argued that childhood conditioning or modelling can account for the complexities of a natural language. On the other hand, scholars like Chomsky (1959), Pinker and Bloom (1990), Pinker (1995) who are in support of **Language Acquisition Device (LAD)**, argue that the ease and speed with which children learn language requires something more[1].

From analysis of brain it is observed that in most mammals, except the human beings, both the hemispheres looked very much alike. Somewhere in humanity's early years, a few people possibly inherited a mutation that left one hemisphere with a limited capacity. Instead of neural connections going in every direction, they tended to be organised more linearly within brain. The left hemisphere could not relate to things in the usual full-blown multi-dimensional way. But surprisingly, that same diminished capacity proved to be very useful for ordering things linearly. And that is exactly what language needs. It needs the ability to convert fully dimensional events into the linear sequences of sounds and vice versa.

While it is certain that human speech has developed much before the advent of writing system, no one knows for certain how human languages originated. There are, however, some speculations as well as some theories which have tried to give explanation about the origin of human languages. Some of these speculations and theories are reported below. Many of these have traditional amusing names as the following speculations and theories show. After referring to the general history of the assumptions about the origin of language, we have discussed in brief the *Divine Theory*, the *Bow-Wow Theory*, the *Pooh-Pooh Theory*, the *Ding-Dong Theory*, the *Yo-He-Ho Theory*, the *Sing-Song Theory*, the *Oral-Gesture Theory*, the *Natural Selection Theory*, the *FOXP2 Speech Gene* and some other short theories related to this assumption.

3.2 The History

The general question of all ages is: when did language begin? Did it begin at the very beginning (4-5 million years ago) when the genus *Homo Sapiens* came into world? Did it start with the advent of the *modern man* (i.e., Cro-Magnon) some 1,25000 years ago? Could the Neanderthal man speak? Although he had a brain that was larger than ours, his voice-box appeared to be positioned much higher in his throat, like that of the apes. This has been an intriguing question for centuries, to which we have no complete answer. Even then the question still lingers: how did we get *language* which is so different from animal vocalisations (e.g., *barks, howls, calls, chirps, tweeters,* etc.)

It is noted that animals often make use of various physical signs, which point to what they can represent, but they cannot use symbols, which are arbitrary and conventional. While examples of physical sign include *sniffles* as a sign of an on-coming cold, *clouds* as a sign of rain, or a *scent* as a sign of territory; symbols include things like the words human uses. For instance, *dog, hund, chien, cane, perro,* etc. are the symbols that refer to the creatures so named, yet each one contains nothing in it by which it can directly indicate that particular creature. In addition, human language is a system of symbols, with several levels of organisation, such as *phonetics* (the sounds), *syntax* (the grammar) and *semantics* (the meanings).

An over-simplified history of human evolution has claimed that the *Homo sapiens* developed as a sub-division in the following stages from the hominoid family:

(a) Three million years ago we had split from the apes.
(b) Two million years ago the tool-using Homo called *Homo Habilis* (i.e., the handy man) emerged.

(c) One and half million years ago *Homo Erectus* (i.e., the upright man) came who was able to use fire.
(d) About three hundred thousand years ago the archaic *Homo Sapiens* (i.e., the archaic wise man) arrived, followed by modern humans – the *Homo Sapiens*.
(e) About fifty thousand years ago the *Homo Sapiens* started using not just stone but also other raw materials such as bone and clay. At this time paintings on cave walls started and living sites increased.

The puzzling characteristic features of grammar of a language, such as the sentence and phrase distinction and the organisation of inflection classes, may provide us clues about the prehistory of a language. When the *Homo Sapiens* led to changes in the vocal tract that favoured syllabically organised vocalisation, this made possible an increase in vocabulary which, in return, rendered advantageous and reliable syntax, whose source was the neural mechanism for controlling syllable structure. Several features of syntax make sense as by-products of characteristics of syllable (for example, grammatical subjects may be the by-products of onset margins). This scenario is consistent with evidence from biological anthropology, ape language studies and brain neurophysiology.

For generations one of the primary questions of mainstream linguistics has been to know how language has come into being or has been invented. Speculations are galore to reply this question. Some people have thought that human language was invented by our earliest ancestors who had genetic and physiological properties to develop complex sounds and organise these into meaning strings to from words and sentences. This theory is known as the **Monogenetic Theory** or **Monogenesis.**

On the other hand, the **Polygenetic Theory** or **Polygenesis** assumes that perhaps language was invented many times by many people at different points in time. Due to this reason, we can try to reconstruct the earlier forms of a language, but can go only a little far through the cycles of change before these have become so obliterate that any possibility of reconstruction becomes impossible. Scholars have argued that we can, at best, go back up to only ten thousand years or so, before the trail is lost for ever in wilderness. So we shall never know what was before this.

In the last century linguists developed a method known as the **Historical Reconstruction**, in which, based on linguistic evidences of modern languages one reconstructs the proto-forms of a language, which are not available today. Some scholars thought that by this process they would be able to trace out the linguistic evidences of the pre-historic periods, linguistic evidences of which are not available to us today. But this hypothetically reconstructed language, at best, can give the phonetic and morphemic patterns of nearly ten thousand years old. This speculation cannot go beyond that. So we have no tool in our hand to determine the origin of language.

Some other linguists imagined that language might have originated from the antique systems of communication and information exchange. To establish their proposition they have emphasised on the similarities observed between the main traits of non-human communication systems with that of the human languages. They have assumed that the calls, shouts and songs of animals might be the sources of human language.

If we agree with this view, then we may say that it is true that language is certainly the evolution of the system of information exchange. In that case the basic question is: what is that system? In the animal world there are some unique systems of communication among them. The bee, for instance, when finds a source of honey goes back to its hive and dances a particular type of dance by which it can convey to its fellow bees about the kind, direction and distance of the source. Gibbons, on the other hand, can give various calls, each one being different from the other and there is always a variety of time gap between the calls. Each call has different connotation, implication or significance to others belonging in the clan. The call about the presence of a predator is different from the mating call or the call for food. It is counted that gibbons living in Northern Thailand are able to produce nine different calls by which they can communicate among themselves.

The 'language' of animals is fundamentally different from that of humans because contrary to the human language, 'language' of animals is genetically inherited and acquired. Moreover, by these fixed number of calls the gibbons can exchange information about nine specific or different situations or events such as position of danger, attack of the predator, location of food, calling a partner for mating, or similar other events. Their 'language' is primarily a closed world confined within nine different calls, which is equally true for the languages of other animals. But human language is an open world free from any kind of confinement. We cannot say surely when and how the language originated but we can firmly say that when this closed world of calls

54

and hints unfolded into an open world only then human language was formed.

3.3 The Divine Theory

The origin of the Divine Theory may be traced in realms of human fears and limitations. Human beings, whenever encounter something they can not fully comprehend and thereby explain, attribute it to the God or some supernatural power. In most of the religious thoughts of the world, there appears to be a divine source that provides humans with language.

In order to discover the origin of language many queer experiments have been carried out in the history (e.g., the *Order of Psammetichus 600 BC or the James IV of Scotland 1500 AD*, etc.). However it appears that children with no access to human speech simply grow up with no language at all and this reality establishes the ground truth: No speech = No language.

In the early days of **philology** minds of the scholars were much occupied with the question of origin of human speech. Several scholars have advanced theories to explain the reason why a particular sound was chosen to express a particular concept and so on. The ancient peoples all ascribed their speech to the Gods. For instance, in India, *Sanskrit* was called the *devabhāṣā* (i.e., the language of God) and in Europe the legend of the *Tower of Babel* ascribed the origin and diversity of all the languages to the direct interference of God[2]. In ancient Greek, it was believed that Hermes[3], the great messenger of God, invented words and speech. Horace, too has described eloquent Hermes who brought language as a means of civilising primitive humans (Gera 2003: 117).

In the medieval age and perhaps even during the renaissance, scholars were highly unscientific towards the problems of origin and development of language. Many scholars were convinced and accepted Hebrew as the first language of the human world. They were more guided by their own religious faith and fanaticism rather than by their rational process of thinking. Some other scholars, who were more patriotic rather than rational, proposed their own mother tongues as the candidates for the status of the first language on earth. For instance, one of the Swedish scholars Andreas Kemke mentioned, *"In the Garden of Eden God spoke Swedish language"*[4].

Superstitions still work strongly behind the belief that human language is a divine blessing for the man on this earth. People are still highly enthusiastic to speculate that while some languages are 'good', some are 'bad' or while some languages are 'divine' some other languages are 'satanic'. There is also naïve belief that the languages, which are spoken today, may have originated in the beginning of the history. These are all wrong assumptions. The theory of divine creation is, no doubt, the most non-conflicting proposition; as it has very little to offer in scientific explanation for the origin of language. Even then, the indomitable curiosity among people is: how is the language originated?

The renaissance scholar Leibniz (1646-1716), who realised the futility of trying to relate all languages to Hebrew or to Biblical Hebrew, was interested in studying relationships among the languages and establishing a linguistic genealogy. So he encouraged his contemporaries to examine and describe the languages and on the basis of the *shared features* to establish a genealogy. He was more concerned with collecting linguistic evidences to identify closeness among the leading languages.

3.4 The Bow-Wow Theory

In this theory it has been assumed that language, at its initial stage of growth and development, began as imitations of natural sounds: *moo-moo, coo-coo, crash, clang, buzz, bang, ding-dong, drim-drum, meow-meow,* etc. Technically, this is referred to as **onomatopoeia** or **echoism** (also called **sound symbolism**). Since people do not know how language originated, as no scholars have ever been able to find out the mystery behind this, a group of scholars argued that language originated following the barking of dogs. This theory is known as the **Bow-Wow Theory** or **Onomatopoetic Theory**. According to this theory, language began when human ancestors started to imitate natural sounds which they found in nature around them. The first speech was onomatopoeic, which was marked by many echoic words such as *moo, meow, splash, cuckoo* and *bang,* etc. It also supposes that objects are named after the sounds they produce. Thus *cuckoo* in English or *miaou* in Chinese are the names of those animals, which produce these sounds. Similarly in Bengali, we get the name of a bird *ghughu,* because the bird sings in this manner. Children always name animals by the sounds they produce. In Bengali **baby talk**, dogs are called *bhau-bhau,* cows are called *hamba* and ducks are called *pyank pyank* because these animals produce these sounds, respectively.

However, this theory can explain only a small portion of the vocabulary of a human language. This theory, therefore, as stated by Max Mueller, "Goes very smoothly so long as it deals with cackling hens and quacking ducks, but round the poultry yard there is a dead wall and we soon finds that it is behind that wall that language really begins". It is true that only limited numbers of words are actually onomatopoeic in a language and these words vary from one language to another. For instance, a dog's bark is heard as *au au* in Brazil, *ham ham* in Albania and *wang, wang* in China. In addition, many onomatopoeic words are of recent origin and not all of these are actually derived from natural sounds.

3.5 The Pooh-Pooh Theory

This theory holds that human speech began with interjections—spontaneous expressions of pain (e.g., *Ouch!*), surprise (e.g., *Oh!*), excitement (e.g., *Wah!*) and many such human emotions. The believers of this theory have argued that interjectional sounds were the first prototypes of language, because all the interjectional sounds like *uh, ah, ouch, uff*, etc. come automatically in the human mouth first as a mode of expression. From these expressions the language has evolved after many methodical and systematic modifications and refinements. This theory (also known as **Interjectional Theory** or the **Tut-Tut Theory**) takes its stand on the psychological fact that the different perceptions excite different feelings and emotions in human mind and body and there are several appropriate sounds to express each one of the all human feelings and emotions. It has been argued that the word *fiend* is perhaps derived from the sound *fie*, which carries an expression of horror.

The main criticism against this theory is that no human language contains so many interjections that can be the sources of all the words available in a language. "The clicks, intakes of breath and other noises which are used in this way bear little relationship to the vowels and consonants found in phonology" (Crystal 1997). So, if we believe this theory to be true, we shall be on a very slippery ground because it is clear that the sounds accompanying different emotions are not the same for all the languages. Thus when the Englishman, being used to repressing his emotions, has a very limited set of interjections to rely upon, other speakers seem to have more interjections to express them. Although it is always possible to let the imagination run riot in search

57

Language and Linguistics

of a solution, this theory, however, sounds nearly impossible as it has no truth in it.

3.6 The Ding-Dong Theory

This theory, which was favoured by Plato and Pythagoras, maintained that human speech arose in response to the essential qualities of objects in the environment. The original sounds people made were supposedly in harmony with the world around them. Even scholars like Max Mueller have pointed out that there was rather a mysterious correspondence between sounds and meanings. While small, sharp, high things tend to have words with high front vowels in many languages, big, round, low things tend to have round back vowels. For instance, let us compare the phrase: *itsy bitsy teeny weeny with moon*, which is usually referred to as sound symbolism. Further extension of this theory claimed that there was a strong and inherent relationship between sound and meaning; and as a result of this, natural things and objects are named after the sounds they produced.

This theory, which is also nick-named as the **Pathogenic Theory**, tries to give some kinds of satisfactory explanations for a certain number of words. It observes that specific kinds of objects so affected the primitive man as to elicit from him or to make use of to bring out of him the correspondingly specific utterances (Max Mueller). The word *zigzag* in English as well as the modern form *jazz*, *dazzle* and such others may be cited as suitable examples. The Hindi word *jagmag* as well as a large number of Bengali *anukār* or *dhvanyātmak* words may come under this head. Also, some reduplicated forms, for the sake of emphasis, can come under this umbrella (e.g., *a big big man*).

It is true that there are onomatopoeic words in every language, i.e. words that echo natural sounds, for example: *cuckoo, splash, bang, thud, rattle, buzz, hum*, etc. However, the main limitation of this theory is that apart from some instances of sound symbolism and idiophone, there is hardly any persuasive and pervasive evidence, in any natural language, that can clearly establish an innate or internal connection between sound and meaning.

3.7 The Yo-He-Ho Theory

Another speculation about the origin of language is the **Yo-He-Ho Theory**, which argues that language has evolved from the grunts, groans and snorts evoked by heavy physical labour. This theory places the development of human language in a social context and states that language has originated in the need to co-ordinate physical efforts. Thus this theory tries to find out a relation between the labour of man and the sounds produced by them when they undertake labour. Language had begun as rhythmic chants, perhaps ultimately from the grunts generated in heavy work (e.g., *heave-ho!*). Linguist D. S. Diamond suggested that since these were perhaps the calls for assistance or co-operation accompanied by appropriate gestures, they may be related to *yo-he-ho* to *ding-dong*, as these words express heavy physical works such as *cutting, breaking, crushing, striking, pulling,* etc.).

It has been noted that whenever we do some heavy collective work, such as carry a palanquin, or row a boat, or pull a big block, etc. we produce some loud vocal sounds. It has also been observed that the verb roots of language express actions which can be performed by human beings. It is the habit with labourers, while doing a heavy bit of work, to utter loud sounds in unison. This undoubtedly lightens the mental fatigue accompanying bodily labour and bodily exhaustion. All sailors, for example, when hauling the anchor shout together *yo-he-ho* and this instance has been cited to explain the first syllable in *heave*. The theory, thus, tries to establish that the action itself is indicated by the sounds that accompany the action.

The basic limitation of this theory is that although physical notions and movements may account for some of the *rhythmic* features of a language, it does not go very far in explaining where words have come from.

3.8 The Sing-Song Theory

Famous Danish linguist Otto Jespersen (1922) has suggested that language might have originated from the sounds associated with love, play, laughter, courtship, cooing, emotional mutterings and especially, from song. Due to its uniqueness in proposition the theory is called as **Sing-Song Theory** or **La-La Theory**. Jespersen has assumed that, contrary to other theories, perhaps some of our first words were actually long and musical in form, rather than being short grunts, as many people had assumed, we started with. For Jespersen, the origin of language was an important question and therefore it should not be avoided in the study of language. He has opined that some clues might be found in the use of language by the infants or in the language of the proto-hominoids.

His expectation was that there might be some cues and hints within the meaningless babblings of new born babies that might help us to understand how language has originated and evolved[5].

Let us assume that there might be some clues in the languages of proto-hominoids. However, linguists have proved that a clan or community can be aboriginal but no language is aboriginal. The speech community we call 'aboriginal' may be backward in respect to technology, scientific discoveries and advancements, but their language is neither backward nor the under-developed one. As the nature of complexities observed in their languages is no less than that of the modern languages, there is hardly any possibility to get information from the language of the proto-hominoids[6].

Jespersen has argued that if we could trail back towards the past from the modern language, we would have seen that in the earlier stage, the language had some specific features, which have been diminished in the present stage. We could assume that those features, at that stage, were clearer and more universal. Those features would be our guide to reach to the earliest stage of the language. In this process we might reach to a stage which we might not call 'language' but could, perhaps, call the **proto-language**, which surely not originated from a void, it must have some material or content for its origin and growth. If we could determine that particular material wherefrom the 'proto-language' originated, we could find a path to trace the origin of language.

Jespersen has noticed that there were some sounds in the language, which were very difficult to utter. Gradually these sounds were either simplified or lost forever from the language. He has also noticed that the pitch, accent and tone are in the process of gradual loss from languages. In the older versions language structure was complicated; sentences were complex; words were structurally long and polysyllabic in form; and speech sounds were hard to articulate. He has assumed that all languages are becoming simplified with the progress of time as many of the complex features of language are made simple in new era. In the earlier period language was immature, non-formed and non-polished and the vocabulary was very small to express thoughts and ideas. Thus Jesperson had the assumption that perhaps language was started in the emotional outbursts, noises and bustles as well as in the sounds and cries of the proto-hominoids.

Modern scholars, however, declined to agree with the ideas of Jespersen, because whatever the distance we can trace back, proofs do not support the **Simplification Hypothesis** proposed by Jespersen. All the natural languages, however old or new they may be, are highly complex in nature and function. There is not a single old tribe or clan whose language was not fully developed. The more important thing is that we can trace back, at best, to ten thousand years following the procedure of Jespersen. It has been proved that those proto-hominoids, who, regarding the size of brain, were less developed than the modern man, were more advanced than apes, which appeared in this world nearly twenty million years ago. Modern archaeologists have also found some cultural evidences among the descendants of these hominoids[7]. Moreover, this theory fails to account for "the gap between the emotional and the rational aspects of speech expression" (Crystal 2005: 122).

3.9 The Oral-Gesture Theory

The supporters of the **Oral-Gesture Theory** (also known as **Ta-Ta Theory**) have proposed an extremely unique connection between physical and oral gestures involving a "specialised pantomime of the tongue and lips" (Paget 1930: 118). Richard Paget, influenced by the evolutionary theory of Darwin, believed that human body movements must have preceded human language. He argued that language began as an unconscious vocal imitation of these movements, like the way a child's mouth would move when it use scissors, or the tongue of the player sticks out when one tries to play guitar. This had led to language to be derived from gestures.

To establish his hypothesis Paget had developed in his book a new theory of language known as the **Oral-Gesture Theory.** According to him, human language must have started from gestures and every tongue position must, so he claimed, be a weakened bodily gesture. He had examined vowels and consonants in detail, taking many words and comparing their meaning with the gestures they convey. Finally, he came to very definite conclusions, such as, for instance, that a high tongue position or gesture—as he preferred to call it—was used for the words meaning little, small, or high (Jones 1935)[8].

The limitation of this theory can be observed in many of our physical gestures when we use body, hands, legs and face, etc. as means of non-verbal communication. These gestures were not used by the ancient people only; these are still being used by the modern man, even with their developed linguistic skills.

3.10 The Natural Selection Theory

The supporters of the **Natural Selection Theory** have argued that there is every reason to believe that language has been shaped by natural selection as it can be understood within orthodox **Synthetic** or **Neo-Darwinian Theory** of evolution (Pinker and Bloom 1990). These scholars have opined that "the only successful account of the origin of complex biological structure is the theory of natural selection, the view that the differential reproductive success associated with heritable variation is the primary organising force in the evolution of organisms" (Pinker and Bloom 1990). Although they did not directly claim that natural languages are definitely the products of natural selection, they have suggested that language may be the side effects of other evolutionary forces such as an increase in overall brain size and constraints of as-yet unknown laws of structure and growth.

These scholars have argued that human language, like other specialised biological systems, evolved by natural selection. Their conclusion is based on two facts that they think would be entirely uncontroversial: (a) language shows signs of complex design for the communication of propositional structures and (b) the only explanation for the origin of organs with complex design is the process of natural selection. Although distinguished scientists from a wide variety of fields and ideologies have tried to cast doubts on this orthodox Darwinian account about the evolution of a biological specialisation for grammar, upon close examination, none of the arguments appear to be quite compelling.

Some of the physical aspects of humans that make the production of speech possible or easier are not shared with other creatures. For instance, human teeth are upright and roughly even in height; human lips have an intricate muscle interlacing them, human mouth is relatively small which can be opened and closed rapidly and contains a very flexible tongue. The human larynx (or voice box) is special as well as the pharynx above the vocal cords which can act as a resonator for any sounds produced there. The human brain is lateralised and has specialised functions in each of the two hemispheres. The functions which are analytic (e.g., tool-using and language) are largely confined to the left hemisphere of the brain for most humans. Moreover, all the languages require the organising and combining of sounds or signs in specific constructions.

The supporters of the **Natural Selection Theory** advocated that there is a wealth of respectable new scientific information relevant to the evolution of language that has never been properly synthesised. Computational theory of human mind, generative grammar, articulatory and acoustic phonetics, study of dynamics of diachronic change and the developmental psycholinguistics can profitably be put into a combination with recent discoveries of molecular, archaeological and comparative neuro-anatomical sciences and with strategic modelling of evolution using insights from the evolutionary theory and anthropology. It is certain, as the supporters of this theory have argued that there are definitely many questions about the evolution of language that we will never get answer for. But we can be optimistic that there are insights to be gained, if only the problems are properly posed.

3.11 The Human Language Gene

Human beings have a deep desire to communicate with animals as it is evident from the way people converse with their dogs, enjoy myths about talking animals or devote lifetimes to teaching chimpanzees how to speak. A delicate, if tiny, step has now been taken towards the real thing: the creation of a mouse with a human gene for language[9]. The gene, known as **FOXP2**, was first identified in the year 1998 as the cause of a subtle speech defect in a large London family, half of whose members have difficulties with articulation and grammar[10]. All those people who were affected with this kind of linguistic deficiency inherited a disrupted version of the gene from one parent. FOXP2 attracted the attention of evolutionary biologists because other animals also possess the particular gene and the human version differs significantly in its DNA sequence from those of mice and chimpanzees, just as might be expected for a gene sculpted by natural selection to play an important role in language.

Scientists at the *Max Plank Institute for Evolutionary Anthropology,* Germany have now genetically engineered a strain of mice whose FOXP2 gene has been swapped with that of human gene. The upgraded mice squeaked somewhat differently from plain mice and were born with subtle alterations within their brain structure. However, since mice and human beings are largely two distant cousins – their last common ancestor lived some seventy million years ago – the human version of the FOXP2 gene evidently was not able to exert a transformative effect on the mice.

However, the most notable finding was that the possession of the human version of FOXP2, in fact, changed the sounds that mice use to communicate with other mice, as well as other aspects of their brain function. A large team of researchers studied three hundred features of the *humanized mice* and observed that FOXP2 gene, whose protein product switches on other genes, becomes important during the development of embryo and plays an active part in constructing many tissues, including lungs, stomach and brain. The gene is so vital that the mice in which both copies of the gene are disrupted die after a few weeks. The team also found that the human version of FOXP2 gene seemed to substitute perfectly for the mouse version in all the mouse's tissues except for the brain.

In a region of the brain called 'basal ganglia' (known in human beings to be involved in language), the *humanised mice* grew nerve cells that had a more complex structure. Baby mice utter ultrasonic whistles when removed from their mothers. The humanised baby mice, when isolated, made whistles that had a slightly lower pitch, among other differences. It has been argued that putting significant human genes into mice is the only feasible way of exploring the essential differences between people and chimps—our closest living relatives. There are about twenty million DNA differences between the genomes of humans and chimps, but most make no physical difference. To understand which DNA changes are important, the genes must be put into another species. As there is no good way of genetically engineering chimps, even if it were ethically acceptable, the mouse is the choice for text.

Researchers have also taken a careful first step towards understanding the role of FOXP2 in the development of the brain, as it has been observed that the gene seemed to have a great effect on pathways of neural development in mice. Such studies show many small effects from the human FOXP2, which fit with the view that FOXP2 plays a vital role in language, probably with many other genes. According to some studies, there are more than twenty thousand genes in the human genome and only a few are more fascinating than the FOXP2—a gene that underlies and controls the faculty of human speech. Although all animals have an FOXP2 gene, but the human version differs at 2 of its 740 units from that of other animals, mostly chimpanzees, suggesting that this tiny evolutionary fix may hold the key to know why people can speak and chimpanzees cannot.

A team of researchers at the *University of California, Los Angeles*, has now completed a parallel experiment in which they had put the chimp version of the FOXP2 into human neurons to observe its effects of human. The human neurons are actually living in laboratory glassware and not in a human brain. They gave a snapshot of FOXP2 only at the cellular level to find that FOXP2 was a maestro of the genome. The gene does not do a single thing but rather controls the activity of at least hundred and sixteen other genes. Like the conductor of an orchestra, the gene quiets the activity of some other genes and summons a crescendo from others. Surprisingly, the chimp version of the gene had a more forceful effect in the human nerve cells than did the human version[11].

Several of the genes under FOXP2's thumb show signs of having faced recent evolutionary pressure, meaning that they were favoured by natural selection. This also suggests that the entire network of genes has evolved together in making language and speech a human faculty. Moreover, some of the genes in network of FOXP2 have already been implicated in diseases that include disorders of speech, confirming its importance in these faculties.

According to the researchers, the FOXP2 network is certainly not the only set of genes that is involved in language, as it has been observed that the FOXP2 is equally active on both sides of human brain, whereas the language faculty is asymmetric. Therefore, they need to study other genes in the FOXP2 network so that they can use FOXP2 as a lever to get a view of the molecular machinery in a biological language circuit. In spite of several limitations in the research, it has been argued that the new finding from the FOXP2 network can be treated as important discovery that can provide a starting point for future studies of the molecular basis of human language and human evolution.

3.12 Some Other Speculations

There are other theories or speculations regarding the origin of language and most of these are skewed in observation and fallacious in argumentation. As all these speculations have serious flaws, none can withstand close scrutiny of present knowledge about the structure of language and about the evolution of our species (Farb 1993: 22). Some of the theories are summed up below.

The **Hey-You-Theory** suggested that we always needed an interpersonal contact, which has played a pivotal role in the birth of language. Language began as sounds to signal both identity (e.g., *here I am!*) and belonging (e.g., *I am with you!*) of speakers with the addressers. We may also cry in fear asking help from others; become angry to express anger to others; or can seek help from others whenever we are hurt by external factors. This theory is more commonly called the **Contact Theory**, because language was first developed as a means of establishing contact with others.

The **Eureka Theory** suggested that perhaps language was consciously invented by humans. Perhaps some human ancestors had the idea of assigning arbitrary sounds to mean certain external things. Clearly, once the idea was germinated, it caught on like wild-fire!

The **Mama Theory** suggested that human language began with the easiest syllables attached to the most significant objects.

The **Pop Theory** imagined that language has just popped into existence all at once at a particular point of time of evolution of human civilisation.

Finally, the **Hocus Pocus Theory** assumed that language may have had some roots in a sort of magical or religious aspect in the lives of our ancestors. Perhaps ancient people began using language by calling out to game animals with magical sounds, which became their names.

3.13 Concluding Remarks

In spite of so many theories and speculations, the question about the origin of language still remains unsolved. Although these assumptions have, no doubt, speculated some possibilities but each one is incomplete and not supported with evidences and proofs. One of the major problems among even the most responsible attempts to speculate about the origins of language has been that the investigators ignore the wealth of specific knowledgebase about the structure of grammar discovered during the past thirty years. As a result of this linguistic competence has been equated with cognitive development, leading to confusions between the evolution of language and the evolution of thought. Also, it has been expediently equated with the activities that leave tangible remnants, such as tool manufacture, art and conquest. Even if we combine all the theories and speculations together, their collective force also fails to explain clearly the whole of the roots of a natural language. Surely there will be many different explanations and counter arguments as there are mental processes which accompany articulate speech.

On the other hand, when scholars argue that the proto-hominoids have created sounds at the time of their works and therefore these sounds can be considered as the first specimens of language, it is clearly understood that this will fail to explain all the facts and features of a natural language. Since our knowledge about the history of the proto-hominoids is incomplete as well as sparse, it will be foolish to say anything about the origin of the language. Whatever is known so far about the proto-hominoids, it is understood that the proto-hominoids had, as other animals had, some calls with their unique sequences, varieties and networks. The number of these calls was limited and properties like *duality of patterning, cultural transmission, arbitrariness, creativity* and *specialisation* were not present in it. At that stage it was **proto-language** and was used for information exchange among them.

The language possibly originated from this *proto-language* when the closed net of the *proto-language* was opened and when the quality of creativity was merged with it. So there was no divine power or blessings of God behind the origin of human language. We shall never know how human languages originated as it was a process happened millions of years ago, but what we know is that language is an open net which evolved from the close net of the proto-hominoids. The evolution of language from the *proto-language* is the greatest event in the cultural history of the mankind.

All these problems regarding the origin of language led modern linguists not to spend time in the imaginative speculations as well as inspired many of them to keep this topic out of their linguistic discussions[12]. In 1886, the *Societe de Linguistique de Paris* passed a resolution barring linguists forming theories about the origin of language, as speculations about the origin of language have been one of the common issues of discussion throughout the 19th century Europe without any conclusive results. This resolution, in this case at least, had the useful result of channelling the energies of investigators towards gathering of more and better information about languages as these are used today. The subsequent progress in understanding the workings of language has been truly remarkable as various related fields have made long strides in the last one century. In the light of these developments there should be no excuse for reopening the issue about the origin of human speech.

Notes and Comments

[1]   The debate between the behaviourists and the generativists appears to be real only for those who prefer to take one or the other of these extreme views. It, however, seems to most that neither of the arguments is the answer. Then the question is: is

there some special neural mechanism for language which is not in the sense of a LAD? We are yet to know the answer to this question.

[2]   This, in paradoxical sense, holds certain amount of truth in the sense that the language is the direct result of God's greatest gift to the whole mankind – the human mind.

[3]   Hermes was a great messenger of gods in Greek mythology and additionally as a guide to the Underworld. Hermes was born on Mount Kellina in Arcadia. An Olympian god, he is also the patron of boundaries and of the travellers who travel across them, of shepherds and cowherds, of the cunning of thieves and liars, of orators and wit, of literature and poets, of athletics and sports, of weights and measures, of invention and of commerce in general. His symbols include the tortoise, the rooster, the winged sandals, the winged hat and the caduceus (given to him by Apollo in exchange for the lyre).

[4]   The 17ᵗʰ century Swedish scholar Andreas Kemke determined that Eden was at least tri-lingual: God speaking Swedish, Adam speaking Danish and the Serpent speaking French. Thomason (1991) has called it as **Kemke Hypothesis.** An interesting study about the origin of all languages from just one language is provided in Mozeson (2006).

[5]   It has been scientifically proved that children generally imitate the language of the adults who live around his world and after some time, due to the feature of linguistic generativity, a child starts producing some words which he had heard never before.

[6]   Jespersen was acquainted with this fact. That is why he has emphasised only on the history of language. He has explained his idea through an analogy. He has said that, as we know in the story, the fox concluded that the lion must be inside the cave and the animals which entered into the cave, did not come out as he found the footprints of the animals to enter into the lion's den and not to return from it. Thus so far the theories are thought about are all about entering into the lion's cave. But we have to think in opposite direction also. We should start from our present day language and walk down towards the past. Then, at last, we would be able to reach to the first stage of language.

[7]   It is, however, agreed that if not language, there must have been some thing like the *proto-language* among those hominoids, if the concept of culture—as claimed by the archaeologists—has to be

believed. Even then, following the methods proposed by Jespersen, it is simply impossible to think of that *proto-language* which might have existed ten million years ago.

[8]   Sir Richard Paget made a general appeal for standard pronunciation of English according to the 'gestural' meaning of the language and had reproved all who conformed to a 'fashion' in pronunciation. His works stood in sharp contrast to accepted etymological and phonetic findings of his time (Jones 1935).

[9]   Report published in *The New York Times* (28th May 2009): "A Human Language Gene Changes the Sound of Mouse Squeaks".

[10]   The FOXP2 came to light in a big London family, half of whose members have severe problems in articulating and understanding human speech. All turned out to have a mutation that disrupted this vital gene.

[11]   Report published in *The New York Times* on 11th November 2009: "Speech Gene Shows Its Bossy Nature".

[12]   Does this mean that questions about the origin of language are unanswerable? Not perhaps. Over the past twenty years or so, scientists from such diverse fields as genetics, anthropology, ethnology and cognitive science have been engaged, in a cross-discipline, multidimensional treasure hunt to find out how language began. It is, for some investigators, the hardest problem in science today. The mystery "lies in the nature of the spoken word. For all its power to wound and seduce, speech is our most ephemeral creation; it is little more than air. It exists in the body as a series of puffs and dissipates quickly into the atmosphere. There are no verbs preserved in amber, no ossified nouns and no pre-historical shrieks forever spread-eagled in the lava that took them by surprise." (Kenneally 2007: 15).

Chapter 4
What Is Linguistics ?

4.1 Introduction

The question 'what is linguistics?' is directly interlinked with the question 'what is language?' In naïve realisation—linguistics is the scientific study of a natural language. This kind of definition is available in almost all of the textbooks on linguistics. Although the definition is quite straightforward, it is not free from ambiguity as it does not exactly explain what the terms *language* and *scientific* mean. Moreover, it triggers the question of pertinence: can we call linguistics *science* in the true sense of the term? The first thing to notice about the question 'what is linguistics' is that it uses the word 'language' in singular sense without an indefinite article, which in return, directly inspires readers to form almost a similar question 'what is language?'.

It is rational to state that the discipline 'linguistics' is much wider in scope, because it takes almost all the aspects of language and its speakers into its area of investigation. Although at the earlier stages of its birth and growth, it had fixed focus only on properties of language and their features, during last one century, it has passed through a conceptual metamorphosis to cover not only language and its properties but also other fields which are directly or indirectly related to language and its speakers.

In the new millennium it appears that linguistics has become much wider in its scope by way of incorporating many new areas of human knowledge which were never thought to be linked with linguistics. Moreover, the introduction of computer science in the study of language(s) has given an unprecedented impetus to linguistics due to which linguistics has become an indispensable part in many areas of **artificial intelligence** and **information technology**. This has been

71

responsible for the generation of a number of sub-fields of linguistics never thought for. If we can relate as well as understand the goals and functions of various sub-fields of linguistics, we shall be in a position to understand if linguistics can be called *science* and how it can leave a lasting impact in understanding the nature of man and its society through the study of language they use.

4.2 The Name of the Discipline

In the ancient period—in Europe as well as in India—there was no separate field for studying language. Therefore, there was no separate discipline such as linguistics. In ancient India, the study of language and its properties was mostly a part of philosophy, theology, or rhetoric where questions related to purity and style in use of language were mostly addressed in a prescriptive fashion. Great Indian sages like — *Pāṇini, Patañjali, Bhartṛhari , Dharmakīrti, Dinaṅga , Gautama, Bhoja, Kumārilabhaṭṭa, Prabhākara, Anandavardhana, Kalidāsa, Vāmana, Bharata, Ratnakīrti,* and others have discussed various aspects and properties of language while discussing grammar or style of creative texts.

Similar trends were also observed in ancient Greece and medieval Rome. Observations on language were found in records of pre-Socratic philosophers and rhetoricians. Great Greek and Roman philosophers like *Plato, Aristotle, Stoics, Analogists, Anomalists, Dionysius Thrax, Speculative Grammarians* and others studied various aspects, forms and features of language mostly from prescriptive perspective as parts of their philosophical, theological or rhetoric enterprises.

In the 18th and the 19th century, the study of languages, their features and their functions were mostly comparative in nature where the main goals were to trace phonological, morphological, semantic and etymological similarities between two or more Languages to establish their typological or genealogical proximities. This kind of study was mostly known as **comparative philology** or **philology**[1]. In the 18th and the 19th century, the term *philology* (it was first attested in 1716) was commonly used to refer to the science of language, which was then predominantly historical in focus.

Famous Swiss scholar Ferdinand de Saussure (1857–1913) is regarded as the *father of modern linguistics*. His innovative ideas related to the study of languages and their properties laid a solid foundation for many significant developments in the 20th century linguistics[2]. The scientific approach he has proposed to adopt in study of language and his insistence on the importance of synchronic and diachronic analysis of language, inspired scholars to shift focus from *philology* to other areas to study grammar, history and literary tradition of languages. With the guiding light provided by Saussure, scholars now became more aware of the intricacies involved in natural languages and decided to explore these with scientific bent of mind. This new approach to the study of language comes to be known in the modern age of science as linguistics or 'the science of language'[3].

4.3 Is Linguistics a Science?

Although the term *linguistics* is narrowly defined as a scientific approach to the study of language, languages can also be studied from various directions to understand how a number of other intellectual disciplines are relevant to it and how these disciplines leave influences on it. For instance, *semiotics* is a field which is concerned with the general study of signs and symbols used in language and in other areas of human existence. Similarly, literary theorists, literary critics and stylisticians study the use of language from purely artistic or stylistic perspective considering language as a medium of expression in literary creations. Also, the study of a language depends on the information drawn heavily from the works of diverse fields such as *sociology, anthropology, ethnology, psychology, speech pathology, folkloristics, informatics, computer science, demography, philosophy, biology, physics, mathematics, statistics, economics, acoustics, human anatomy* and *neuroscience*.

In general, linguistics can be understood as a science in both general and specific senses. When we use the term *science* for any discipline of human investigation, we assume that the discipline is based on clear, systematic and rational understanding of the elements included in it. This general frame of reference can lead us to speak about *science of politics, science of cooking* or *science of directing*. Also we use the term *science* for systematic study of the phenomena—natural or simulated— that may enable us to define principles, states or theories regarding the phenomena. This kind of study needs to pass through examination of verifiable data and information obtained through careful observation of phenomena and experimentation. In other words, it has to be *empirical* and *objective*. Also, scientific studies are meant to provide explanation after adequate observation of data and analysis of information, which should be *consistent* (i.e., there should be no contradiction between different parts of the explanation or statement) and *economical* (i.e., a precise and non-redundant statement has to be provided).

We can now apply all these criteria of science to linguistics to understand and evaluate if linguistics is scientific in its approach and if it adheres to the principles and practices used in science.

(a) **Science studies observable phenomena:** Linguistics studies language as an observable social phenomenon, which is *objective* and *variable*. Like natural phenomena in the physical world, like the organisms in the living world, language has also a concrete shape and occurrence. A physicist observes natural materials, measures their physical properties, examines their forms and functions, etc. to determine their nature, composition and properties. In the same way a linguist studies components of a language, observes occurrences of various speech sounds, examines how words and sentences are formed and used, investigates how meaning is conveyed by subtle use of linguistic items in sentences, etc. Thus a linguist is objective in approach as he analyses the observable elements of a language with the mechanism necessary for the tasks. He uses ears to hear sounds; observes how vocal organs are in movement at the time of generating sounds; and observes texts produced in written form to know how letters and words are formed and used in formation of sentences and texts.

(b) **Scientific studies depend on analysis and classification:** In most of the fields of science, each observable phenomenon needs to be given a precise explanation as well as its nature needs to be described completely. Thus, for example, the biologist classifies the organisms into genres and species, into plants and animals, etc. Further classifications are made according to the characteristic features of living organisms belonging to different sub-classes, classes and categories, etc. In case of linguistics a linguist does the same thing. He observes the languages, collects data from the languages and classifies their features and properties based on different factors, etc. For example, he collects the sounds used in a language, observes manners and places of their articulation, identifies their types and classifies them based on their nature, properties and functions. Moreover, he collects words and other lexical items used in a language; classifies them based on their forms, structure and function; categories them to particular class or part-of-speech; as well as identifies particular classes of words on the basis of similarities or differences in their meanings. After all these works are done, a linguist takes up sounds or words—either in isolation or in groups—to define their nature and form their definitions.

(c) **Scientific studies are empirical:** All the branches of physical and natural sciences are, to a large extent, empirical in nature. Physics, chemistry, biology, geography, zoology and others observe minutely all empirical events and phenomena for their investigations. Linguistics is not different from this pattern. Linguistics not only shares the characteristic features of empirical sciences, but also appears to be a special kind of science, which studies language as a unique form of social behaviour manifested in the interactions between human beings living within a speech community.

(d) **Scientific studies are experimental:** All the natural and earth sciences also depend on experiments when scientists find that mere observation of empirical evidences does not help them much in their investigation. So, as and when required, they make experiments to understand the nature and form of the phenomena they are investigating. Linguistics also adopts this approach or strategy as and when required. Since human language is the result of a highly complex mental process, it cannot be considered just as an objective phenomenon. Following the methods of observation and experimentation used inductively in empirical sciences, linguistics tries to make experiments to identify patterns and forms of language use and tries to draw faithful deductions from the experiments, as practised in several areas of linguistics such as *speech pathology, psycholinguistics, neurolinguistics* and *cognitive linguistics*.

(e) **Scientific studies are deductive:** A true scientific study does not believe in preconceived ideas or theories. Rather, it verifies symptoms, observes features, analyses data and carries out experiments to deduct inferences and formulate theories. This has been the norm in the history of scientific studies. However, there is another method, namely the subjective or the intuitive method[4], which goes directly against this method. Linguistics, as an area of scientific investigation, does not depend much on intuition or speculation, although some areas of modern linguistics are found to tilt towards intuitive generalisations[5]. To promote a neutral position, one can, however, reconcile with these two procedures. There are definitely certain elements in languages, which a linguist can observe empirically and which can offer reliable as well as authentic instances of objective and verifiable data. On the other hand, a linguist may need to formulate some tentative or working hypotheses to explain the empirical databases, which he may accept, reject, or modify as he proceeds with his investigation. If required, he can collect more data to attest or to refute preconceived ideas and assumptions. Thus, with an interface between the inductive and the deductive procedures, a linguist arrives at explanations, which meet the requirements of science—exhaustiveness, consistency and precision.

The above discussion shows that linguistics is a unique science that tries to combine methods used in natural sciences and social sciences. Therefore, we should call linguistics a **human science,** as it is concerned with human and his language—two most dynamic elements of a living human society. It includes within its periphery not only language, people and its roles in a society; but also the language manifested in other media of human interaction like *literature, advertisement* and *music*. When a linguist tries to understand a natural language, he tries to understand the people who use it as well as the society where the language is used. In fact, understanding people and their society can never be complete if the language used by particular class of speakers in a particular society is not understood properly.

Linguistics is such a unique field of study on which all other branches of human knowledge have to depend for exchange of information. As every branch of human knowledge is destined to use language as suitable and convenient medium of information exchange, debate regarding the identity of linguistics as science, art, or humanities becomes entirely irrelevant. To refer to Lyons (1981)—linguistics has natural links with a wide range of academic disciplines. To say that linguistics is a *science* is not to deny that, by virtue of its subject matter, it is closely related to such eminently human disciplines as philosophy and literary criticism (Lyons 1981: 45).

4.4 Levels of Linguistic Analysis

Every natural language has several levels in its structure and it is interesting to know how each and every level is interfaced with the other to give to the language a complete holistic form. While studying a language it is necessary to sub-divide its domains and study these domains in minute details in order to study the language in analytical and systematic manner.

All languages have hierarchical structures. This implies that languages are made up of units, which themselves are made up of smallest indivisible units. From a sentence if we start a backward journey of breaking larger units into smaller ones—we shall eventually reach to those single, unbreakable and distinguishable units, which are called **phonemes**. On the other way round, if we start an onward journey of combining single phonemes together to form larger linguistic units, we shall gradually get morphemes, words, phrases and ultimately, sentences. Meaningful combination of phonemes will generate larger meaningful units called **morphemes**; which again can be combined together to form larger units called **words**; words can be combined to form larger units called **phrases** and phrases can be combined together to generate far more larger units called **sentences**. If we want to go a little further we can combine several sentences in a coordinated way to produce a unified piece of speech or writing, which we can call **text** or **discourse**.

What is the most important thing here is that the process of combining smaller units in formation of larger units is not at all an arbitrary or a random affair. At every stage (or level), there are certain language specific rules that operate *inherently* and these rules which permit occurrence and combination of smaller units in generation of larger units. For instance, rules of phonology determine and permit occurrence and combination of particular phonemes in generation of morphemes; the rules of word-formation can allow permissible combination of morphemes in formation of words; and the rules of sentence determine and dictate the terms of combination and positioning of words in formation of sentences. Each level is a **system** in its own right.

It is, therefore, important to keep in mind that, because of the existence of rules at every level of linguistic representation, we need to analyse each level independently of the other and if required, at the time of analysing each level we can show its relational interface with the other level. For example, while we are studying the level of phonology or the sound system of a language, it is not mandatory to relate it with another level, but can refer to morphology to show how phonemes are actually realised in morphemes. Similarly, we can study morphology in its own right as well as can show how it builds up close interface with syntax; and study syntax on its own and show its relationship with morphology. Although these levels are layered in such a way that one is lower to another in hierarchy and the higher level includes the lower level, each level is independent because it has its own rules of operation that can be described, analysed and understood. We can have some ideas from the flow chart given below (Fig. 4.1) how each level of linguistic representation is independent in its own right as well as how each level is interfaced with the other level.

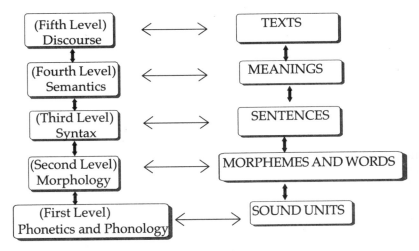

Fig. 4.1: Levels of linguistics and their interfaces

A minute investigation into the above representation (Fig. 4.1) can show that the levels of linguistic representation are not completely separate from each other, since there are important linkages between the levels. In earlier years, when language was not studied in such a rigorously structured manner, it was assumed that each level is actually free from interference of other level. That means phonology, which deals with forms and functions of sound units of a language, has no relation whatsoever with morphology that deals with forms and functions of morphemes and words, or with semantics that represents meaning of words and sentences. However, researches and investigations in last few decades have shown that there are indeed strong relations between the levels and most of these relations are so fine and complex in nature that it is not easy to predict these relations. Even then, it is rational to look at each level separately to understand how each level actually works in its own right before we explore their inter-level relationships.

4.4.1 First Level: Phonetics and Phonology

The first level of linguistic representation is phonetics and phonology. In its own right phonetics studies a language to identify the sound units used in it; how the sound units are articulated by speech production mechanism and received by auditory mechanism; how these sound units are characterised, distinguished and differentiated by their places and manners of articulation; and how these sound units are actually used in production of speech.

Phonology, on the other hand, studies the patterns of combination of the sound units into organised units of speech, the formation of syllables, foot and larger units. It also describes the sound system of a particular language and the combination and distribution of sounds which occur in that language. Furthermore, it makes classification of sound units on the basis of the concept of phoneme (i.e., a distinctive, contrasted sound unit), e.g., /a/, /e/, /i/, /o/, /u/, /k/, /p/, /j/, /e/ m/, /r/, /t/, /f/, /v/, /s/, /h/, etc. These distinct sounds usually enter into combination with others to form morphemes and words. It also studies how the rules of combination of the sound units can differ from language to language and how there are some similarities among the sound units despite notable differences among the languages. Though phonology is often treated as a superficial level of language as it is more concrete in treatment of sound units (not abstract as in the case of meaning), there are indeed some aspects of phonology, such as tone and intonation, which faithfully contribute in understanding meaning of utterances.

4.4.2 Second Level: Morphology

Morphology investigates nature, form, type and functions of the meaningful building blacks used in a language for the purpose of forming words, phrases and sentences. In general, morphemes are identified as combination of sounds (or phonemes) into minimal distinctive units, which have explicit or implicit meanings. In principle, it is not possible to break a morpheme into smaller units because if it is done, it will no longer make any sense as it will lose its meaning. For instance, the morpheme *pin* is actually made of three sounds: /p/, /i/ and /n/. The unique combination of these three phonemes makes up a single morpheme *pin* which has a special meaning. If we break it, it will no longer carry the meaning and the unit will lose its entity as a morpheme.

Words can be made of a single morpheme such as *pin* or a combination of more than one morpheme such as *pins*. For instance, the word *pins* is made up of two morphemes: pin + -s (where *pin* is a morpheme with a unique meaning and the *-s* is a bound morpheme with a sense of plurality). Since there is no restriction in the use of number of morphemes in a word, one can go as far as one's language permits. For instance, let us consider the following words in English where each word is formed by one to eight morphemes in a very systematic order.

(a)	Prodisantiestablishmentarianisms	= 8 morphemes
(b)	Disantiestablishmentarianisms	= 7 morphemes
(c)	Antiestablishmentarianisms	= 6 morphemes
(d)	Establishmentarianisms	= 5 morphemes
(e)	Establishmentarianism	= 4 morphemes
(f)	Establishmentarian	= 3 morphemes
(g)	Establishment	= 2 morphemes
(h)	Establish	= 1 morpheme

Morphology not only deals with the rules for combination of morphemes to form words, it also explores how these morphemes are actually combined in the process of word formation. It shows how suffixes, infixes, prefixes, case markers, plural markers, tense markers, aspect markers, number markers, gender markers, etc. are attached with base morphemes to form words of different parts-of-speech. It also studies the changes that take place in the structure of words when words undergo grammatical or semantic changes. For instance, the morpheme *do* changes into *did* and *done* when it is used in the past and in the past participial forms respectively. These changes signify a change in tense.

The level of morphology is related with phonology on the one hand and to semantics on the other. It is clear from the above example that *do* changed into *did* by way of introducing two changes: the first change is the change of vowel *o* into *i* and the second change one is the addition of consonant *d* with the string. It also shows change in the meaning of the morphemes. The first form *do* denotes the action of doing in the present tense, while the second form *did* denotes the action of doing in the past tense, as the sense of change in tense is reflected by alternation of the first form (i.e., *do*). It implies that the change at morphological level often involves changes both in sound and meaning. In essence, morphology is a wide area of a linguistic investigation which covers processes like *derivation, compounding, reduplication, sandhi* and many other word formation processes found to be highly operational in a language.

4.4.3 Third Level: Syntax

Syntax is the third level which studies how words are syntagmatically arranged and combined to form phrases; how phrases are combined to form clauses; and how clauses are joined together to make sentences. Besides these basic questions the study of syntax also involves the description of grammar of a language, i.e., the rules of positioning of various elements in sentence such as nouns and noun phrases, verbs and verb phrases, preposition and prepositional phrases and adverbs and adverbial phrases, etc. Also it tries to understand what kinds of transformation take place in sentences when we try to convert simple descriptive sentences into interrogative ones or affirmative sentences into negative ones, etc.

The rules of grammar say that sentences must be composed with sentence formative elements arranged in a particular order. And based on these rules one can attempt to describe how these elements function in the sentence, i.e., what is their role in the sentence. For elucidation, let us consider the following examples, which show how a word can act either as a noun or as an adjective based on its role within a sentence:

(a) The cook$_{[1]}$ can cook$_{[2]}$ good food for one and all.
(b) The head$_{[1]}$ has agreed to head$_{[2]}$ the discussion.
(c) It is good$_{[1]}$ that you can differentiate between good$_{[2]}$ and bad.

In the sentences given above we can find that the words *cook, head* and *good* are used in two different parts-of-speech. In sentence (a), the first use of the word is a noun (cook$_{[1]}$), while the second use of the word is a verb (cook$_{[2]}$). In sentence (b) the first use of the word is a noun (head$_{[1]}$), while the second use of the word is a verb (head$_{[2]}$). Similarly, in sentence (c), the first use of the word is an adjective (good$_{[1]}$), while the second use of the word is a noun (good$_{[2]}$).

Also, the rules of grammar show how a particular word can play different syntactic roles within sentences. For instance, the word *man* is a noun, which can function either as a subject or an object in sentence as the following examples can show:

(d) The *man* lives in this city.
(e) Everybody likes this *man* for his work.

In sentence (d), the word *man* functions as the subject of the sentence, while in sentence (e), it functions as the object.

The rules of grammar show that sentences can be accepted in a language if sentences are both grammatically right and logically valid. This opens for us four possibilities for forming sentences, as the following rules show:

(1) Sentences may be grammatically right and logically valid.
    Example: An old man is walking slowly on the road.

(2) Sentences may be grammatically wrong but logically valid.
    Example: He cannot do nothing.

(3) Sentences may be grammatically right but logically invalid.
    Example: Colourless green ideas sleep furiously.

(4) Sentences may be grammatically wrong and logically invalid.
    Example: Ideas green furiously sleep colourless.

The rules of syntax consider sentence (1) as the only acceptable form in a language like English. They also consider sentence (2) acceptable because in our normal linguistic interactions we often form many sentences, which are not grammatically accurate but are able to convey message or information. We do not generally raise strong objections against such sentences. The sentence (3) may also be considered acceptable if our fanciful imagination gives us liberty to roam in a utopian world where logic and rationality of this world have no relevance. This usually happens in *science fictions, fairy tales, child literature* and similar fanciful texts. However, such sentences are not usually accepted as normal sentences in a language. On the other hand, sentence (4) is never considered acceptable as it has grossly deviated from grammaticality and logicality. The rules of syntax of a language have to be comprehensive to explain and elaborate how the acceptable sentences, which are grammatically and logically valid, can be constructed.

4.4.4 Fourth Level: Semantics

Semantics is the fourth level that deals with meaning in a language. In general, it tries to analyse how meaning is embedded within a construction –either a word or a sentence. This is, perhaps, one of the most interesting levels of linguistic representation as decipherment of meaning from a surface form is a real tricky thing. It tries to understand how meaning is assigned to words; how words are similar or different in meanings, how words are treated as *synonyms, antonyms, homonyms, polysyms, hypernyms, hyponyms,* etc. It also attempts to show the inter-relationships among words through forming 'categories' and through sub-categorisation of categories.

In essence, it tries to give an account of both word and sentence meaning; formulate theories; explores different levels of meanings words and sentences denote (e.g., *referential, denotative, connotative, figurative, emphatic,* etc.); and attempts to analyse and define that elements which are considered to be abstract. It is easy to define meanings of **concrete words** such as *road, table, horse, book* and *girl,* etc.; but it is difficult to define meanings of **abstract words** like *love, faith, honesty, courage* and *ego,* etc. as well as the **function words** like *to, up, in, by, for, at,* etc. This is why semantics is considered as one of the less clearly definable areas of language study.

4.4.5 Fifth Level: Discourse

Discourse is the fifth level of study of linguistic representation that takes chunks of language, which are bigger than a sentence, into consideration and tries to understand the information embedded within them. At this particular level, we may try to analyse the inter-sentential links that form a connected or **cohesive text** that carry not only individual meanings of formative elements but also a total meaning, which may or may not be extracted from meanings of the formative elements. **Cohesion** is the relation of information established within a sentence between it and the sentences preceding and following it, by the use of connectives such as *and, though, also, but, then, either, therefore, else,* etc. and by the manner in which reference is made to the other parts of the text by devices such as repetition of words, use of pronouns, definite articles, etc. By studying the elements of cohesion we can understand how a sentence is connected with other sentences within a text as a text contains greater or larger meaning more than the sum-total of the individual sentences it contains. Discourse is made up with all the levels of linguistic representation that work in a combined manner in decipherment of information loaded within a piece of text, while semantics incorporates analysis of meaning at the level of words (i.e., word meaning) and at the level of sentence (i.e., sentence meaning).

4.4.6 Other Levels

In addition to these levels of linguistic representation and analysis, we have also some less important levels such as **graphology**, which studies the shapes, sizes, directions and manners of using characters in writing a text in a language and the conventions used in representing speech in writing, e.g., the formation of letters. Another level of language analysis is **lexicography**, which studies the manner in which lexical items (e.g., words, affixes, idioms, phrases, proverbs, etc.) are used in a language. Also, it records and presents these linguistic elements in a systematic order in the form of compilation of dictionaries. The extension of the study of meaning or semantics is identified as a new level called **pragmatics**, which deals with the contextual aspects of meaning in particular situations taking into the account various important factors that trigger formation of a piece of sentence or a text. As distinct from the study of sentences, pragmatics considers utterances, i.e., the sentences actually uttered by the speakers of a language in particular situations. The strategies generally adopted for understanding pragmatics involve finding answers to the questions: who has said, to whom it is said, what is said, when it is said, where it is said, how it is said, in which context it is said and why it is said.

4.5 Core Areas of Linguistics

Linguistics is concerned with describing and explaining the nature, form and function of human languages. In the history of study of languages, scholars have been able to identify a few major areas, the investigations of which have become indispensable in the study of any language. If we want to have some basic ideas of a language, we need sufficient information and data from all these major areas, without which our knowledgebase about the language is bound to be skewed and insufficient. Although linguistics has several sub-fields, which are independently concerned with the particular aspects of linguistic data, information, scope, structure, meaning and style, etc., for our present discussion, we intend to focus on those five major primary areas of linguistics that include *phonetics and phonology, morphology, syntax, semantics* and *etymology*.

4.5.1 Phonetics and Phonology

By a simple definition **phonetics** is the empirical study of human speech sounds with close reference to their physical properties, while **phonology** is the study of human speech sounds as discrete and abstract elements in the speaker's mind that distinguish meaning. The term *phonetics* is derived from Greek word *phōnē* meaning 'sound' or 'voice'. Phonetics studies the physical properties of the speech sounds (i.e., phones), as well as the processes of their physiological production, auditory reception, as well as neuro-physiological perception.

History shows that phonetics was first studied as early as 2500 years ago in ancient India when great Indian sage *Pāṇini* presented a highly scientific account about the place and manner of articulation of Sanskrit consonant sounds in his famous treatise, *Aṣṭādhyāyī*, written in the 5th century BC[6]. During the last one century phonetics has become one of the major areas of linguistic research and application in language teaching, speech repairment, speech recognition and speech technology. In general, phonetics has three main branches:

(a) **Articulatory phonetics** is concerned with the articulation of speech sounds. It studies the position, shape and movement of the *articulators* or the speech producing organs, such as the glottis, lips, tongue, larynx, pharynx, uvula, velum, vocal folds, palate, teeth, etc.

(b) **Auditory phonetics** is concerned with the science of speech signal reception and perception. It investigates how sounds are received by the outer part of ear, how these sound signals are passed through the inner part of ear and how these sound signals are actually perceived by the brain of a listener.

Language and Linguistics

(c) **Acoustic phonetics** is concerned with the acoustics or the physics of speech sounds. It investigates the properties of sound waves, such as frequency, amplitudes, bass, harmonics, undulation, pitch, accent etc. when these sound units are produced by human speech organs.

The term **phonology** is derived from Greek words *phōnē* meaning 'voice, sound' + *lógos* meaning 'word, speech and subject of discussion'. Linked with phonetics, phonology is a sub-field of linguistics, which aims at studying the sound system of specific languages (or particular languages). While phonetics discusses the physical production and perception of the sounds of speech, phonology describes the way the sounds actually function within a given language or across languages.

An important area of phonology is feature-based study that tries to identify the distinctive sound units within a given language. For instance, in English /p/ and /b/ are two distinctive units of sound which are different from each other due to their unique set of distinctive features. Since these are two distinctive as well as different sound units, we consider them **phonemes** as their difference is **phonemic** or **phonematic**. This claim is substantiated with a minimal pair: *pit* and *bit*. This implies that by replacing the sound *p* by the sound *b*, we can have two different words, which have different meanings due to difference in only one sound.

On the other hand, the phoneme /p/ can be pronounced differently in different ways depending on its position relative to other sounds within a word. Yet these different pronunciations are still considered by the native speakers to be the 'same sound'. For example, the phoneme /p/ is slightly aspirated in *pin*, but not aspirated in *spin* and *nip*. In many other languages like Thai, Bengali, Oriya, Hindi, etc., the difference between aspiration and non-aspiration causes difference between the phonemes. That means in these languages aspirated /pʰ/ and non-aspirated /p/ are two different phonemes, not the allophones of the same phoneme.

In addition to analysis and investigation of minimal meaningless sounds (i.e., phonemes), phonology also studies how sounds alternate, such as the /p/ in English described above; investigates segment redundancy strategies used in formation of morphemes and words; and discusses the phonological factors such as syllable structure, stress, accent and intonation are used in speech of a language[7].

4.5.2 Morphology

Morphology[8] is the study of morphemes used in a language and their role in formation of words in accordance with word formation rules used in a language. Also, it is that field of linguistics, which tries to explore the internal structure of morphemes, words and other formative units used in a language[9]. In a systematic manner it identifies, analyses and describes the structure of morphemes, as well as other units of meaning used in a language such as words, affixes, compounds, part-of-speech, intonation, stress and implied context, etc.[10].

Words in morphology are generally accepted as being the smallest units of sentence. It is however, clear that in many languages, words can be related to other words by rules of grammar. For example, English speakers recognise that the words *dog* and *dogs* are actually the same form differentiated only by the plurality morpheme -*s*, which is found to be bound to nouns and it is never used separately. Speakers of English can recognise these relations from their tacit knowledge of the rules of word formation used in the language. They infer intuitively that the relation between *dog* and *dogs* is almost similar to that of between *cat* and *cats*. The rules understood by the speaker reflect on the specific patterns or regularities in the way words are formed from smaller units and how those smaller units interact in speech.

Morphology is an indispensable branch of linguistics that inspires us to study the forms and functions of morphemes, the patterns of word formation within and across the languages and the nature of rules that can model the knowledge of the speakers of the languages. In sum, morphology is the study of morphemes, where 'morpheme' is a generic term that includes all kinds of lexical units of a language formed with phonemes—morphemes, words, word stems and affixes. Though morphemes are often treated as units of meaning, these are actually considered as parts of syntax or grammar of a language.

Based on morphology we can make differences between the languages which are identified as **isolating** (e.g., *Chinese, Indonesian,* etc.), **agglutinating** (e.g., *Turkish, Finnish, Tamil,* etc.) and **inflexional** (e.g., *Russian, Latin, Arabic,* etc.). While the isolating languages use grammatical morphemes which are actually separate words; the agglutinating languages use the grammatical morphemes in the form of attached syllables called affixes; and the inflexional languages may go one step further and change the word at the phonemic level to express grammatical morphemes.

4.5.3 Syntax

It refers to the study of rules of how words combine to form grammatically and logically acceptable sentences[11]. In traditional linguistics, it describes the types (e.g., *simple, complex, compound,* etc.) and kinds (e.g., *declarative, assertive, interrogative, exclamatory,* etc.) of sentences constructed in a language as well as the rules used to form these sentences. It also studies the form and nature of phrases and clauses used in sentences, as well as subject, object, predicate and other properties used in sentences.

Critical analysis on the syntactic or the grammatical rules was presented long before the advent of modern syntax. The *Aṣṭādhyāyī* of *Pāṇini* is often referred to as one of the finest examples of pre-modern work on syntax that approaches the sophistication of a modern syntactic theory. In the Western world, the school of thought that came to be known as **traditional grammar** began with the work of Dionysius Thrax[12].

In the 19th century, with the advent of historical/comparative linguistics, linguists were able to observe syntactic diversities among the languages and this led scholars to question about some of the fundamental assumptions that wanted to establish structural relationships between language and logic. Gradually, it became apparent that there was no such thing as a most natural way to express a thought and logic could no longer be relied upon as a base for studying the structure of a language.

The modern research into syntax has changed its goal to a large extent to describe languages not only in terms of such syntactic or grammatical rules, but also in terms of finding out the general rules which may be applied to all the languages. Since the field of modern syntax attempts to explain the grammatical judgments of the speakers of a language and does not try to provide these to the users, it is unconcerned with the linguistic prescriptions of a language that may vary with regard to individual understandings.

In the last century, with intensive studies on structure of sentences carried out by the structuralists and the generative grammarians, the central role of syntax within theoretical linguistics became clear and understandable[13]. In this century several theories and models are proposed by scholars not only to understand the surface forms of sentences but also to understand how these surface forms are generated, produced and understood by the speakers. Although all the theories of syntax use humans as their object of study, there are some basic significant differences in their outlooks. While some theories adopt a more **Platonistic view** considering syntax as the study of an abstract formal system of a language or variety (Gazdar *et al.* 1985); other theories want to consider grammar as a **taxonomical device** to reach to the broad generalisations among the languages (Greenberg 1963) and some other theories want to consider syntax as a **branch of biology**, since they conceive syntax as the study of linguistic knowledge as embodied in the human mind (Chomsky 1972).

4.5.4 Semantics

Semantics[14] is the study of meaning of words and other forms used in a language. Within its broader purview it takes **lexical semantics** (i.e., meaning of words) and **phraseology** (i.e., meaning of fixed word combinations) to understand how words can combine together to form meanings of sentences. It also investigates meanings of sentences used in a piece of communication. In modern linguistics, it is the study of interpretation of linguistic signs used by the agents or communities within particular circumstances and contexts.

Meaning, as the studies on language through the history show, is inherent at the levels of words, phrases, sentences and larger units of discourse (referred to as *texts*). The basic area of study is the meaning of signs and their relationships underlying different linguistic units used in sentences or texts. At lexical level it tries to identify, explore and define *homonymy, synonymy, antonymy, polysemy, paronymy, hypernymy, hyponymy, meronymy, metonymy, holonymy* and other relations among words; and at the sentence or discourse level, it studies how the sentences are constructed to elicit different layers of senses and meanings within a piece of text.

Another key concern of semantics is to understand how meaning is being attached to larger chunks of text, possibly as a result of the composition from smaller units of meaning. Thus semantics includes the study of *connotative sense and denotative reference, truth conditions, argument structure, thematic roles, discourse analysis, pragmatics* and the linkages of all of these to text. At the text level, from the functional point of view, it tries to understand the *conceptual meaning, referential meaning, denotative meaning, connotative meaning, thematic meaning, intended meaning, interpreted meaning, associative meaning, collocative meaning, affective meaning, reflected meaning, stylistic meaning,* etc.

Modern semanticists differ to a large extent from traditional semanticists to count on what constitutes meaning in an expression. For instance, in a sentence like *"It is the head"* the word *head* may refer to the object itself, which is its literal meaning or *denotation*. It may, however, refer to many other figurative senses and associations, which may be its *connotation* and which can be understood from the context of its use within a piece of text. Although traditional views want to restrict semantics to its literal meaning only and relegate all the figurative associations to pragmatics, the distinction, however, is increasingly becoming difficult to defend as modern theories are interested to merge information obtained from text with that of semiotics, pragmatics, discourse and the extralinguistic world in proper cognition of meaning of spoken and written texts.

4.5.5 Etymology

Etymology[15] studies the history of origin and development of words used in a language. It is known that each and every language has large number of words, some of which are obtained from its mother language or ancestors, while others are indigenously created and some other words are borrowed from various neighbouring and distant languages at different points of time. The goal of etymology is to trace how words are incorporated in a language, at what point of time and in which manners. It systematically explores which words are borrowed into a language; when these words have come to be used; from which sources these have come; and how their forms and meanings have been changed over time in the borrower language.

For the languages like Greek, English, Sanskrit and Tamil which have a long and detailed history of their origin and growth, etymologists make use of **philology**, to study how words change from culture to culture or language to language over time. Also etymologists apply methods of **comparative linguistics** to reconstruct information about the languages that are too old for any direct information (e.g., writing) to be known. By analysing the related languages with a technique known as **comparative method**, the linguists can make inferences, about their shared parent language and their vocabulary. In this way, word roots have been found which can be traced all the way back to the origin of, for instance, the **Indo-European** language family.

Even though etymological researches grew from the ancient philological tradition, at the present context etymological researches are done in language families, where little or no early documentation is available. The general theories of etymology argue that words are originated through a limited number of mechanisms such as the followings:

(a) **Borrowing,** in which words from foreign and neighbouring languages are adopted in a language as *loanwords, loan translations, loan shifts* and *loan blends,* etc.
(b) **Word formation** by which words are generated in a language through deployment of word formation processes like *derivation, compounding, inflection, reduplication, euphonic combination,* etc.
(c) **Onomatopoeia and sound symbolism** by which words are created in a language through imitation of external physical or natural sounds.

While the history of origin of newly emerged words is often more or less transparent, it tends to become obscured through time due to the following factors:

(a) **Sound change:** For instance, it is not clear at first sight that English *set* is actually related to *sit* (the former is originally a causative formation of the latter) and even more less so that *bless* is related to *blood* (the former was originally a derivative with the meaning 'to mark with blood or the like').
(b) **Semantic change:** For instance, the English word *bead* originally meant 'prayer' and it has acquired its modern sense through the practice of counting prayers with beads.

In search of etymological history, an etymologist often needs to combine etymological mechanisms of various types. For example, the German word *bitte* (please), the German word *beten* (to pray) and the Dutch word *bidden* (to pray) are related through sound and meaning to the English word *bead*. The combination of sound change and semantic change often creates etymological connections that are impossible to detect by merely looking at the new forms of words. For instance, the English word *lord* comes from Old English *hlāf-weard*, meaning literally 'bread guard'. The components of this compound, in turn, yielded modern English *loaf* and *ward*.

The etymologists may apply a number of methods or strategies together to study the origins of words. Most of these methods are, however, often used in comparative method of reconstruction.

(a) **Philological investigation:** It refers to the changes in form and meaning of the word that can be traced with the aid of older texts, if such databases are available.

(b) **Making use of dialectological data:** It refers that the form or meaning of words might show variations between the dialects or the older form and meaning may be stored in dialects. Such data and information may yield vital clues for the earlier history of words.

(c) **The comparative method:** This is an acknowledged method in historical linguistics, where by a systematic comparison among related languages one can detect which words are derived from common ancestor language and which words were later borrowed from another language.

(d) **Study of semantic change:** Etymologists often make hypotheses about changes of meaning of particular words. Such hypotheses are tested against general knowledge of semantic shifts. For example, assumption of a particular change of meaning can be substantiated by showing that the same type of change has occurred in many other languages as well.

4.6 Concluding Remarks

It has always been an issue of great trouble to define the term *linguistics* in a scientific manner, as the discipline *linguistics*, over the centuries, has changed in its scope and vision. Over the centuries, it has been observed that the scope of linguistics has been expanded more and more by way of introducing new areas of investigation within its realm. Even half a century ago, it was beyond our vision that areas like *computer technology, ecology, geography, sociology, psychology, biology, neurology* and *cognitive science* would become important domains of modern linguistics and their interfaces with linguistics would give birth to new fields like *computational linguistics, mathematical linguistics, ecolinguistics, biolinguistics, psycholinguistics, sociolinguistics, neurolinguistics, geolinguistics* and *cognitive linguistics,* etc. The birth of these new fields has put linguistics as a field of science; and the question 'whether linguistics is science or not' has become nullified.

What Is Linguistics?

Once the nature of the discipline has been defined, it becomes necessary to identify its scope and role in the context of human knowledge and here lies the importance of levels of analysis of linguistics as well as identification of the basic domains of linguistics where it actually contributes for the growth and advancement of human knowledge about life, society and its people. In this chapter an attempt has been made to address all these issue in a very systematic manner.

Notes and Comments

[1]   This kind of comparative studies among the languages inspired many scholars to postulate the concept of proto-language, which may be considered as the forgotten mother of the languages that show linguistic similarities.

[2]   The dichotomies proposed by Saussure have not only made linguistics as an independent field of investigation, but also have made monumental impacts in other fields of humanities and social sciences.

[3]   Although the term *linguist* in the sense of 'a student of language' dates back to 1641, the term *linguistics* was first attested in 1847. It is now the usual academic term among the scholars engaged in scientific study of languages.

[4]   Also there has been opposite tradition—the tradition of rationalism—which holds that mind forms certain concepts or ideas beforehand in terms of which it interprets data of observation and experience. According to the tradition, deductive procedure is employed in which we have a preliminary hypothesis or theory in mind. We try to prove this hypothesis by applying it to data. According to empirical scientists, this procedure is unscientific because pre-existent ideas can influence the kind of data we obtain and analyse. That means in this approach, we search for only those kinds of data that may fit into the theory and disregard others. In the true sense of science, this is not an objective method, but a subjective method.

[5]   In support of subjective investigation and apriori theorisation thinkers like *Karl Poper* have argued that no observation, however empirical it may appear, can be free of some theory; it cannot be totally neutral.

93

[6]   All the major Aryan scripts have ordered the arrangement of alphabets, letters and other orthographic symbols used in the scripts according to the scheme of classification proposed in *Pāṇini*. Although some of the modern Aryan scripts like *Devanāgarī, Bengali,* etc., have tried to redesign the order of consonants to address the demands of the new age, the basic pattern of arrangement of the letters, however, remains the same.

[7]   The principles of phonology are also applied to analyse sign languages, even though the phonological units used in sign languages do not consist of sounds. The principles of phonological analysis are applied here independent of modalities because these are designed to serve as general analytical tools and not as language-specific principles and theories.

[8]   The term morphology was first coined by August Schleicher ("For the science of word formation, I choose the term 'morphology'": *Mémoires Academia Impériale* 7/1/7, 35). However, the history of morphological analysis dates back to the ancient Indian linguist *Pāṇini,* who had formulated 3,959 rules of Sanskrit morphology in his famous treatise, namely, *Aṣṭādhyāyī*. Also Greco-Roman grammatical tradition discussed morphology in some details.

[9]   Since words as lexical or linguistic units are the members of the lexicon and the subject matter of lexicology and lexicography, they are not discussed in details here. The identity of words as the different conceptual entities are discussed in details elsewhere (Dash 2011: *Bengali Words: An Empirical Investigation*).

[10]   Morphological typology represents a way of classifying languages according to the ways by which morphemes are used in a language. From the analytic point of view, languages use isolated morphemes, agglutinative morphemes, bound morphemes (i.e., affixes) and polysynthetic morphemes in formation of single word forms.

[11]   The term syntax is derived from Greek *syn-* 'together' + *táxis* 'arrangement'. It refers to the rules of a language that show how the words of that language are to be arranged to make acceptable sentence of that language. The term is also used to refer to these rules themselves, as in 'the syntax of English'.

[12]   For a few centuries, works in syntax were dominated by a framework known as *Grammaire Générale,* first expounded in 1660 by Antoine Arnauld in a book of the same title. This system took,

as its basic premise, the assumption that natural languages are direct reflections of thought processes and hence, there are most natural ways to express thoughts.

[13]   Due to this reason, the last century is reasonably called 'century of syntactic theory' as far as linguistics is concerned (Graffi 2001).

[14]   The term semantics is derived from Greek *semantikos* 'significant' from the term *semainein* 'to signify, mean', which is again derived from *sema* 'sign or token'. The term, in its modern sense, is considered to have first appeared in French as *sémantique* in Michel Breal book *Essai de sémantique* (1897). In the *International Scientific Vocabulary* the term *semantics* is called *semasiology*.

[15]   The word etymology comes from the Greek words *etumologia* < *etumon* 'true sense' + *-logia* 'study of', from *logos* 'speech, oration, discourse, word'.

Chapter 5
Dimensions of Linguistics

5.1 Introduction

During the last five decades modern linguistics has evolved as a discipline, which is more concerned with application of linguistic data, information and observations in various domains of human enterprise. This has been possible due to change in attitude of people engaged in the discipline as well as due to origin of several new fields of linguistics the existence of which is related to direct utilisation of linguistic data and information, such as, sociolinguistics, computational linguistics, corpus linguistics, cognitive linguistics, language teaching, dictionary compilation, translation, etc.

The birth of these new fields has made it possible to look at the languages from different perspectives, due to which it has been possible to present new accounts about languages as well as to trace differences existing in context-bound use of languages. As a result of this, the undefined conflict between the traditional and the modern linguistics, which continued to haunt linguists for generations, has become almost irrelevant due to change in attitude and approach of linguistics.

Even then, one can trace finer traits of difference between the two types, if one wants to understand why there was debate for generations between the two approaches. If one investigates meticulously, one can find out several differences that occur with the objects and goals of research of the traditional and modern linguistics. In general, these are summarised in the following manners:

(a) The focus of the traditional linguistics lied in describing and defining the language use and changes that occurred in the past ages of a language or a language family. Modern linguistics, on the contrary, focuses on the present state of language change, tries to identify and analyse the causes or motivations behind such changes, as well as wants to look at the people and their mind through the language they use. It also explores the nature of spread and the modality of language change.

(b) The traditional linguistics mainly concentrated on a language and its changes regarding internal factors. The modern linguistics, on the other hand, puts its focal point on external factors, e.g., the social surroundings that are responsible for language change. It believes that synchronic change observed in a language is a key factor in the diachronic study of a language. It argues that the beginning of a language change is variation.

(c) For traditional linguistics, structures and systems of a language were more important factors than other elements, because systematic analysis of these things could provide vital clues in understanding a language. In modern linguistics, however, language use and language users are more important, as it claims that the grammar of a language is actually shaped by discourse and texts of a language as changed by its speakers.

(d) The traditional linguistics was mainly interested in describing phonology, morphology and comparative linguistics between the languages with no or less focus on their syntax, semantics, discourse and pragmatics. The modern linguistics, on the other hand, is distinctly inclined towards syntax, semantics, pragmatics and discourse, although traditional fields are not ignored altogether. In fact, it tries to shed new lights on the patent areas of traditional linguistics with new insights obtained from detailed analysis of linguistic data actually used by the speakers.

(e) The traditional linguistics was mainly based on intuitive analyses and/or individual observations. It was mostly particular in observation, skewed in generalisation and qualitative in assessment. The modern linguistics, on the other hand, is experimental than observational, analytical than descriptive and both qualitative and quantitative in interpretation.

(f)   The traditional linguistics dealt mostly with languages that have written forms. It had hardly paid any attention to those languages, which have no writing system or script for representing speech. The modern linguistics is, however, more concerned with the spoken form. Also, it is interested to trace mind that actually operates behind the usage of language in various situations controlled by different linguistic and extralinguistic factors.

Although the modern linguistics has been drastically different from the traditional linguistics in approach, attitude, methods, orientation, subject matters and focus, it has not yet succeeded to ignore the basic dimensions of linguistics, without which linguistic study of any kind is bound to be skewed, incomplete and insignificant. The basic dimensions are as the followings:

(a)   Descriptive linguistics and prescriptive linguistics.
(b)   Theoretical linguistics and applied linguistics.
(c)   Microlinguistics and macrolinguistics.
(d)   Synchronic linguistics and diachronic linguistics.

In the following sections of the chapter I have made an attempt to discuss all the four major dimensions of linguistics, the understanding of which will provide us the knowledge to comprehend various factors, features, issues and events related to both traditional and modern linguistics.

5.2 Descriptive Linguistics and Prescriptive Linguistics

The first dimension relates to distinction between *descriptive linguistics* and *prescriptive linguistics*.

5.2.1 Descriptive Linguistics

Descriptive linguistics or language description, in the study of language, is a kind of study that objectively analyses and describes how language is used in all kinds of activity related to it and other things. In case of analysing and describing speech, for instance, it studies how a language is spoken by a group of people of a particular speech community. On the other hand, in case of describing and analysing writing systems, it studies how the people of a language community use their writing system in linguistic activities where writing is used as one of the indispensable methods for information storage, information transfer, information exchange and language education.

All research and investigation activities in linguistics are descriptive in nature, because like all other sciences, the primary goal of linguistics is not to prescribe about what people should do or should not do, but to observe how people use language in their linguistic activities. And it does so without the bias of any preconceived idea about how a language ought to be. A linguist observes and records how a language is being used in practice by the people in all their language-related activities and this is the basis of all linguistic studies. Serious scholarly descriptive works are usually based on texts or language corpora analysis, or on field studies, while non-rigorous descriptive studies include each individual's observations of their own language usage. In each case, a descriptive linguist, unlike a prescriptive linguist, abstains himself from value judgements and makes no recommendation.

Linguistics, in the history of its birth and growth, has always tried to use a process known as *description*, which involves observing languages as well as creating conceptual categories for it without establishing rules for language use. However in the 16th and 17th century, when the modern linguistics started to acquire a formal shape, the works of lexicography tended to be prescriptive to provide the basis for 18th and 19th century comparative works—mainly for the classical languages. By the early 20th century, the focus was shifted to modern languages as descriptive approach of analysing speech and writings became more formal and acceptable norm.

In all spheres of language investigation, *descriptive* method was always used prior to *prescription* as it was generally considered to be the key to any kind of linguistic research. The reason for this priorhood of description is attested in the argument that linguistics, as any other branch of science, requires observation and analysis of natural phenomena, such as the patterns of use of sounds in speech or the order of words in communication, which may be done without adopting any strategy for prescribing rules. Thus, in descriptive linguistics, it has been logically accepted that the non-standard varieties of a language should receive equal amount of attention as that of the standard variety. Within the descriptive frame, the observational methods are considered to be far more accurate and objective than prescriptive methods, because the outcomes of descriptive methods become inputs of prescriptive methods.

Since the inception of the discipline of linguistics, it has been concerned with describing and documenting languages previously unknown to the discipline. Starting with Edward Sapir (1921), Franz Boas (1940) and others, descriptive linguistics became the main strand within linguistics until the rise of formal structural linguistics in the middle of the 20th century (Hockett 1958). The rise and growth of descriptive linguistics was the result of the concern for describing languages of indigenous peoples that were moving rapidly towards extinction. The focus of descriptive linguistics necessitated the development of several disciplines such as *dialectology, sociolinguistics, anthropological linguistics* and *ethnolinguistics* and others, which intended to investigate the relations between language, people, culture and society. With the advent of corpus linguistics (Svartvik 1992), the emphasis on language description and documentation has become an important area at the present global context, since documentation of rapidly dying indigenous languages has become a primary focus in many of the world's linguistic programmes[1].

In the modern age, descriptive linguistics has been much dependent on a structural approach to language study, as shown in the works of Bloomfield (1933), Hockett (1958) and others, which has given birth to a new idea known as **descriptivism** that argues that authentic description of a language and its properties is much more significant or important than prescribing it in case of understanding a language, teaching a language and developing resources for language planning. This has led modern scholars working in the areas of *corpus linguistics* (Dash 2007) and *cognitive linguistics* to argue that the basic task of a linguist is to describe and explain the features of language without making any kind of subjective judgment on whether a particular feature is 'right' or 'wrong'[2] .

Since it is really difficult to present accurate description of real speech in its true self, linguists often tend to reduce description to approximations. This implies that almost all the linguistic theories so far available in linguistics have their origin in practical problems of descriptive linguistics. The theories of phonetics and phonology, for example, are developed from proper and minute analysis and description of phonemes, which are used to understand function and interpretation of sounds in a language. Similarly, the theories of syntax have been developed from the analysis and interpretation of the rules concerning how words are related to each other in order to form sentences.

The extreme 'mentalist' viewpoint denies that the linguistic description of a language can be done by anyone but a competent speaker. Such speakers have internalised something called **linguistic competence**, which gives them the ability to extrapolate correctly from their experience the new but correct expressions and to reject unacceptable expressions.

There are thousands of linguistic descriptions for thousands of languages that are prepared by people without adequate linguistic training. Even then their linguistic descriptions can be considered descriptively adequate if they achieve the following goals of descriptive linguistics:

(a) Adequate description of phonology of the language in question.
(b) Faithful description of morphology of words belonging to that language.
(c) Reliable description of syntax of well-formed sentences of that language.
(d) Systematic description of lexical derivations used in formation of words in that language.
(e) Authentic documentation of vocabulary that includes at least one thousand lexical entries.
(f) Methodical description of word meanings both in their lexicographic and text-based environments.
(g) Reproduction of a few genuine text books and reference materials based on the description of phonology, morphology, syntax and vocabulary.

5.2.2 Prescriptive Linguistics

Prescriptive linguistics, contrary to descriptive linguistics, refers both to the codification and the enforcement of rules governing how a language should be used by the people of a particular speech community. These rules may come from all the spheres of linguistics, such as those rules that cover the topics as standardisation for spelling, grammar and syntax and the rules for what is deemed socially or politically correct or proper, etc. The rules may also include mechanisms for establishing and maintaining an interregional language or a standardised language system including pronunciation and spelling.

It can also include declarations of what particular groups consider to be of good taste socially acceptable in terms of formality and informality. If these tastes are conservative, prescription may be resistant to language change of any kind, or if they are radical, prescription may be productive of neologism. Prescription also includes recommendation for effective language usage taking into consideration genres and domains of language use.

For some practical purposes, linguistic description becomes associated with linguistic prescription, which is found especially in language education, language promotion and in publishing. In these cases, at least, prescription tries to define the standard language forms and gives advices on effective language use, which may be realised as presentation of fruits of descriptive research in a learnable form, although it draws on more subjective aspects of language aesthetics.

Linguistic prescription, in *sociolinguistics*, makes an attempt to promote particular linguistic usages over others, often favouring a particular dialect or acrolect. This may have the aim of establishing a linguistic standard, which can aid communication over large geographical areas. It may also, however, be an attempt by speakers of one language or dialect to exert influence over the speakers of other languages or dialects for political and socio-cultural advantages. This leads to generation of a concept known as **prescriptivism**. An extreme version of prescriptivism can be found among the censoring authorities, who attempt to eradicate words (such as *slang*) and structures which they consider to be destructive to a society or culture, which eventually leads to the birth of **purism** in language use.

Prescriptive approach in language use becomes far more evident in case of *language planning*, when the authority makes concerted effort to standardise script, orthography, grammar and language use for the people of a speech community. The power-game of socio-economic tensions becomes crucially instrumental in shaping the form of a language through conscious and careful use of means of mass communication and motivation such as newspapers, television, radio, school curriculum and other devices which have direct and lasting impacts on the mass of a speech community.

Language description and prescription, are however, complementary to each other as they usually exist in a dynamic tension. Many commentators on language description show elements of both prescription and description in their thinking and several popular debates on language issues frequently revolve around the question of how to balance between the two. Although descriptive and prescriptive linguistics are complementary to each other, they have indeed different priorities and motives, as a result of which sometimes they are seen to be in conflict. Prescription and description are often seen as opposites, in the sense that one declares how a language *should be* while the other declares how a language *is*.

5.3 Theoretical Linguistics and Applied Linguistics

The second dimension relates to distinction between *theoretical linguistics* and *applied linguistics*.

5.3.1 Theoretical Linguistics

Theoretical linguistics is an approach that is most concerned with developing models and theories of linguistic knowledge. Generally, it refers to the core fields of linguistics, which attempts to establish the characteristics of the system of language itself by postulating models of linguistic competence common to all humans. Briefly, theoretical linguistics studies a particular language as well as a group of languages with a view for constructing theory of their structure and functions without regard to any practical applications that the investigation of language and languages might have (Lyons 1981: 35). It is taken for granted by most of those who use the term *theoretical linguistics* that the goal of the theoretical linguistics is the formulation of a satisfactory theory of the structure of language in general. The fields that are generally considered the core of theoretical linguistics are *phonology, morphology, syntax* and *semantics*. Although phonetics contributes data and information to phonology, it is often excluded from the purview of theoretical linguistics, along with *psycholinguistics, sociolinguistics* and *computational linguistics,* since these fields of linguistics are usually considered to be observational as well as experimental.

An important goal of theoretical linguistics is to search explanations for linguistic universals to establish the proposition that some of the linguistic properties are actually common to all the human languages. The supporters of theoretical linguistics, however, are not reluctant to pay attention to other areas of linguistic investigation such as *sociolinguistics, language acquisition, psycholinguistics* and *historical linguistics,* as they envisage that understanding the basic characteristic aspects of these areas in depth will not only enrich the discipline but also will help in formation of new theories and rules to achieve linguistics universality in the long run.

5.3.2 Applied Linguistics

Applied linguistics is an interdisciplinary field of inquiry that identifies, investigates and offers solutions to language-related real-life problems. It tries to address a broad range of language-related issues in order to improve the lives of individuals and conditions of society. It has as its concerns the application of the concepts and findings of linguistics to a variety of practical tasks, including *language teaching, dictionary compilation, textbooks preparation, language planning, computer application, language processing* and others (Lyons 1981: 36). The emphasis of applied linguistics is solely on language users and the ways in which they actually use languages, contrary to theoretical linguistics which studies the language in the abstract form not referring it to any particular context or language (e.g., *Generative Grammar* as made by Chomsky).

As far as applied linguistics is concerned, it is clear that it draws on both the general and the descriptive branches of the subject. It draws on a wide range of theoretical, methodological and educational approaches from various disciplines—from the humanities to the social, cognitive, medical and natural sciences—as it develops its own knowledge about language, its users and uses and their underlying social and material conditions. Some of the academic fields related to applied linguistics are *language education, computer assisted language teaching, computer-mediated linguistic communication, sociolinguistics, psycholinguistics, anthropolinguistics, ethnolinguistics, ecolinguistics, dialectology, bilingualism and multilingualism, lexicography, computational linguistics, corpus linguistics, conversation analysis, contrastive linguistics, language assessment, stylistics, discourse analysis, language pedagogy, second language acquisition, language planning and policies, pragmatics, semiotics, forensic linguistics* and *translation*. Thus, applied linguistics becomes an umbrella term that covers a wide set of areas of study connected with the focus on the language that is actually used.

Applied linguistics has established itself as a response to the narrowing of focus in linguistics with the advent of **generative linguistics** in 1950s. It has always maintained clearly a socially accountable role demonstrated by its central interest in language problems of each and every speech community. Thus, although it started from Europe and the United States, it has rapidly flourished internationally because language-related problems are vital issues directly linked with survival and growth of societies and civilisations.

Initially, applied linguistics was concerned with principles and practices on the basis of linguistics. In the early days, it was thought as the 'linguistics-applied'—at least from the outside of the field. In the 1960s, however, it was expanded to include issues like language assessment, language policy and second language acquisition. As early as the 1970s, it became a problem-driven field as it included solutions to language-related problems in the real world. By the 1990s, it broadened its sphere by including critical studies and multilingualism. Thus the goals of applied linguistics are changed to the theoretical as well as empirical investigation of real world problems in which language is a central issue (Brumfit 1997: 87)[3].

Interestingly, even among applied linguists, there are many differences in opinion with regard to scope, domains and limits of applied linguistics. After the introduction of the term 'applied linguistics' it was associated mainly with first, second and foreign language teaching. However, now-a-days, it is seen as more interdisciplinary branch of science. Although in certain parts of the world language teaching remains the major concern of applied linguists, issues such as speech pathologies and determining the levels of literacy of societies, or language processing along with differences in communication between various cultural groups - all have gained strong interest in applied linguistics. There are many new issues investigated by applied linguists such as discourse analysis, use of sign language, stylistics and rhetoric as well as language learning by children and adults, both as mother tongue and second or foreign language. Also, research on correlation of language and gender as well as the transfer of information in media and interpersonal communication are also included in applied linguistics. Besides, *forensic linguistics, language interpretation, language documentation, language planning, language change* and *translation,* etc. have come within the broad area of applied linguistics.

In most countries, the primary focus of applied linguistics is on the issues connected with language policy of multilingual community. The primary aim is to keep the balance in fulfilling the need for *lingua franca* and maintaining smaller languages in order to save them from extinction. This is a pressing need as with the migration of people within and across the country and from outside its boarders, since the mixture of languages is getting more and more complex. Thus, the focus of applied linguistics is more on linguistic analysis[4] (i.e., the analysis of language attitudes, adopting common language policy, creating teaching textbooks and other materials, etc.).

There are many trends in applied linguistics—some are interconnected, while others are not having too much in common. There are, however, some very general tendencies among the applied linguists to put more effort on certain investigations such as languages of wider communication, corpus analysis and critical applied linguistics[5]. When it comes to languages of wider communication it is clear that with increasing numbers of international travels and technological advances the need for an international language rises. As English is used as the *lingua franca*, the applied linguists attempt to include language policy and language planning in their interests. They are equally concerned with analysing language and identity as well as special educational needs. Applied linguists take both quantitative and qualitative approach to the study of language and focus on identification of patterns of language use depending on social context, audiences, genres and settings.

There are debates if other disciplines are as important as linguistics for applied linguistics. For instance, psychology enters into many courses of applied linguistics, as it is noted in language education, particularly the ideas about language testing and learning. To some applied linguists, the discipline can draw on any subject with anything to say about language teaching or language learning. To others, linguistics is the sole source of ideas in applied linguistics. To many others, applied linguistics is for applying the theoretical issues to actual language data. Hence the construction of dictionaries or the collection of language corpora of millions of words of a language are applied linguistics, as are descriptions of social networks or of gender differences. Thus, the scope of applied linguistics becomes wider as it includes many areas starting from the study of first language acquisition to computational linguistics.

Applied linguistics has shown enormous growth in the last few decades. With utmost orientation, it has been concerned with classroom language acquisition because of its implications on psychological models of language and language processing and on social models of interaction and identity. Another dimension of applied linguistics is seen as providing data to test out linguistic theories rather than to increase our knowledge of a language itself. It also explores how the language is used for referring things by people who have said as well as to trace how the knowledge of people is carried through language.

107

Applied linguistics means many things to many people. Discovering what a book or a course in applied linguistics is about involves reading the small print to discover its orientation. Those with an interest in linguistic theory feel frustrated when bombarded with classroom teaching techniques; those who want to handle large amounts of spoken or written data will be disappointed by single example of sentences or experiments.

Today, computers are widely used in many areas of applied linguistics. For instance, works on *speech synthesis* and *speech recognition* use phonetic and phonemic knowledgebase to provide voice interfaces to computers. Also, application of computer in machine translation, computer assisted teaching and natural language processing are areas of applied linguistics, which have come to the forefront. The influence of these new fields has an effect on the theories of syntax and semantics, because modelling syntactic and semantic theories on computers have faced many constraints.

In principle, the apparent distinction between the theoretical and the applied linguistics is independent of the other two distinctions drawn so far. In practice, there is little difference between the terms *theoretical linguistics* and *applied linguistics*: it is taken for granted by most of those who use the term *theoretical linguistics* that the goal of theoretical linguistics is the formulation of a satisfactory theory of the structure of language in general. As far as *applied linguistics* is concerned, it is clear that it draws on both the general and the descriptive branches of the subject (Lyons 1981: 37).

5.4 Microlinguistics and Macrolinguistics

The third dimension looks into the interface underlying *microlinguistics* and *macrolinguistics*, which are discussed below.

5.4.1 Microlinguistics

The distinction between *microlinguistics* and *macrolinguistics* is actually related to the narrower and broader view of the scope of the discipline. Since there is no universally accepted terminological distinction for this purpose, one can use generalised terms such as *microlinguistics* and *macrolinguistics* to measure the scope of the discipline in better perspective. It can be said that while in *microlinguistics* one adopts the narrower view, in case of *macrolinguistics* one is inclined to adopt a broader view.

Linguists often differ in their views on what precisely should be the scope of linguistics or linguistic studies. Some of the scholars argue that the primary concerns of linguistics should be confined to the levels of phonetics and phonology, morphology and syntax. This is called the *microlinguistics* perspective.

The term *microlinguistics* was first used in print by George Trager (1949) in an article published in *Studies in Linguistics: Occasional Papers* (OED 1989). In this article it has been argued that *microlinguistics* is a branch of linguistics that concerns itself with the study of language systems in the abstract form, without any regard to meaning or notional content of linguistic expressions. Language, in *microlinguistics*, is reduced to abstract mental elements of syntax and the physical elements of phonology. It contrasts with *macrolinguistics* that includes meanings of various types and especially with sociolinguistics, which studies how language and meanings function within human social systems (Matthews 2002).

At its narrowest view *microlinguistics* is concerned solely with structure of a language system, without any regard to the ways in which languages are acquired, stored in brain, or used in various functions, without regard to the interdependence of language and culture; without regard to the physiological and psychological mechanisms that are involved in language behaviour; and without regard to *ethnolinguistic* or *stylistic factors* involved in linguistic activities, etc. In short, *microlinguistics* looks at language without regard to any thing other than the language-system, considered in itself or for itself, as noted in the dichotomies proposed by Saussure (Lyons 1981: 35).

According to Bell (1976) these are broad terms which refer to two major types of linguistics. While *microlinguistics* refers to phonetics, phonology, grammar and semantics; *macrolinguistics* covers sociolinguistics, discourse analysis, pragmatics and other related disciplines. In sociolinguistics, the micro level is often equated with variation and face-to-face communication, whereas macro level involves language planning and sociology of language (Bell 1976: 252).

5.4.2 Macrolinguistics

Some scholars are interested to take a broader view of linguistics to include besides the levels of language analysis mentioned above (i.e., *phonology, morphology* and *syntax*) other aspects of language within the scope of linguistics. They argue that many areas of human activity, which are directly or indirectly linked with language and linguistics, should also come under the purview of linguistics. This view is generally known as *macrolinguistics*. At its broadest view, *macrolinguistics* is actually concerned with everything that pertains in any way at all the things to language and linguistics. As many disciplines other than linguistics are also concerned with language, it is not surprising that many interdisciplinary areas are identified in *macrolinguistics* and given distinct names such as *sociolinguistics, psycholinguistics, cognitive linguistics, ethnolinguistics, computational linguistics, stylistics, mathematical* or *statistical linguistics*, etc. (Lyons 1981: 35).

The distinction between *microlinguistics* and *macrolinguistics*, however, is not free from the distinction drawn between *theoretical linguistics* and *applied linguistics*. Since there is theoretical aspect in every branch of *macrolinguistics*, in applied linguistics it becomes essential to take a broader view rather than a narrower one about the structure and functions of languages. This is why linguists are willing to incorporate what is here called *microlinguistics* within applied linguistics (Lyons 1981: 37).

Since the scope of *macrolinguistics* is wider than that of *microlinguistics*, linguists study languages, their properties and their users in a much broader perspective with a scientific bent of mind required for studying the human languages. They not only try to answer what language is, but also deal with the structure of languages to describe and explain their nature and function in accordance with other disciplines directly or indirectly related to languages. They try to discover the language universals; put the linguistic elements into theoretical frameworks; investigate all major domains of *microlinguistics* such as *phonetics* (production of sounds), *phonology* (use of sounds), *morphology* (word formation) and *syntax* (sentence and phrase formation) to understand how these fields are interfaced with other fields such as *semantics* (meaning), *pragmatics* (effect of situation) and *discourse* (texts).

The scope of *macrolinguistics*, within the last few years, has expanded to such an extent that linguists are now at their liberty to take majority of issues of *theoretical linguistics, sociolinguistics, psycholinguistics, historical linguistics, applied linguistics, computational linguistics, neurolinguistics, anthropolinguistics, pragmatics, cognitive linguistics, semiotics, forensic linguistics* and others under their research and investigation. To study these fields of linguistics, linguists adopt scientific approaches and methods to be explicit, consistent and systematic—three indispensable qualities of any scientific study. They select aspects of languages to be studied; standardise specific procedures to be adopted for study; and restrict themselves from accepting intuitive beliefs, hypothesis and guesses. With objectivity, they apply critical approaches with an open-mind and use valid, acceptable and standard resources to deal with the languages of every period, speaker and community.

In the context of acknowledging importance of language and linguistics to so many disciplines, linguists are bound to take the broadest possible view about its subject matter. However, the problem is that modern linguistics has not yet developed a satisfactory theoretical framework within which we can view language simultaneously from a psychological, a sociological, a cultural, a stylistic, an aesthetic, a mathematical, an applied and a neuro-physiological point of view. Most linguists now-a-days would say that it is *theoretical synchronic microlinguistics* that constitutes the core of their discipline and gives it whatever unity and coherence it has. Almost half of the present study is devoted to this central core; the rest is concerned with historical linguistics and with selected areas of *macrolinguistics* (Lyons 1981: 37).

5.5 Synchronic Linguistics and Diachronic Linguistics

The last dimension deals with the distinction between *synchronic linguistics* and *diachronic linguistics*.

5.5.1 Synchronic Linguistics

Synchronic linguistics is an approach of linguistics that analyses the structure of a language or languages as static phenomenon. It is the study of a language at a given point in time. The time studied may be either the present or a particular point in the past. Synchronic analyses can also be made of the dead languages, such as *Latin, Greek, Avestan* and *Sanskrit*. It is the study of the phonological, morphological, syntactic and other features of a language at a stated time. In essence, synchronic description of a language is non-historical (or non-evolutionary) as it tries to present an account of the language as it is manifested at some particular points in time.

Ferdinand de Saussure is regarded the father of this dimension, which adds a new perspective in the study of language. In his *Course in*

111

General Linguistics (1916), Saussure examines the relationship between language used at a particular given point of time and the evolution of language over the years. He defines linguistics as the study of language, as well as the study of the manifestations of human speech. He says that linguistics is also concerned with the history of languages and with the social or cultural influences that shape the development of language. He distinguishes between *synchronic* (i.e., static) *linguistics*, which is the study of language at a particular point in time and *diachronic* (i.e. evolutionary) *linguistics*, which is the study of the history or evolution of language.

Synchronic linguistics is also called as **descriptive linguistics**. In the 20th century, synchronic description of language has come to be regarded as prior to diachronic description, as the latter presupposes that synchronic studies at various stages of development of a language have already been carried out. The goal of *synchronic linguistics* is to analyse as well as describe the language actually used now, or in the past, by a group of people. Accurate synchronic description of actual language use in speech and writing is, indeed, a very difficult proposition and linguists have often been reduced to very inaccurate approximations.

Almost all the linguistic theories have their origin in practical problems of descriptive linguistics or synchronic linguistics. For instance, phonetics (and its theoretical developments such as phonemes) has been dealing with how to pronounce languages. In a similar manner we can say, syntax is meant to describe what is going on in construction of phrases and sentences by way of using words once phonetics has been reduced to a control level; and lexicography is meant to show how 'words' in a language, at a given point in time, are actually used in multifaceted linguistic activities.

5.5.2 Diachronic Linguistics

Diachronic linguistics is contrasted with and distinguished from synchronic linguistics, because it studies a language or languages over the periods of time. It regards linguistic phenomena in terms of their development and evolution through time. Diachronic linguistics is called **historical linguistics**, since the diachronic analysis of language is the main concern of historical linguistics, while most other branches of linguistics are concerned with some forms of synchronic·analysis of language data and information.

Throughout last two centuries, linguists were very much concerned with investigating the details of historical development of languages to formulate hypotheses and rules about language change. The branch of the discipline that dealt with these matters was known as the diachronic or the historical linguistics. A diachronic description of a language can trace the historical developments of the languages and records the changes that have taken place in it between successive points in time: *diachronic linguistics* is equivalent, therefore, to *historical linguistics* (Lyons 1981: 36). It is obvious that in *diachronic linguistics*, as in *synchronic linguistics*, one may be interested to study language in general or in particular languages.

According to Ferdinand de Saussure, the diachronic change of languages actually originates in social activities of speech. Changes occur in individual patterns of speaking before becoming more widely accepted as a part of a language. Speaking is an activity, which directly involves oral and auditory communication between the individuals. According to Saussure, nothing enters into written language without being attested in speech (Saussure 1966: 168). Language changes by rearranging and reinterpreting its units. He has also argued that the units of language could have a synchronic or diachronic arrangement (Saussure 1966: 121).

Diachronic linguistics (or historical linguistics) studies the history and evolution of languages through the **comparative method**. Often the aim is to classify languages in different language families, which have descended from a common ancestor. This leads to comparison of the elements in different languages to detect possible cognates in order to be able to reconstruct how different languages have changed over time. This also involves the study of *etymology*, the study of the history of single words.

Diachronic linguistics (or historical linguistics) was among the first linguistic disciplines to emerge and was the most widely practised form of linguistic studies in the late 19th century. The shift in focus to synchronic perspective started with Saussure and gradually it became quite predominant in western linguistics with Chomsky's emphasis on the study of synchronic and universal aspects of language. Diachronic linguistics, within its scope, has five main concerns as the followings:

(a) To describe and account for observed changes in particular languages;

113

(b) To reconstruct pre-history of languages and determine their relatedness, grouping them into language families (comparative linguistics);

(c) To develop general theories about how and why language changes;

(d) To describe the history of speech communities; and

(e) To study the history of words, i.e., etymology[6].

Modern diachronic linguistics dates from the late 18th century. It grew out of the earlier discipline known as **philology**, which was mainly concerned with studying the ancient texts and documents dating back to antiquity. At first, diachronic linguistics was called **comparative linguistics**[7], as scholars were primarily concerned with establishing relation of language families and reconstructing the prehistoric proto-languages using the strategies such as **comparative method** and **internal reconstruction**. The focus was initially on the well-known Indo-European languages, many of which had long written histories. Since then, there has been significant comparative linguistic works which expanded outside the European languages as well. The comparative linguistics is now, however, only a limited part of a more broadly conceived discipline of diachronic linguistics. Initially, modern linguistics was primarily diachronic in orientation as the study of modern dialects involved looking at their origins.

A purely synchronic linguistics was not possible for any period before the invention of gramophone, as written records always lagged behind speech in reflecting linguistic developments. Also, the works of sociolinguistics on linguistic variation have shown that synchronic states are not uniform: the speech habits of older and younger speakers as well as the speech habits of people belonging to different ethnicity, profession, gender, etc. differ in ways that point to language change over time (Labov 1966, Labov 1972, Trudgill 1974 and Milroy 1987).

Synchronic and diachronic approaches to study language can come to quite different conclusions. For example, a strong verb in English like *sing: sang: sung* is irregular when viewed synchronically. Native speaker's brain processes these as learned forms, whereas the derived forms of regular verbs are processed quite differently, by the application of productive rules. This is an insight of psycholinguistics, relevant for **language didactics**[8], both of which are synchronic disciplines. However a diachronic analysis will show that the strong verb is the remnant of a fully regular system of internal vowel changes, as diachronic linguistics seldom approves 'irregular verb'.

5.6 Concluding Remarks

The discussion presented above shows that languages—either in general or in particular—can be studied from different angles, perspectives and points of view. Therefore, the field of linguistics as a whole can be divided into several sub-fields or domains according to the points of view that are adopted or the special emphasis that is given to the one set of phenomena, or assumptions, rather than the other. As a holistic discipline, linguistics studies language as a human phenomenon taking various extralinguistics issues within its realms of investigation.

When language is treated as a human behaviour, a linguist is set to study and describe how physical movements and acts are involved into it; how people acquire and learn languages; how human cognitive system works behind the comprehension and production of speech sounds. When language is viewed as social phenomenon or social identity, linguists try to understand what happens in linguistic conversation; how a language becomes a valuable possession for social group identity; how people can interact, relate, cooperate and maintain social status with the use of language; how language becomes a medium for expressing personalities, views, beliefs, attitudes, solidarity and knowledge of world; and how language succeeds to denote spatial, deictic, telic and temporal features. When language is considered as a formal system, linguists treat language as a system; aims to explain its structure; classifies its forms and properties; and verifies if it belongs to social science or natural science.

In essence, linguistics is both theoretical and applied; both intuitive and empirical; both descriptive and prescriptive; both synchronic and diachronic; and both cognitive and computational. A linguist has no right to make value judgment about the languages or language varieties (e.g., dialects, sociolects, idiolects, pidgins and creoles, etc.). He has to acknowledge the existence of written and spoken forms and contrast and compare dichotomies (e.g., form and class, langue and parole, system and use, syntagmatic and paradigmatic, code and message, competence and performance, theories and applications, micro structure and macro structure, diachronicity and synchronicity, etc.). He has to define the future of linguistic research; identify the branches of specialisation and study the language as a whole 'system of systems'. To a linguist, language is both speech and writing; language is what the native speakers say; and languages can be different in genealogical, typological and geographical parameters. He has to consider social and situational contexts, understand the intentions and perceptions of speakers; and attest the role of context in language use. Thus a linguist can provide satisfactory conceptual representation of language to be applied to describe not only the language(s) he studies, but also the other languages which are not yet studied.

Notes and Comments

[1]   Language description is a work intensive endeavour usually requiring years of field work for linguists to learn a language sufficiently well to develop a reference grammar of it. Further task of language documentation requires the linguist to collect a preferably large corpus of texts and recordings of sounds and videos in the language and to arrange for its storage in accessible formats in open repositories where it may be of the best use for further research and application by other researchers.

[2]   This idea is analogous to practices in other sciences. For instance, a zoologist studies the animal kingdom without making subjective judgments on whether a particular animal is better or worse than another; or a botanist who studies the world of plants without any prescriptive bias to claim that a particular plant is better than the other.

[3]   In the new millennium, linguists are largely concerned with linguistic findings and describing the generalities and varieties both within particular languages and among all languages. Applied linguistics takes the result of those findings and applies them to other areas. Although the term *applied linguistics* is often used to refer to the use of linguistic research in language teaching only, the results of linguistic research are used in many other areas as well, such as lexicography and translation. *Applied linguistics* is, therefore, a misnomer, since it focuses on making engineering solutions for real-world linguistic problems, not simply applying existing technical knowledge from linguistics.

Moreover it applies knowledge from many other sources and disciplines, such as sociology, conversation analysis and anthropology.

[4] Linguistic analysis is a sub-discipline of applied linguistics used by many countries to verify the claimed nationality of migrating people seeking asylum who do not hold the necessary documentation to prove their claim. This often takes the form of an interview by personnel in an immigration department. Depending on the country, this interview is conducted in either the asylum seeker's native language through an interpreter, or in an international *lingua franca* like English. Australia uses the former method and Germany employs the latter; the Netherlands uses either of the methods based on the languages involved. Tape recordings of the interview then undergo language analysis, which is usually done by either private contractors or within a department of the government. In this analysis, linguistic features of the asylum seeker are used by the analysts to make a determination about the speaker's nationality. The reported findings of the linguistic analysis can play a critical role in the government's decision on the refugee status of the asylum seeker.

[5] Critical applied linguistics is interested in those social problems, which are connected with language such as unemployment, mass illiteracy and language pedagogy (Brown 2005).

[6] Etymology is the study of history of words—when these entered a language, from what source and how their form and meaning have changed over time. A word may enter a language as a *loanword* (i.e., as a word from one language adopted by speakers of another language), through *derivational morphology* by combining pre-existing elements in the language, by a hybrid of these two processes called *phono-semantic matching,* or in several other minor ways.

[7] Comparative linguistics (originally called *comparative philology*) is a branch of historical linguistics that is concerned with comparing languages in order to establish their historical relatedness and antiquity. Languages may be related by convergence through borrowing or by genetic descent, thus languages can change and are also able to cross-relate.

[8]   Language didactics refers to second language acquisition or learning, which intends to develop learners in such a way that learners become highly skilled in using a second language. It also refers to the process by which learners learn a second language in addition to their native language(s). Since it refers to what the learner does; and does not refer to what the teacher does, it studies both the psychology and sociology of the learning process.

Chapter 6
New Branches of Linguistics

6.1 Introduction

Natural languages, in general and in particular, can be studied from different perspectives, purposes and reasons. That means, the discipline linguistics as a whole, can be divided into several sub-fields in accordance with the goals and missions of language study. At the present moment, linguistics has been trying to cross over its old-age traditional divisions of *phonetics and phonology, morphology, syntax, semantics* and *etymology* to enter into new arenas of study with accumulation of new linguistic data and information. It has been trying to present new analyses and interpretations to shed new lights on languages, speakers and societies.

This change in approach or strategy in language study has become highly beneficial to the whole mankind. We are now in a better position to realise that language is not only a useful means of communication, but also a highly reliable resource for understanding human mind, human societies, human behaviour and human cognition. Moreover, understanding form and texture of language data in new light has become valuable input for mass literacy and language education. For instance, analysis and interpretation of newly accumulated data and information of language use has made a sea change in the approach and strategies used in language teaching and planning—two important areas of applied linguistics, which are considered indispensable in the backdrop of mass literacy and progress of societies.

It may appear to some that the new fields of linguistics are separate from each other completely and there exists hardly any link between these fields. In reality, however, these fields are not at all isolated from each other. Rather, these are interdependent as their common resource

119

Language and Linguistics

is nothing but language. Even then, independent status of each field cannot be ignored, as each field has its own core concepts to foster significant scholarly inquiry and research. In the following sections an attempt is made to discuss a few new branches of linguistics (in alphabetical order) without reference to older branches, which are often discussed in any general book on linguistics.

6.2 Anthropological Linguistics

Anthropological linguistics refers to the study of relations between language and culture, which culminates from the relations developed among human biology, cognition and language. This field quite often overlaps the field of **linguistic anthropology**, which is a branch of anthropology that tries to study humans *through* the languages they use. This field has created a major impact in the studies of human visual perceptions (especially colour) and bioregional demography, both of which are concerned with distinctions that are made in languages about perceptions of the surroundings.

Anthropological linguistics has registered implications for sociology and self-organisation of people. The study of the Penan[1] people, for instance, has revealed that their language employs six different and distinct words, all of which can be translated into English as 'we' (Davis *et al.* 1995: 15). This gives an opportunity to a linguist not only to study these distinctions but also to relate these to types of societies and to actual bodily adaptation to the senses. Furthermore, a linguist can study distinctions made in languages with regard to the colours of the rainbow: seeing the tendency to increase the diversity of terms, as an evidence that there are distinctions that bodies in environment *must* make, leading to **situated knowledge**[2] and perhaps a **situated ethics**[3], whose final evidence is the differentiated set of terms used to denote 'we'.

Anthropological linguistics, in general, seeks to understand the processes of human communication (both verbal and non-verbal), variation in language use across time and space, the social uses of language and the relationship between language and culture. It is the branch of anthropology that brings linguistic methods to bear on anthropological problems, linking the analysis of linguistic forms and processes to interpretation of socio-cultural processes. While working on anthropological linguistics, researchers often tend to draw on related

120

fields including *sociolinguistics, ethnolinguistics, sociology, cognitive linguistics, semiotics, discourse analysis, pragmatics* and *narrative analysis.*

Anthropological linguistics is broadly divided into four major sub-fields: (a) *descriptive linguistics,* which works for developing grammar and lexicon for the unstudied languages; (b) *historical linguistics,* which tries to reconstruct the past languages from which the current languages have descended; (c) *ethnolinguistics* which studies the relationship between language and culture; and (d) *sociolinguistics,* which studies the social functions of language. Also, sometimes, *anthropological linguistics* is linked with it to study the evolution of the parts of human brain that deals with language.

6.3 Cognitive Linguistics

Cognitive linguistics has evolved from the works of several researchers active in the 1970s who were interested in finding out the relation between language and human mind and who were not ready to follow the prevailing practice of explaining language patterns by means of applying structural properties internal to specific languages. Rather than attempting to isolate syntax from the rest elements of language, this line of research was interested to examine the relation of language structure to the things of the outside world. It wanted not only to understand the cognitive principles and the mechanisms specific to language, but also the principles of human categorisation; the pragmatics and interactional principles; and the functional principles in general, such as, iconicity and economy in linguistic expression.

Cognitive linguistics, in general, intends to understand language *creation, cognition* and *usage* as best explained with reference to human cognition, in general. It adheres to three central propositions:

(a)   It denies that there is an *autonomous linguistic faculty* in human mind.
(b)   It understands grammar in terms of *conceptualisation.*
(c)   It claims that knowledge of language arises out of *language use.*

It does not believe that the human mind has any module for language acquisition, which is unique and autonomous (and which stands in contrast to the arguments furnished in generative grammar). Although the supporters of cognitive linguistics do not necessarily deny the fact that human linguistic ability is innate, they certainly deny that it is a *separate* entity from the rest of cognition. Thus they argue that knowledge of linguistic phenomena (such as, phonemes, morphemes, words and syntax, etc.) is essentially conceptual in nature. Also, they argue that the storage and retrieval of linguistic data is not significantly different from the storage and retrieval of other knowledge and the use of language in understanding employs almost similar cognitive skills and methods used in other non-linguistic activities. Deviating from the world of **truth-conditional semantics,** cognitive linguists intend to view meaning in terms of conceptualisation by human mind. That means, instead of viewing meaning in terms of models of the world, they want to view it in terms of mental spaces. This leads them to argue that language is both embodied and situated in specific environments[4].

In general, cognitive linguistics can be divided into three major domains of study:

(a) Cognitive phonology that deals mainly with cognition of speech sounds and their conceptualisation.
(b) Cognitive grammar which mainly deals with morphology, syntax and other grammar-oriented issues.
(c) Cognitive semantics that mainly deals with lexical semantics.

The issues of cognition that are of interest in cognitive linguistics covering all the broad domains, include construction grammar and cognitive grammar, conceptual metaphor and conceptual blending, conceptual organisation, force dynamics, image schemas, metonymy, frame semantics, iconicity, construal and subjectivity, gesture and sign language, linguistic relativism, cognitive neuroscience, etc. Related domains that maintain interface with the above areas include conceptual semantics[5], computational models of metaphor and language acquisition and psycholinguistic research.

Recent works on cognitive linguistics (Chafe 1980, Fillmore 1997, Lakoff 1987, Langacker 1991, Talmy 2000) have developed individual approaches to language description and linguistic theory and have focused on particular sets of phenomena. However, the most important assumption shared by all is that meaning is so central to language that it should be of primary focus of any study of cognitive linguistics. Since linguistic structures serve the function of expressing meanings, mappings between meanings and forms are a prime subject of linguistic analysis and investigation in this field. Moreover, since all linguistic forms are closely linked to semantic structures, semantic structures of all the meaningful linguistic units can be and should be investigated. These arguments are in direct opposition to the ideas that develop within Chomskyan linguistics, in which meaning was 'interpretive' and 'peripheral' to the study of language[6].

During the 1990s, cognitive linguistics became widely recognised as an important field of specialisation within linguistics. Several works on this area developed background for formation of theories and establishing connection with **construction grammar** (Croft 2001) to adopt representational eclecticism while maintaining basic tenets of cognitivism. By the mid-1990s, it has turned out to be known as separate field of investigation characterised by a defining set of intellectual pursuits practiced by its adherents (Geeraerts 1995):

"Because cognitive linguistics sees language as embedded in the overall cognitive capacities of man, topics of special interest for cognitive linguistics include: the structural characteristics of natural language categorisation (such as prototypicality, systematic polysemy, cognitive models, mental imagery and metaphor); the functional principles of linguistic organisation (such as iconicity and naturalness); the conceptual interface between syntax and semantics (as explored by cognitive grammar and construction grammar); the experiential and pragmatic background of language-in-use; and the relationship between language and thought, including questions about relativism and conceptual universals" (Geeraerts 1995: 111-112).

The above mentioned statement establishes a strong connection between cognitive linguistics and the research activities of functional linguistics, psycholinguistics, linguistic descriptions, pragmatics and discourse studies. At present, for many cognitive linguists, the principal interest in cognitive linguistics lies in its provision of a better-grounded approach to and a set of theoretical assumptions for syntactic and semantic theories than generative linguistics can provide. For others, the appeal of cognitive linguistics lies in the opportunity for linking the study of language and mind to the study of human brain.

Language and Linguistics

6.4 Computational Linguistics

Computational linguistics is a discipline that operates between linguistics and computer science. Although it is concerned with the computational aspects of the human language faculty, it is strongly linked with cognitive sciences and overlaps with artificial intelligence —a branch of computer science that aims at computational models of human cognition. So, one can say computational linguistics is an interdisciplinary field that deals with statistical and/or rule-based modelling of natural language from a computational perspective. It develops formal models simulating aspects of the human language faculty and implements them as computer programme. These programme constitute the basis for the evaluation and further development of the theories. In addition to linguistic theories, findings from cognitive psychology play a major role in simulating linguistic competence[7]. Although traditionally computational linguistic tasks were carried out by computer scientists who had specialised in application of computer to the processing of natural languages, at present, experts from many areas are working together in this interdisciplinary field: linguists, language experts, mathematicians, computer scientists, cognitive scientists, logicians, cognitive psychologists, psycholinguists, anthropologists, neuroscientists and experts in artificial intelligence— to mention a few.

Computational linguistics has two major domains: (a) theoretical issues and (b) application. *Theoretical computational linguistics* takes up the issues of theoretical linguistics and cognitive science to deal with the formal theories about the linguistic knowledge that a human being needs for generating and understanding a language. Today these theories have reached a degree of complexity that can only be managed by using computers. On the other hand, *applied computational linguistics* focuses mainly on the practical outcomes of modelling human language use. The methods, techniques, systems, tools and strategies applied in this area are often put under **language engineering** or **language technology**.

Although the existing systems of computational linguistics are far from being successful in achieving the human ability, these have opened numerous applicational possibilities. The goal has been to develop software which have some knowledge of human language and which can be used as products to provide support for human linguistic tasks. The main hurdle in improving human-machine interaction is a communication problem between human and computer. Today's computers do not understand human language and the computer language is difficult to learn by human as it does not correspond to the structure of human language. Even then, it is expected that once machine succeeds in understanding human language and the methods how it works, it will be able to perform more sophisticated tasks that will enable people to use software to enhance their linguistic activities.

Initial activities of computational linguistics started in the United States in the 1950s when scientists began to use computer to automatically translate texts from foreign languages (particularly from Russian scientific journals) into English. Since computers can make arithmetic calculations much faster and more accurately than humans, it was thought to be only a matter of time when technical details could be taken care of to allow quick translation from one language to another. However, when machine translation failed to yield accurate translation outputs right away, processing of human languages was recognised as a far more complex task than it had been originally assumed. It led scientists to formulate a new field of study for developing algorithms and software for intelligently processing human language data. When **Artificial Intelligence** came into being in the 1960s, computational linguistics became a branch of it to deal with the human-level comprehension and production of natural languages.

With regard to machine translation it was clearly understood that in order to translate from one language to another, one has to understand grammars of the both languages, including *morphology* (grammar of word forms) and *syntax* (grammar of sentence structure). Also, in order to understand syntax, one has to understand *semantics, lexicon, discourse* and *pragmatics* of language use. Thus what started as an effort to translate between languages eventually evolved into a separate discipline devoted to understanding how to represent and process human languages by using computer.

Computational linguistics is divided into several areas depending on the medium of language being processed (spoken or textual); and upon the tasks being performed (language analysis, recognition, synthesis or generation). While speech recognition and synthesis deal with how spoken language can be understood or created using computers, parsing and generation deal with, respectively, taking syntactic components apart and putting them together. Machine translation on the other hand, deals with employing computer to translate between the languages. Mentioned below some of the major areas of research of computational linguistics:

(a) Understanding complexities of natural languages with reference to the context-free and context-sensitive grammars.
(b) Understanding semantics which comprises defining the principles for linguistic meaning representation, automatically constructing them and reasoning with them for sense disambiguation.
(c) Electronic language corpora generation and language processing.
(d) Design of parsers, chunkers and concordancers for natural languages.
(e) Design of tagging systems for parts-of-speech (POS) tagging.
(f) Information retrieval from natural language databases.
(g) Automatic translation between languages with application of linguistic and computational tools and systems.
(h) Man-machine interface development for E-Governance.
(i) Educational technology.

6.5 Corpus Linguistics

Corpus linguistic is not a new branch of linguistics. In simple term, it is a new approach to language study which aims at analysing most reliable linguistic data and information for all branches of linguistics. To achieve this mission, it faithfully collects linguistic data and information from different domains of language use and studies these scientifically and systematically. The term *corpus* refers to a statistically sampled large language data, which is designed for the purpose of investigation, analysis, description and application in all branches of linguistics. Due to large language database, diverse text types, varied linguistic data and information, confirmed referential authenticity, wide representation, easy accessibility and unquestionable verifiability, a corpus becomes indispensable in all branches of linguistics. In any branch of linguistics, a scholar can refer to corpus database to verify if earlier data and examples are valid, previous information and explanations are authentic; and intuitive evidence and arguments are appropriate with regard to evidences of actual language use (Dash 2007: 30)[8].

In corpus linguistics, *corpus* holds a special connotative sense. According to Crystal (1995) it refers to "a large collection of linguistic data, either written texts or a transcription of recorded speech, which can be used as a starting point of linguistic description or as a means of verifying hypotheses about a language". In a different way, it refers to "a body of language texts both in written and spoken form. It represents varieties of a language used at each and every field of human interaction. Preserved in machine readable form it enables all kinds of linguistic description and analysis" (Crystal 1997). But Kennedy (1998: 3) does not agree with this definition, since according to him, such a one-dimensional definition may fail to represent the contrasts and varieties involved in the process of corpus generation. Therefore, in the present context of linguistics, *corpus* should be used in the sense of "a large collection of texts assumed to be representative of a given language, dialect, or other subset of a language, to be used for linguistic analysis" (Francis 1982: 7). Although the definitions stated above try to encompass the sociolinguistic components induced within a language, it miserably fails to divert attention to the linguistic criteria considered necessary for designing a corpus.

This need is addressed in the definition where it is argued that, a corpus is a collection of 'pieces' of language that are selected and ordered according to some explicit linguistic criteria in order to be used as sample of the language (Sinclair 1996: 3). It usually refers to a large collection of naturally occurring language texts presented in machine-readable form gathered in a scientific manner to characterise a particular variety or use of a language. It is methodically designed to contain many millions of words compiled from different texts across various linguistic domains to encompass the diversity a language usually exhibits through its multifaceted use. It may refer to any text in written or spoken form. A corpus, which contains constituent 'pieces' of language that are documented as to their origin and provenance are encoded in standard and homogenous way for open-ended retrieval tasks (Sinclair 1991: 172).

Some other scholars, on the contrary, prefer to classify the term *corpus* in finer scheme of classification characterised by some salient features. According to them, a corpus can refer to: (a) (loosely) any body of text (b) (most commonly) a body of machine-readable text and (c) (more strictly) finite collection of machine-readable texts, which are sampled to be maximally representative of a language or a variety (McEnery and Wilson 1996: 215).

127

The definition of *corpus* made by Hunston (2002) is different from others. According to Hunston, "Linguistics have always used the word 'corpus' to describe a collection of naturally occurring examples of language, consisting of anything from a few sentences to a set of written texts or tape recordings, which have been collected for linguistic study. More recently, the word has been reserved for collections of texts (or parts of texts) that are stored and accessed electronically. Because computers can hold and process large amounts of information, electronic corpora are usually larger than the small, paper-based collections previously used to study aspects of language" Hunston (2002: 2).

Two important issues, which are relevant in corpus linguistics in general, come out from the above deliberations: (a) composition of a corpus and (b) usage potential of a corpus. It is not a big deal to collect samples of texts of a language. But mere collection of samples does not stand for *corpus* unless it is marked with some specific properties. A corpus requires data from each and every domain of actual language use without any prejudice and restriction. Theoretically, it has to be infinite in number of data which will faithfully reflect on the varieties normally observed in regular use of language. In sum, it has to be a reliable replica in which all types of language use are honestly manifested.

It has been argued that a corpus should contain a large collection of representative samples of texts covering wide varieties of language use from every domain of linguistic interaction. That means, a corpus should have the following features:

(a)   It should contain large amount of texts of actual language use.
(b)   It should be systematic in formation and text representation.
(c)   It should be truly representative of the source language.
(d)   It should be compatible to computer.
(e)   It should be processeable by both man and machine.
(f)   It should be operational in research and application.

When one tries to develop a general corpus, one needs to keep in mind that it should be designed for faithful study of the linguistic properties of a natural language. Thus, a systematically compiled corpus should contain the following properties:

(a)   It should faithfully contain both common and special linguistic features of a language from where it is designed and developed.

(b)   It should be large in size to include texts from different disciplines. The directional varieties of language use noted in various domains should have proper representation in it.

(c)   It should be a true replica of the physical texts found in spoken and printed documents of a language.

(d)   It should faithfully preserve various forms of words, spelling variations, punctuation marks and other orthographic symbols used in the source text.

(e)   It should represent all the linguistic usage variations in a proportional manner to give a general impression about the language.

(f)   Text samples should be authentic, verifiable and referential for future linguistic works.

(g)   It should be available in machine-readable form for quick access and reference by end-users.

(h)   It should enable users to access language data in multiple tasks starting from simple descriptive study of language to statistical analysis, to language processing, to teaching, to translation, etc.

(i)   Texts should be developed both in annotated and non-annotated forms with provision for removal of annotations.

(j)   Both linguistic and extra-linguistic information should be preserved in a systematic way along with the texts.

Unless defined otherwise, let us consider that a corpus should possess all the properties stated above[9]. In essence, a corpus is an empirical standard, which acts as a benchmark for validation of usage of linguistic properties found in a language. If one analyses a corpus database, one can retrieve the following information about a language or variety:

•   Information about all properties and components used in a language, e.g., sounds, phonemes, intonation, letters, punctuations, morphemes, words, stems, bases, lemmas, compounds, phrases, idioms, set phrases, reduplications, proverbs, clauses, sentences, etc.

•   Grammatical and functional information of letters, morphemes, words, phrases, sentences, idiomatic expressions, proverbs, etc. relating to their structure, composition, patterns of using affixes and inflections, patterns of constituent structure, contexts of use, usage patterns, etc.

129

- Usage-based information of letters, phonemes, morphemes, words, compounds, phrases, sentences, etc. relating their descriptive, stylistic, metaphorical, allegorical, idiomatic and figurative usages, etc.
- Extralinguistic information relating to time, place, situation and agent of language events, social-cultural background of linguistic acts, life and living of target speech community, discourse and pragmatics, as well as of the world knowledge of the language users, at large[10].

It is understandable that developing a corpus in accordance with these conditions mentioned above is really a tough task. However, we can simplify the task to some extent if we redefine the entire concept of corpus generation based on object-oriented and work-specific needs. Since it is known that all types of corpus should not follow the same set of designing and composition principles we can have liberty to design a corpus keeping in mind the works we are planning to do with it (Dash 208: 47). The underlying proposition is that the general principles and conditions of corpus generation may vary depending on the purpose of a corpus developer or user.

There are a number of areas where language corpus is directly used as in *language description, study of syntax, phonetics and phonology, prosody, intonation, morphology, lexicology, semantics, lexicography, discourse, pragmatics, language teaching, language planning, sociolinguistics, psycholinguistics, semiotics, cognitive linguistics, computational linguistics* —to mention a few. In fact, there is hardly any area of linguistics where corpus has not found its utility. This has been possible due to great possibilities offered by computer in collecting, storing and processing natural language database. The availability of computers and machine-readable corpora has made it possible to get data quickly and easily and also to have this data presented in a format suitable for analysis.

Corpus linguistics is, however, not the same as mainly obtaining language data through the use of computer. It is the processing and analysis of the data stored within a corpus. The main task of a corpus linguist is not to find data, but to analyse it. Computer is a useful and sometimes indispensable, tool for carrying out these activities.

6.6 Discourse Analysis

Discourse analysis[11] or the study of discourse is a general term used to refer to a number of approaches adopted to analyse written, spoken and sign language. The basic objectives of discourse analysis are to analyse written texts, speeches, conversations, mediations, negotiations and dialogues, etc. as events of communication and identify those factors, which play phenomenal roles in defining these texts in terms of coherent sequences of sentences, propositions, speech acts and turn-takings in conversations. Contrary to the traditional concepts of linguistics, a discourse analyst tries to study language use 'beyond the boundary of sentence' with close reference to the 'naturally occurring language use', without any reference to the invented or intuitively generated examples. Discourse analysis is used as a powerful method in a variety of disciplines of social science, including *linguistics, anthropology, sociology, cognitive psychology, social psychology, literature, stylistics, international relations, communication studies* and *translation studies*—each of which treats discourse as an area of investigation with its own assumptions, dimensions of analysis and methodologies.

In linguistics, the focal area of discourse analysis is any form of written or spoken language, such as conversations, dialogues, mediations, newspaper articles, advertisements, informative texts and imaginative texts, etc. Since the main goal is to understand the underlying socio-cultural frame of a society, discourse analysts try to know how a social structure is assumed or displayed within spoken or written texts. They are also interested to evaluate the roles of the tools and strategies people use when engaged in communication, such as slowing down one's speech for emphasis, use of metaphors, the choice of particular words, dictions and phrases for creating impacts and so on. In essence, a discourse analyst examines how people use language to construct versions of their own experiences and how they draw on from their cultural and linguistic resources in order to construct their talk in certain ways to have certain effects. So a discourse analyst seeks to find answers how the accounts of the identities of the people are constructed and what is gained from these constructions.

A discourse analyst also tries to identify categories, themes, ideas, views, roles and so on operating within the text itself. Moreover, attention is given for tracing the functions of linguistic forms used in text, the role of context in interpretation of texts, representation of discourse content within the topic, representation of discourse structure at various stages of text, the structure of information, the nature of reference in text and in discourse and the nature of coherence in interpretation of a discourse (Gillian and Yule 1983). The aim is to identify the commonly shared discursive properties (i.e., shared patterns of talking) used to develop conversation or a piece of text.

Information obtained from discourse analysis of a text helps an analyst to answer questions related to various issues under investigation, such as, how people construct their own versions of an event, how they utilise discourse to maintain social relations, how they adapt the linguistic means for achieving goals and how they construct their own identity in relation to others. In case of conversation analysis, the analyst uses transcripted texts of conversation as source materials and analyses these to retrieve valuable data and information about the roles played by the interactants. For instance, one can transcribe the conversations of a street hawker and a customer to focus on those situations that generate interest, query, negotiation, bargain, settlement and eventual (dis)satisfaction.

In general, the common topics of interest to discourse analysis include the followings:

(a) Various dimensions of spoken discourse (such as, accent, intonation, rhetoric, gesture, syntax, lexicon, style, meanings, speech acts, moves, pauses, strategies, turns and other aspects of verbal interaction).

(b) Various levels of written discourse (e.g., orthography, words, syntax, passage, text, style, meaning, strategies, metaphors, pictures, figures, tables, diagrams and few other aspects of written texts).

(c) Genres of discourse (such as various types of discourse used in politics, mass media, advertisement, education, science, technology, business, legal proceedings, sports, etc.).

(d) Relations between discourse and the emergence of sentence in texts.

(e) Relations between texts (discourse) and contexts.

(f) Relations between discourse, social relation and power,

(g) Relations between discourse and interaction.

(h) Relations between discourse, cognition and memory.

Whereas earlier studies of discourse, for instance in text linguistics, have often focused on abstract structures of written texts, recent studies, especially those influenced by social sciences, favour a more dynamic study of spoken (or oral) texts produced in dialogic interaction.

6.7 Ecolinguistics

Ecolinguistics is an interdisciplinary and interactive field of linguistic study in which several disciplines such as, *biology, ecology, geography, history, culture, philology, philosophy* and *sociology* are interrelated. An ecolinguist starts with a collective view of all these disciplines to fabricate a linguistic world interfaced with ideas, principles and findings of these disciplines. Since the central goal of this new field of study is based on interdependence, collective knowledge sharing, information networking, interrelation, dialectics and diversities, an ecolinguist is hardly interested to develop any methodology, which is one-dimensional in application and any theory, which is skewed in approach.

The discipline *ecolinguistics* emerged in the 1990s as a new paradigm of linguistic research which takes into account not only those social contexts in which a language is embedded, but also those ecological and geographical contexts in which a society is embedded. It has been argued that Halliday's paper (1990) on applied linguistics should receive credit for providing the necessary stimulus to linguists for considering ecological contexts and issues in understanding the consequences of language in a society. In the present global situation, it has been a real challenge for the linguists to establish the importance of linguistics to the ecological issues and concerns of the 21st century, particularly in the context of widespread destruction of the global ecosystem. For example, Halliday has described how the orientation of the English language with regard to unmarked terms such as *large, grow, tall* and *good* has given rise to a positive aspect in the society, in spite of the negative ecological consequences. Starting with the initial comments of Halliday, the field of *ecolinguistics* has evolved considerably —a recent development is the application of *ecolinguistics* to education for sustainability of a society.

At present, *ecolingusitics* is broadly divided into two main domains as the followings (Fill 1996):

(a)   Eco-critical discourse analysis.
(b)   Linguistic ecology.

The *eco-critical discourse analysis* includes application of critical discourse analysis to texts about the environment and environmentalism in order to reveal the underlying ideologies (Harré *et al.* 1999, Stibbe 2005a, 2005b). In its fullest form, it tries to analyse a discourse, which has potential consequences for the future of ecosystems, such as neo-liberal economic discourse and the discursive constructions of consumerism, gender, politics, agriculture and nature (Goatly 1996, 1997). In essence, *eco-critical discourse analysis* does not just focus on the exposing potentially damaging ideologies, but also searches for the discursive representations, which can contribute to a more ecologically sustainable society.

On the other hand, *linguistic ecology* uses metaphor of an ecosystem to describe the relationships and the interactions among the diverse forms of language found in the world and the groups of people who speak these languages (Haugen 1972). In fact, a healthy linguistic ecology consisting of a wide diversity of forms of language is claimed to be indispensable for healthy ecosystems, since local ecological knowledgebase is built into local language varieties.

An extended dimension of linguistic ecology is observed in **ecological learning** (Bastardas-Boada 2002, Stibbe 2005) which makes an attempt to understand learning not just by analysing and describing the psychological mechanisms that mediate learned behaviours, but also by understanding how these mechanisms might have evolved, which selection pressures might have contributed to this evolution and what biological functions that learning serves. The primary goals of this attempt are to make a comparative analysis among the basic learning processes, analyse biological function of various learning processes, discuss the ways in which evolutionary processes and selection pressures might have shaped different learning capacities and to describe some of the proximal mechanisms (mainly cognitive) that mediate different forms of learning (Makkai 1993; Fill, Penz and Trampe 2002; Bang and Door 2007).

6.8 Ethnolinguistics

Ethnolinguistics is a new field of linguistics, which studies the language of a particular ethnic group or a culture. This particular area of investigation has often been associated with the minority linguistic communities living within a frame of larger population, such as the ethnic communities living in Indian subcontinent. The scholars of ethnolinguistics normally study the usage of the minority languages within the context of major languages as well as the perception of the people about the minority languages within the broader spectrum of the major or standard languages.

An ethnolinguist studies how the perception and conceptualisation of the members of a speech community can influence language and how these can be linked to different cultures and societies. An example is the way how the **spatial orientation** is expressed in various cultures. In many societies, words for the cardinal directions like East, West, North and South are derived from the terms used for sunrise and sunset. Even in some societies where such terms are not used, cardinal directions as well as time of a day are determined in accordance with the direction and position of the sun[12]. The nomenclature, however, for the cardinal directions for the Eskimo speakers of Greenland is based on geographical landmarks such as the river and one's position on the coast. Similarly, the *Native American Yurok* people lack the idea of cardinal directions and they orient themselves with respect to their main geographical feature, the Klamath River (Heine 1997).

Another notable area of investigation of this field is the interpretation of relationship between language and culture and understanding the means different ethnic groups employ to perceive their inner and outer world. For instance, a well-known (but highly controversial) subject of ethnolinguistics is the **Sapir-Whorf Hypothesis**[13], which argues that perception of the external world is limited and proportional to what can be described in one's own language.

6.9 Forensic Linguistics

Forensic linguistics is an area of linguistics that studies the interface existing between language, law and crime. It includes, as its domains of investigation, texts obtained in courtroom discourse, voice identification, comprehensibility of legal documents, courtroom interpretations, comprehensibility of police cautions issued to suspects, trademark law, interviews with children in legal system, use of linguistic evidences in court, cases of authorship attribution and the readability of written text documents and translations. Because of its direct application in various areas of social and governmental activities, it is considered as an area of applied linguistics (McMenamin 2002).

The range of topics within forensic linguistics is diverse but most of the research works are carried out in the following areas (Olsson 2004, Coulthard and Johnson 2007, Gibbons and Turell 2008):

(a)   Investigation of trademarks and other intellectual property disputes.
(b)   Voice perception, disambiguation and speaker identification.
(c)   Identification of social and regional accents and dialects.
(d)   Telephone speaker recognition.
(e)   Disambiguating speech from background noise.
(f)   Interpretation of expressed, intended and inferred meanings.
(g)   Courtroom interpretation and document examination in forgery cases.
(h)   Software forensics.
(i)   Dissolving disputes of meaning and use of words, terms and phrases in text documents.
(j)   Identification of author of anonymous texts (e.g., threat letters, mobile phone texts, emails, etc.)
(k)   Identifying and solving cases of plagiarism and authorship attribution.
(l)   Investigating language of the asylum seekers and attesting their actual linguistic identity.
(m)   Reconstructing texts used in conversations in mobile phones.
(n)   Providing linguistic resources for reforming legal language.
(o)   Examining language used in legal activities (e.g., cross-examination, judge's direction, police cautions, police interviews, etc.).

Besides these areas mentioned above we can visualise the application of forensic linguistics in analysis of speech and language used by terrorists and anti-nationals who often use encoded language for exchange of information. In such cases, decoding written or verbal texts to extract the original message can be a real challenge for forensic linguists. Moreover, identifying whether a particular individual has said or written something is based on the analysis of his or her idiolect, choice of words and dictions, patterns of use of words, patterns of intonation, patterns of sentence formation and patterns of stylistic use of language of that individual. That means critical analysis about the use of vocabulary, terms, sounds, accents, phrases, collocations, pronunciation, spelling, grammar and style of writing, etc. is necessary for identification and recognition of actual criminals. Systematic analysis and investigation of such linguistic data may supply vital information for identifying a criminal or an offender. It is, however, important that a forensic linguist must utilise such linguistic materials carefully and cautiously, because most of these materials not only vary from person to person, but also present serious quick-sands in the process of reconstructing individual identity of criminals.

6.10 Lexicography (Computational)

Computational lexicography—a reformed version of traditional lexicography—aims at making dictionaries in fully digital form, which will have far better description and presentation of linguistic information for lexical items used in a language. It aims at using computational methods and tools designed to assist various lexicographical tasks, such as the collection of lexical entities from various sources (mostly from digital corpora), editing of lexicological information for lexical entries, storing of lexical items in a structured manner, preparation of lexicographical information in presentable form, as well as presentation of information in an appropriate manner to the dictionary users. Present availability of digital corpus in processed form as well as advanced facilities of computer have made it possible to develop dictionaries of all types in electronic form keeping in mind the possible areas of their utility in machine translation, machine learning, information retrieval and language teaching.

The connection between computers and dictionaries was first established in the 1970's when computer entered the printing and publishing world for typesetting and production of dictionaries. Gradually, dictionary making task developed a lasting relation between computer and lexicographer at all levels right up to the final production of a dictionary. This interface gave birth to a new form of dictionary known as Electronic Dictionary (ED) along side the existing 'printed' dictionary. This new technology made it possible for the lexicographers to add or revise the lexicographic information in a dictionary easily and quickly, which was not possible in case of printed version. Also, it provided a scope for easy revision of typeset, information, instructions, font, special symbols, notation, illustration, etc. in an electronic dictionary, which was not possible in case of a printed one.

The introduction of computer in dictionary compilation has converted lexicography into a work of 'art, craft and science in dictionary

Language and Linguistics

compilation' (Landau 2003). The traditional definition of *lexicography* is changed drastically because computational lexicography not only deals with the collection and analysis of forms and meanings of the lexical units, but also constructs a user-interface for lexical entries in such a manner that a user can extract all kinds of linguistic and extralinguistic information related to any lexical entry from the dictionary. Computer plays crucial role in formation of such a dictionary, since it makes possible for the dictionary compilers to accelerate the work of dictionary compilation, store unlimited data and information for each lexical item and design the system in such a manner that it becomes highly user-friendly for people of different requirements, orientations, professions and backgrounds.

A computer provides great aids in the job of a lexicographer. It has been introduced into compilation of dictionary due to the fact that it enables a dictionary maker to manage large amount of language data in accumulation, storage, sorting, processing and management. The interaction between a computer and a lexicographer can be seen in all stages of development of a dictionary. In fact, the advances which have been accomplished in the field of lexicography can be realised when we examine the English dictionaries available in electronic form. The merits and advantages of computer-based electronic dictionary are realised due to the following factors:

(a) Modern linguistics has changed its attitude towards a direction, which aids lexicographers in preparation of electronic dictionaries.
(b) Introduction of computer has made it possible to process linguistic data and information efficiently. It has revolutionised lexicographical works, which were once considered impossible.
(c) Electronic dictionary has opened many new applications of dictionaries, since new ways of presenting and disseminating linguistic information succeed to address the needs of new areas such as machine translation, speech-to-text and text-to-speech conversion, dictionarial support for on-line language teaching, spelling checking and language education.

In general, every dictionary—either prepared in printed or digital form—has three main stages: (a) stage of planning, (b) stage of compilation and (c) stage of production. While thirty per cent (30%) of time and energy is spent on planning, fifty per cent (50%) of time and energy is spent on compilation and remaining twenty per cent (20%) of time and energy is spent in production. In case of electronic dictionary, both lexicographers and computers play crucial roles as they interact in all stages of dictionary making. Since a computer can deal with vast amount of information quite elegantly, it provides better mode for accessing information. A computer can be involved at different stages of dictionary making in the following manner:

(a)   Collecting language data of different kinds from digital corpora.
(b)   Storing of language data in easy accessible format.
(c)   Making fast access of linguistic data, materials and information.
(d)   Carrying out text processing operations on the database.
(e)   Carrying out consistently complex repetitive tasks with great precision.
(f)   Selecting the final list of lexical entries for the dictionary.
(g)   Arranging the entries in a systematic order (mostly alphabetically).
(h)   Constructing elaborate definitions for each entry word.
(i)   Supplying all kinds of information for the entry words.
(j)   Ensuring consistency and completeness of information in use.

A computer is highly efficient when it comes to editing a text database. It enables one to handle the database easily and reorganise the texts in various ways. For instance, searching through a large database to trace every sense of a word is a highly laborious task for an individual but a simple job for a computer. A simple tool like **concordance** can search each and every instance of use of a word from a large database without any fail within a very short time and present these before a dictionary maker with full contextual and / or sentential information. Moreover, it can rapidly access all words and their information; make change to text through a single command; sort out words alphabetically and numerically, verify and correct errors in the database after compilation (e.g., spelling, brackets, section, etc.), can lemmatize inflected words; extract words from running texts; divide words according to different linguistic categories, cite contextual and collocational information of words; and show the distributional patterns of words in formation of larger linguistic units like phrases, idioms and proverbs, etc.

The presentation of information related to each entry word needs to be structured efficiently so that maximum number of queries of a dictionary user is addressed. In this regard, the type of information included in an electronic dictionary are: form of the headwords, spelling variations, pronunciation and stress patterns, part-of-speech, grammatical information, inflectional variants, derivational forms, sense indication by definitional meaning, cross reference to synonyms, examples of the different ways a word is used, expressions and collocations in which a headword commonly occurs, usage notes and special uses and illustrations, etc.

The practical lexicographic works also involve several other activities. The compilation of an electronic dictionary requires careful consideration of all or some of the following issues:

(a) Identifying the target users and their requirements.
(b) Defining the communicative and cognitive functions of the dictionary.
(c) Selecting and organising the components of the dictionary.
(d) Choosing appropriate structures for presenting data in the dictionary (i.e., frame structure, distribution structure, macro-structure, micro-structure and cross-reference structure, etc.).
(e) Selecting words and affixes for systematisation as headwords.
(f) Selecting collocations, phrases, idioms and proverbs, etc. for citation.
(g) Choosing lemma forms for each affixed or inflected word or the parts of word to be lemmatised.
(h) Defining entry words and organising their definitions.
(i) Specifying pronunciations of each headword and entry word.
(j) Labelling definitions and pronunciations of the head words based on their register and dialect variations, where appropriate.
(k) Selecting equivalents in bilingual and polylingual cognate forms.
(l) Describing collocations, reduplications, idioms, phrases and proverbial examples of words.
(m) Designing the best way in which users can access the data in printed and electronic form.

Besides addressing all the issues, an electronic dictionary developer needs to keep a close vigil on the overall lexicographic information costs incurred by dictionary users as low as possible. It is assumed that all the issues become relevant for a lexicographer when compiling a dictionary, as these can affect the users' impression and the actual use of specific dictionaries.

It is evident that lexicographers consider computer as a vital tool used in the manipulation of vast amounts of information without which the level of difficulty of their task will increase along with the amount of time which will be spent compiling a dictionary. Computer has revolutionised the work of lexicography to an enormous extent in the sense that dictionary-related tasks have been fast, consistent, accurate and innovative. Computer is evolving in a favourable direction when we can consider the long, complicated, enduring, time consuming and expensive task of dictionary making is changing into a short, simplified, easy, elegant and user-friendly enterprise. In essence, the utilisation of computer in dictionary making has resulted in the production of new types of dictionaries with new ways of presenting linguistic data and information to meet the new needs of the new age.

6.11 Neurolinguistics

Neurolinguistics[14] is a branch of linguistics, which is concerned with human brain mechanism that works behind comprehension, production and abstract knowledge of language — spoken, signed or written. As an interdisciplinary field, it has fabricated a wide spectrum covering linguistics, cognitive science, neurobiology, psychology and computer science — among others. Scientists have joined this field of research from variety of backgrounds, bringing along with them a variety of experimental techniques, strategies and theoretical perspectives. Several studies on neurolinguistics have identified the special role of that part of the human brain known as **Broca's area**, which play crucial role in human language understanding and usage, mainly, the sentences: the component of language that involves recursive application of grammatical rules underlying every valid syntactic construction.

In earlier years the investigation related to **aphasiology** (i.e., the study of language disorder caused from physical damage of brain) was considered to be the core area of neurolinguistics. However, in recent years, the scope of neurolinguistics has been considerably expanded due to advent of many new technologies which are being used in the study of human brain. As a result, language is used as a fundamental area of interest in cognitive neuroscience and several modern techniques used in imaging of human brain have made remarkable contribution in understanding the anatomical organisation of the linguistic functions in human brain[15].

Although, till date, the results of application of these techniques have not yet contradicted the existing results obtained from research in aphasiology, these techniques, however, do not allow for high temporal resolution of brain activity as comprehension or production of sentences unfolds. As temporal resolution is of utmost importance in these activities, researchers also deploy the electrophysiological techniques such as **Electroencephalography** (EEG)[16] and **Magnetoencephalography** (MEG)[17] for achieving more accurate results from their experiments.

Although these techniques can provide resolution during milliseconds, the exact nature of brain mechanism generating the electrical signals on the scalp is not yet known, which make the entire scenario of understanding the human brain a difficult task. EEG and MEG techniques are primarily used to constitute theories about cognitive or computational architecture of language, without any regard to their precise neurobiological implication. For example, one might suspect that out of three categories of words that are used at the end of a sentence, two are actually tapping into the same mechanism, but the third one is represented differently. Showing that these two categories elicit an identical electrophysiological response, which is different from that of the third one, will support such a hypothesis.

Neurolinguistics is closely related to **psycholinguistics** or **psychology of language**, which refers to the study of the psychological and neurobiological issues that enable humans to acquire, use and understand a language. Initial research activities in psycholinguistics were largely philosophical in nature, because there was a deficit of cohesive database on which experiments could have been carried out to understand how human brain operated in cognition of language. However, this deficiency is being gradually made up with data faithfully retrieved from linguistically challenged informants with necessary support from computer technology.

Modern researches in neurolinguistics make use of biology, neuroscience, cognitive science, psychology and information theory to study how human brain actually processes language. As a result, modern neurolinguists have been trying to include the cognitive processes that make it possible, to a large extent, to generate a grammatical and meaningful sentence out of vocabulary and grammatical structures, as well as the processes that make it possible to understand linguistics utterances, words and texts, etc.

At present there are several areas of neurolinguistics, which try to explore the components used in formation of human language. Within a broader spectrum it investigates several issues, including those areas where language information is processed, how language processing unfolds over time, how brain structures are related to language acquisition and learning and how neurophysiology contributes to speech and language pathology. In sum one can identify the following domains as primary areas of neurolinguistics:

(a) Localisation of Language Processes

Many recent works in neurolinguistics have been related to investigation of the locations of specific language 'modules' within human brain. The basic questions of investigation include what kinds of linguistic information is passed through the brain when language is being processed (Hickock and Poeppel 2007), if there are particular areas which are responsible or specialise in processing particular sorts of linguistic information (Embick et al. 2000), how different regions of human brain interact with one another in the task of language processing (Brown and Hagoort 1999) and which parts or locations of brain are activated in producing or perceiving a language other than the first language of a language user (Wang et al. 2003).

(b) Time Course of Language Processes

Another important area of investigation of neurolinguistics is related with the application of electrophysiological techniques for analysing the rapid processing of language in human brain (Philips and Sakai 2005). It has been investigated that temporal ordering of specific peaks in human brain activity may reflect on discrete computational processes that the human brain undergoes at the time of language processing. With regard to sentence parsing and processing in brain it has been claimed that there are three different parts of human brain which are actually responsible for producing three different steps in syntactic and semantic processing of language (Friederici 2002).

(c) Language Acquisition

For last two decades or so, neurolinguistics has been concerned with defining the relationships between the structures of brain and the

143

processes employed in language acquisition (Caplan 1987: 11). So far several research outputs in the area of first language acquisition have already established the fact that infants from all linguistic environments pass through similar and predictable stages (such as *cooing, babbling,* etc.) of language acquisition. Moreover, some neurolinguistic researches have attempted to find out the correlations existing between several stages of language development with stages of development of brain (Caplan 1987: 12), while other researches have made investigations to observe the nature of physical changes that the brain undergoes (known as **neuroplasticity**) during second language acquisition, when adults learn a new language (Sereno and Wang 2007).

(d) Language Pathology

Neurolinguistic techniques are also used to study disorders and breakdowns in language cognition and usage (Van Lieshout *et al.* 2007). There are several types of linguistic disorder, like *aphasia, dyslexia, schizophrenia, anomia, apraxia, autism, dysphagia,* etc. which ask for serious clinical investigations into the problems for identifying the nature of disorder and for prescribing necessary remedies for recovery. Thus the scope of neurolinguistics is largely expanded to include traumatic brain injury, developmental delays, stroke, cranial nerve damage, learning disabilities (speaking and listening), autism spectrum disorders (including **Asperger syndrome**[18]), genetic disorders that adversely affect speech, language and/or cognitive development, injuries due to the complications at birth, craniofacial anomalies that adversely affect speech, language and/or cognitive development, cerebral palsy, augmentative alternative communication disorders and many other problems related to language cognition and use. Also there is a serious need to identify how these disorders are related to the physical characteristics of the brain (Caplan 1987: 12). Proper assessment of the linguistic outputs of the linguistically impaired people suffering from these disorders also requires specialised investigation, analysis and examination of the symptoms and phenomena.

6.12 Pragmatics

Pragmatics is very much the study of how to do with language (McMenamin 2002:23). It is the study of the aspects of meaning and language use that are dependent on the speaker, the addressee and other features of the context of an utterance. The effect that has on the choice of expression of a speaker and the interpretation of an utterance by an addressee mostly depends on the context of utterance. And the context is generally governed by the principles of communication, goals of the speaker, programmatic concerns, such as the treatment of given versus new information, including presupposition, deixis, speech acts especially illocutionary acts, implicature, the relations of meaning and the functions between the portions of discourse or turns of conversation.

Since the basic goal of pragmatics is to deal with the *utterances* made in specific situations and events, it takes into consideration the intentional acts of the speakers at times and places, typically involving language. Logic and semantics, on the other hand, deal with the properties of *types* of expressions and not with the properties that differ from token to token, or use to use, or from utterance to utterance and vary with the particular properties of types that differentiate them. Pragmatics differs from logic and semantics in this case because it is characterised for dealing with the effects of *context* in speech events. Thus pragmatics becomes equivalent to the issues of dealing with the utterances, in reference to all the facts that vary from utterance to utterance as 'context.'

Within the broader scheme of pragmatics, different theorists have focused on different properties of utterances. Researchers usually consider utterances as paradigmatic and declarative sentences, where a speaker *says* something. To bring in clarity in the idea of pragmatics, scholars have made a distinction between the two types of pragmatics:

(a) Near-side pragmatics.
(b) Far-side pragmatics.

Near-side pragmatics is concerned with the nature of certain facts that are relevant to determining what is being said. It includes, but is not limited to resolution of ambiguity and vagueness, reference of proper names, indexicals and demonstratives, anaphors and some issues involving presupposition. In all of these cases researchers need to know the facts about an utterance, which are beyond the expressions used and their meanings. One can make divisions of these facts into several categories. The **indexicals** such as *I, now* and *here*, etc. are the basic facts about an utterance, which are required to identify the agent of an utterance and when and where the utterance has taken place. For understanding other indexicals and demonstratives, the intention of speakers is also relevant. While it appears that the use of the referent *you* is meant for the person addressed by the speaker, it opens the scope for relating to several possible addressees to sum up the intention of speaker. For instance, within syntactic and semantic constraints, anaphoric relations are largely a matter of speaker's intent, because the intention of a speaker and the way the speaker is connected to the wider external world by way of causal or historical chains of reference, become relevant to the reference of proper names.

Far-side pragmatics, on the other hand, concentrates on what we do with language, *beyond* what we have (literally) said. That means, it focuses on what happens *beyond saying*: what speech acts are performed *in* or *by* saying what is said, or *what* implicatures are generated by saying what is said. Based on this strategy, it is up to semantics to tell what someone is literally saying when he or she is using expressions of a given type in an utterance. On the contrary, it is up to pragmatics to explain the information one conveys and the actions one performs, in or by saying something in the utterance.

Pragmatics, as a sub-field of linguistics, studies the ways in which context contributes in understating meaning of an utterance or expression. In general, it covers **speech act theory, conversational implicature, talk in interaction** and some other approaches to language behaviour in philosophy, sociology, linguistics and discourse (Mey 1993). It also investigates how an event of successful transfer of meaning depends not only on the linguistic competence (e.g., phonological, grammatical, lexical, etc.) of the speaker and listener, but also on the factors related to communicative competence of the interactants (e.g., context of an utterance, knowledge about the social status and relation of those involved, the inferred intent or motive of the speaker and so on). The knowledge of pragmatics elucidates how the language users can succeed to overcome the apparent ambiguities of utterances, because the meaning of an expression relies not only on what is conveyed but also on manner, place, time, situation, context, motive, etc. of an utterance (Mey 1993: 13)[19].

Pragmatics studies various facts and issues related to different domains of linguistic knowledge representation in the followings manners:

(a)   It studies meaning in context and the influence that a given context can have on a message. It requires knowledge about the identity of speaker and the information of place and time of an utterance. That means it studies objective facts of utterance, including the factors such as who is the speaker, when the utterance has occurred and where the utterance has taken place, etc.

(b) It focuses on the intentions of the speaker and studies the meaning a speaker wants to convey, not focusing on the phonetic or grammatical forms of an utterance, but instead focusing on what intentions and beliefs of the speaker are. On the *near side*, it investigates what language a speaker intends to use, what meaning he intends to convey, whom he intends to refer to with various shared names, whether a pronoun is used in a demonstrative manner or anaphorically and the like. On the *far side*, it studies what a speaker actually intends to achieve by saying what he does.

(c) It studies implicatures, i.e., the things that are communicated with an utterance even though these are not explicitly expressed. It relates to the study of what is not meant, as opposed to the intended meaning, i.e., that which is unsaid and unintended, or unintentional.

(d) It studies the beliefs of speakers and those with whom they are engaged in speaking as well as the conversations in which they are engaged in. It also investigates what beliefs they do share; what is the central focus of their conversation and how do they develop the cource of their talk, etc.

(e) It studies the significance of relative distance, both social and physical, existing between the speakers in order to understand what determines the choice of what is said, how it is said and what is not said.

(f) It investigates relevant social institutions, such as promising, marriages, negotiations, mediations, debates, quarrels, assurances, judiciary oaths and the like, which affect what a person accomplishes in or by saying what he does.

(g) It intends to analyse **information structure**, which relates to the study of how utterances are marked at different junctures of a conversation in order to efficiently manage common ground of referred entities between the speaker and the hearer.

In general, pragmatics is believed to be interfaced with different kinds of *reasoning* than semantics. It involves perception augmented by some types of 'ampliative' inference —inference to the best explanation, Bayesian reasoning (MacKay 2003) and application of principles special to communication (Grice 1991: 78-79). But in any case, a sort of reasoning is bound to go beyond the application of rules and it makes inferences beyond what is established by the basic facts about what expressions are used and their meanings.

Pragmatics is considered as one of the challenging aspects for language learners to grasp, since it can only be learned through experience. Also, there is a considerable overlap between pragmatics and sociolinguistics, as both the areas share an interest in linguistic meaning as determined by usage at certain contexts within a speech community. However, while sociolinguists tend to be more oriented towards variations within such communities, pragmatics tries to understand the relationship between the signs and their users (Morris 1966). On the other hand, semantics tends to focus on the actual objects or the ideas to which a word refers to. Thus semantics is the literal meaning of an idea, whereas pragmatics is the implied meaning of the given idea.

By now it is clear that successful communication of intended meanings (i.e., pragmatics uses of language) depends on reference to non-linguistic information such as the identity and social relationships of speaker or writer and the listener or reader; the place, time and topic of conversation; the purpose of the communication and the language used, etc. Without this contextual information, the intended meaning of a sentence may be misinterpreted or remain unknown (McMenamin 2002: 23).

6.13 Concluding Remarks

Alongside these newly evolved fields of study in linguistics, there are many other fields within the realm of traditional linguistics, which are separated by different reasons and factors in the study of language. These include **applied linguistics** that explores language-related issues applied in everyday human life such as language planning, language policies and language education, etc.; **biolinguistics** that studies the natural and human-taught communication systems in animals, compared to human language; **clinical linguistics** that studies the application of linguistic theories to the field of speech-language pathology; **developmental linguistics** that studies development of linguistic ability in individuals, particularly the acquisition of language in childhood; **geolinguistics** that investigates the distribution of languages and linguistic features in different geographical locations; **linguistic typology** that studies the common properties of diverse unrelated languages, properties that may, given sufficient attestation, be assumed to be innate to the human language capacity; **stylistics** that studies linguistic factors and stylistic issues that place a discourse in a broader context of communication; and **semiotics** that treats language as a system of sign or symbol with the world as its actual place for representation and investigates the relationship between the signs and what they signify.

Notes and Comments

[1]   The Penan people are nomadic and aboriginal hunter-gatherers living in the northern part of Sarawak, the Malaysian part of the Island of Borneo. They are one of the last such peoples remaining. Although many have now been settled, some Penans still lead a completely nomadic life in the forest. Even the settled Penans continue to rely heavily on the forest. They have an egalitarian society without any hierarchy. Sharing is taken for granted in their society: there is no Penan word for 'thank you'. They are noted for their practice of 'molong' which means a hunter must not eat a single bite more than he gives to others, however small his catch. The forest provides them with everything they need to survive. In particular, they rely heavily on sago, which they use for building houses, making baskets and as food. They love to eat it fried in pig fat and mixed with pig blood. They eat plants, which are also used as medicines and animals and use the hides, skin, fur and other parts for clothing and shelter.

[2]   *Situated knowledge* is a kind of knowledge which is specific to a particular situation. For example, the knowledge of a *tree* is a situated knowledge as it is situated in 'space' and has three dimensional properties. This knowledge is not a knowledge that we can 'forget', even if someone suffers from amnesia. Some methods of generating knowledge, such as those by trial and

error or through learning from experience create situational knowledge. Situated knowledge is often found to be embedded in language, culture and traditions. Scientific methods and experiments generate less situated knowledge.

[3] *Situated ethics* (often confused with *situational ethics*), is a view of applied ethics in which abstract standards from a culture or theory are considered to be far less important than the ongoing processes in which one is personally and physically involved, e.g. climate, ecosystem, etc. It is one of those theories of ethics within the *philosophy of action*. It emphasises on the actual physical, geographical, ecological and infrastructural state an actor is in and these states determine the actor's actions or range of actions. It denies that there is any point of view which can be applied as standard or authority. This makes such theories unpopular with authority and popular with those who advocate political decentralisation.

[4] This approach of cognitive linguistics may be considered as moderate offshoot of the Sapir-Whorf Hypothesis in the sense that language and cognition can mutually influence one another and both are embedded in the experiences and environments of its users.

[5] The conceptual semantics pursued by noted generative linguist Ray Jackendoff (1983, 1990) is directly related to cognitive linguistics because of its active *psychological realism* and the incorporation of prototype structure and images.

[6] Since the central object of interest within Chomskyan frame of linguistics was syntax, structures of language were not driven by meaning, but instead were governed by the principles, which were essentially independent of meaning. Thus, semantics associated with morpho-syntactic structures did not receive any importance for investigation, as the main focus was on language-internal structural principles as explanatory constructs.

[7] The *Association for Computational Linguistics* defines computational linguistics as "a scientific study of language from a computational perspective. It is interested in providing computational models of various kinds to different linguistic phenomena".

[8] Etymologically, *corpus* is derived from Latin *corpus* meaning "body". Although it is randomly applied to various non-linguistic collections of data and samples in other branches of human

knowledge, in linguistics, it occupies an esteemed status with an orientation towards large collection of language samples. It has been informed (Francis 1992: 17) that in the 16th century, the emperor Justinian formed the *Corpus Juris Civilis*, which is nothing more than "a compilation of early Roman laws and legal principles, illustrated by cases and combined with explanation of new laws and future legislation to be put into effect" (*World Book* 10.168). However, closer to the sense in which the term *corpus* recently used is the Latin *Corpus Glossary* of the 18th century, which assembled "hard Latin words arranged in alphabetical order and followed by easier Latin synonyms or equivalent in Anglo-Saxon" (Starnes and Noyes 1946: 197).

[9]   Exception may be noted in historical corpus, which, due to its diachronic form and composition, is neither unlimited nor synchronic. Such a corpus is not a serious concern for us, since a historical corpus is mostly confined within a peripheral area of application, which has marginal importance in the on-going activities of empirical language research.

[10] Extralinguistic information obtained from a corpus may be analysed along with intralinguistic information obtained from linguistic data to understand how a piece of text is composed, how the text is used, in which context it is used and how does it serve the purpose of the users, etc.

[11] The term *discourse analysis* first entered in general use as the title of a paper published by Zellig Harris in 1952 although that paper did not offer a systematic analysis of linguistic structures 'beyond the sentence level'. As a new discipline, *discourse analysis* began to develop in the late 1960s and 1970s in most of the humanities and social sciences, more or less at the same time and in relation with, other new (inter- and sub-) disciplines, such as semiotics, conversation analysis, psycholinguistics, sociolinguistics and pragmatics.

[12] In the childhood days of our education we used to identify cardinal directions by turning our face towards sun. The instruction was like this: "In the morning turn your face to the sun. This is East. Your back side is West. Your left-hand direction is North and your right-hand direction is South".

[13] The *Sapir-Whorf Hypothesis* is also known as *linguistic relativity*, which postulates that an individual's thoughts are influenced by the language(s) available to him or her for expressing them.

That means, a particular language's nature can influence the habitual thought of its speakers. As a result, different language patterns yield different patterns of thought. This idea challenges the possibility of representing the world perfectly with language, because it acknowledges that the mechanisms of *any* language condition the thoughts of its speaker community. This theory has been strongly criticised on the basis that Whorf supposedly claimed that *language determines thought*. However, Whorf himself wrote that 'language provides 'habits' of thought that influence cognition'.

[14]   Historically, the term *neurolinguistics* has been most closely associated with *aphasiology*, the study of linguistics deficits and spared abilities, occurring as the result of brain damage.

[15]   Modern brain imaging techniques such as the *Positron Emission Tomography* (PET) and *Functional Magnetic Resonance Imaging* (FMRI) provide high spatial resolution images of energy utilised in various regions of brain during a course of language processing. The images acquired through these techniques have contributed greatly in understanding the anatomical organisation of linguistic functions in human brain.

[16]   *Electroencephalography* (EEG) is the recording of electrical activity along the scalp produced by the firing of neurons within the brain. In clinical contexts, it refers to the recording of the brain's spontaneous electrical activity over a short period of time (usually 20-40 minutes), as recorded from multiple electrodes placed on the scalp. In neurology, the main diagnostic application of EEG is in the case of epilepsy, as epileptic activity can create clear abnormalities on a standard EEG study.

[17]   *Magnetoencephalography* (MEG) is a technique for mapping brain activity by recording magnetic fields produced by electrical currents occurring naturally in the brain, using arrays of SQUIDs (superconducting quantum interference devices). Applications of MEG include localising regions affected by pathology before surgical removal, determining the function of various parts of the brain and neurofeedback.

[18]   *Asperger syndrome* is an autism spectrum disorder which is characterised by significant difficulties in social interaction, along with restricted and repetitive patterns of behaviour and interests. It differs from other autism spectrum disorders by its relative preservation of linguistic and cognitive development. Although

not required for diagnosis, physical clumsiness and atypical use of language are frequently reported in this linguistic disorder (McPartland 2006).

[19]   The ability to understand the intended meaning a speaker wants to convey by his or her utterance is called *pragmatic competence*. An utterance that describes the pragmatic function is called *metapragmatic utterance*. Pragmatic awareness is regarded as one of the most challenging aspects of language learning, as it is acquired through experience as well as through the amount of exposure to the varieties of situations in the external world.

Chapter 7
Functions of Language

7.1 Introduction

Human language is used in various ways for different purposes and hence, it has many functions. Our general idea is that the main function of language is communication—that means language is primarily used to communicate among people within and across speech communities. Although by using language we can easily share and exchange information, it has many more functions. By way of using language we can share feelings, refer things, get information about different elements and events of external world, express minds, exchange emotions and experiences, release tension, maintain social relationships, learn lessons and develop friendships. Also, we use language to learn about the events of distant past, fill up the embarrassing situations of silence, remember forgotten events or items and recapitulate past memories and activities. But the most vital function of language is not communication but thinking, because it is through language that we formulate and generate our thoughts as well as establish a relation between our internal self with the world we live in. Thus, language, through its multidimensional functions, helps us to establish ourselves as thoughtful, civilised and cultured people.

In this chapter I have made an attempt to describe in short the observations and arguments made by earlier scholars regarding the functions of language in general, as well as the functions of specific components and properties of language in overall understanding the roles of language both as a means of communication and as a symbol of manifestation of social identity of the language users. The chapter is built up in the following manner: in Section 7.2, I have recorded the observations made by the early thinkers of the medieval Europe with a short discussion on the traditional views and the views expressed by Karl Bühler. In Section 7.3, I have referred to the ideas and views expressed by modern thinkers such as Ludwig Wittgenstein, Roman Jakobson, Dell Hymes, M.A.K Halliday and others. In Section 7.4, I have focused on the interface existing between the observations of Halliday with that of some other thinkers of the last century. In Section 7.5, I have referred to the observations made by some Indian scholars. In Section 7.6, I have discussed in short the arguments and explanations presented by some recent scholars, who ask us to consider the functions of language from the perspectives of Darwinian principle of Natural Selection.

7.2 Early Observations

7.2.1 John Locke

In the medieval era, the great empiricist and philosopher of Europe, John Locke (1632-1704) tries to define the importance and function of language in the following way that the comfort and advantage of a society may not be achieved in its full form if it has to sustain without any communication of thoughts. It was, therefore, necessary that man should find out some external sensible signs or means, where the invisible ideas which his thoughts are made of, might be made known to others (Locke 1997: 307).

John Locke devotes *Book III* of *An Essay Concerning Human Understanding* to investigate the nature and functions of language. He understands that the issues about the functions of language are of considerable importance in attaining knowledge. Words, according to him, stand for ideas and therefore these should be distinguished according to the categories of the ideas. There should be words for the ideas of substances, simple modes, mixed modes, relations and so on. There are also many particles and words in language that signify the connection that the mind gives to ideas, or propositions, one with another.

7.2.2 Traditional Views

The traditional concept, before 1930, regarding the functions of language is that there are mainly three basic functions of language: informative function, expressive function and directive function[1].

The *informative function* is also known as *cognitive* or *referential* function, which essentially, signifies the communication of information, thoughts and ideas. It affirms or denies propositions, as in science or statement of a fact; describes the world or reason about it (e.g., if a state of affairs has occurred or not); and asserts if sentences have truth value (i.e., sentences are either true or false).

The *expressive function* is known as *emotive* or *affective function*, which reports feelings and transmits attitudes of the writers (and speakers) and evokes feelings and emotions in readers (and listeners). Although poetic and literary texts are the best examples of expressive function of language, simple ordinary texts of discourse are also able to express emotions, feelings and attitudes. Two salient aspects of this function are generally identified: (a) expressing feelings and (b) evoking feelings.

The *directive function* is known as *evaluative function* in which language is used for the purpose of causing (or preventing) the overt action of any kind. It is most commonly observed in commands and requests although directive language is not normally considered to be true or false in nature. A sentence like *You are smoking in a non-smoking area* is directive in function although it appears to be declarative in form.

A list of examples presented below (Table 7.1) can sum up the basic three functions of language as envisaged in traditional linguistics.

Basic Function	Informative	Expressive	Directive
Declarative	The day in bright.	I am happy.	I want some food.
Interrogative	Are you going?	Isn't that great?	Don't you like it?
Imperative	Bring the book.	Have a nice time.	Close the door.
Exclamatory	Life is ruined!	How happy I am!	Oh! You are late!

Table 7.1: Three basic functions of language in traditional view

Undoubtedly, identifying just three basic functions of language is simply an oversimplification. However, awareness about these functions is a good introduction for understanding the complexities involved in defining the functions of language. Besides these functions, scholars are also interested to include the following functions in the general frame postulated in traditional linguistics.

(a)   **Ceremonial Function:** It refers to the ritualistic use of language. It is something quite different from simply mixing expressive and directive functions because the performative aspects of language are included in it, e.g., *Friends, we gather here to witness the holy matrimony of* ....

157

Language and Linguistics

(b) **Performative Function:** It refers to those linguistic utterances which are meant to perform the action they report, e.g., *I declare you before the God as my wife for life.* Here the use of 'I declare' acts as a performative verb. In fact, verbs used in **speech acts** such as *accept, apologise, congratulate, condemn, think, promise, despise, hate, declare, object,* etc. denote an action which is performed by using the verb itself in the first person. Nothing more is needed to be done to accomplish the action. The performative utterances are, therefore, not normally subject to hearsay rules, since they imply an action taken.

(c) **Phatic Function:** It refers to those **street-corner conversations** that are used to accomplish a social task. The notable thing is that it involves the subtle transition from verbal words such as, *Hi* or *How are you?* to body language such as a nod or wave of hand.

7.2.3 Karl Bühler

Karl Bühler (1879-1963) is best known for his contribution to the scientific study of language, particularly the function of language in a given language community. Bühler (1934) considers that the basic functions of language are of three types[2]:

(a) **Function of expression:** It refers to the psychological condition or the mental state or attitude of the speaker,

(b) **Function of appeal:** It refers the impact created upon an addressee after he or she is communicated with, and

(c) **Function of reference:** It refers to the content of the text, i.e., what is being communicated from an addresser to an addressee.

While the first two functions serve the emotive purposes of the speakers, the third one conveys the factual content of language. Bühler argues that all these functions are solely responsible for stylistic differentiations of language or an expression while the functional adequacy is the main criterion by which the correctness of a word or a phrase is measured.

7.3 Modern Observations

7.3.1 Ludwig Wittgenstein

Ludwig Wittgenstein, a great philosopher of modern times, defines functions of language from a new perspective (Wittgenstein 1953). He puts forth the view that conceptual confusions surrounding language use are at the root of most of the philosophical problems. The problems can be traced within a set of related assumptions about the nature of language, which by themselves, presuppose a particular conception about the essence of language. He argues that the individual words in language name objects and sentences are the combinations of such names. In this picture of language, one finds the roots of the following idea: Every word has a meaning. This meaning is correlated with the word. It is the object for which the word stands[3].

In the view of Wittgenstein, language is inextricably woven into the fabric of life and as part of that fabric it works relatively unproblematically. We do not, when speaking ordinarily, worry about how our words mean what they do. Philosophical problems arise when language is forced to leave from its *proper home* into a metaphysical environment, where all the familiar and necessary landmarks and contextual cues are removed, specifically for the purpose of *pure philosophical examination*. He describes this metaphysical environment as like being on frictionless ice: where conditions are apparently perfect for a philosophically and logically perfect language, where all the philosophical problems can be solved without confusing and muddying the effects of everyday contexts; but where, just because of the lack of friction, language in fact, do no actual work at all.

To review the multiplicity of functions of language Wittgenstein observes the following examples:

- Giving orders and obeying them...
- Describing the appearance of an object, or giving its measurements...
- Constructing an object from a description (a drawing)...
- Reporting an event...
- Speculating about an event...
- Forming and testing a hypothesis...
- Presenting the results of an experiment in tables and diagrams...
- Play-acting...

159

Language and Linguistics

- Singing catches...
- Guessing riddles...
- Making a joke, telling it...
- Solving a problem in practical arithmetic...
- Translating from one language to another...
- Asking, thanking, cursing, greeting, praying...

Since Wittgenstein deals largely with the difficulties of language and its meaning, he views language as a tool, which is fundamentally simple and he believes that philosophers obscure this simplicity by misusing language as well as by asking meaningless questions. His methods for perceiving the language lead to the summary of his argument in the following manners: meaning *is* just use, i.e., words are not defined by reference to the objects or things which they designate in the external world nor by the thoughts, ideas, or mental representations that one might associate with them, but rather by how they are used in effective, ordinary communication. For example, there is no need to postulate that there is something called *good* which can exist independently of any particular 'good deed'. A further example is 'A *spade* is to dig', inasmuch as a *spade* is used *to dig*.

Summing up of the propositions of Wittgenstein produces the following categories about the functions of language: **(a) cognitive (informative) function** and **(b) non-cognitive (non-informative) function.** The *non-cognitive function* also includes another three different sub-categories of function, namely, the *emotive function*, the *directive function* and the *performative function*.

7.3.2 Roman Jakobson

The well-known model about the functions of language is introduced by the Russian-American linguist Roman Jakobson (1960: 350-377). His model for the functions of language distinguishes six primary elements or factors that are necessary for linguistic communication to occur. These are:

(a)   **Context:** the co-text, that is the verbal signs of a message and the world in which the message takes place.
(b)   **Addresser:** a sender or enunciator who sends the message.
(c)   **Addressee:** a receiver to whom the message is addressed.

(d) **Contact:** link established between the addresser and the addressee.

(e) **Code:** which is mutually intelligible to both the members involved in an event of communication.

(f) **Message:** which is communicated by the addresser to the addressee.

In an event of successful communication, each of the factors stated above is the focal point of a relation or function that operates between the message and the factor. The functions, according to Jakobson, may operate always in the following order:

(a) **Referential Function:** It corresponds to the factor of context and describes a situation, object, or mental state. It is oriented towards the context where the dominant function is a message. The descriptive statements of a referential function can consist of definite descriptions and deictic words, e.g., *The winter leaves have fallen* or *The sun rises in the East,* or *Water boils at 100 degrees.*

(b) **Emotive Function:** It is known as *expressive* or *affective function,* which is oriented towards an addresser as expressed in interjections. It relates to the addresser and is best exemplified by interjections and other sound changes that do not alter the denotative meaning of an utterance but add information about the internal state of an addresser, e.g., *Wow, what a view!* or *Ah! At last I have reached!* etc.

(c) **Conative Function:** It is oriented towards the addressee with forms of imperatives and apostrophes. It engages the addressee directly and is best illustrated by vocative and imperatives, e.g., *Dear, can you come here and sit beside me?* or *Call my name and I am for you,* etc.

(d) **Phatic Function:** It is the language for the sake of interaction and, is therefore, associated with the contact factor. In communication, it is used to serve to establish, prolong, or discontinue communication. It also serves to confirm whether the contact is still there. In case of phatic function of language one uses familiar and fixed formulae (e.g., *hello, hi, good morning,* etc.). It is used in case of greetings and casual discussions with strangers or known persons, e.g., *Hello! Have you ever been to London? How was the weather?*

(e)   **Metalingual Function:** It is also known as *metalinguistic* or *reflexive function*. It refers to the use of language (what Jakobson calls 'code') to discuss or describe itself. It is used to establish mutual agreement on the code, for example, a definition, *What do you mean by 'I fall'?*

(f)   **Poetic Function:** It is the message for its own sake (Jakobson 1960: 356). It is the operative function in poetry as well as in slogans, e.g., *Hail to thee blithe spirit! Bird thou never wert!*

Following the model of Jakobson when the functions of language are analysed for any given linguistic unit (e.g., a word, a sentence, or a piece of text), it is generally specified which functions are present or absent in it and the characteristics of these functions, including the hierarchical relations and any other relations that may operate between them. Since each factor is the focal point of a function that operates between the message and the factor, it yields six different functions. In brief, these six functions can be described as follows (Table 7.2)[4].

Function No.	Target Factor	Source Factor	Function
1	Context	Message	Referential
2	Addresser	Message	Emotive
3	Addressee	Message	Conative
4	Contact	Message	Phatic
5	Code	Message	Metalingual
6	Message	Message	Poetic

Table 7.2: Factors of communication and functions of language

According to Jakobson, when the aspect of a piece of text is focused on the addresser the function is *emotive* or *affective*. The feelings, liking, thinking and the mental state of the addresser is expressed through this function. When the addressee is focused, the function is *conative*, where the addresser orders or requests the addressee to do something and the addressee does the work. The context refers to the statement of different facts and the different contexts are expressed through *referential*, *cognitive* or *denotative* functions. In this function neither the addresser nor the addressee gets importance. The internal message of the speaker or the writer is expressed through the *poetic function* of the language. The literal message reaches to the readers through *poetic function*. The social contact is the main aspect of the *phatic function* of language where the interaction or the management of information become important. Finally, language is a code through which one can communicate information to others. This code is understood by *metalinguistic functions* of language. The model suggested by Jakobson regarding factors and functions of language may be represented in the following manner (Fig. 7.1).

To explain the diagram (Fig. 7.1) presented below, it can be said that the *Addresser* typically uses 1st person and some times 3rd person (e.g., *I requested him to come and meet me*). The *Addressee* is typically indicated by 2nd person, name of the addressee, a title or sometimes by 3rd person (e.g., *Mr. Johnson, are you sure this person is honest?*). The elements of the *Context* may be persons, animals, things, or any other object than the addresser and the addressee and it can be reflected in the 3rd person (e.g., *There lies the book you are looking for*). A *Message* is a *spoken* or a *written* text that is formed in a particular structure or sequence in a language (e.g., *Well, you are really good at cricket.*) It is the *Code* in which the vast system of message in the form of spoken or written text is built up. *Metalanguage* is the language used to talk about the language (e.g., *sentence, noun, verb, sign,* etc.). Finally, the *Contact* involves both a physical channel and a psychological connection. The most obvious contact signals are *hi, hello, good morning, please, dear,* etc.

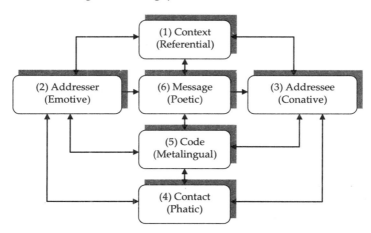

Fig. 7.1: Six factors of an effective verbal communication

It has been observed that in the *poetic function* of language there is some amount of innovation. The possible indications of the *poetic function*, among other things, may be the followings:

(a) **Linguistic Deviance:** The key role of *linguistic deviance* is reflected in the figure of speech known as *metaphor*. It is a special kind of linguistic innovation, which acts as a factor for generating impact through a piece of text in the poetic function. The age-old saying attributed to Aristotle records that metaphor consists in giving the thing a name that belongs to something else, which shows the nature of innovation or deviance in case of the *poetic function* of language, as in, *The moonbeam kisses the sea* or *The night sings the songs of solitude!*

(b) **Verbal Patterning:** Jakobson refers to it as 'the well-ordered shape' of a text, which may involve *sound, shape* and *sense*. While sound patterning appears in alliteration (e.g., *She sails on the sea shore,* etc.) and in rhyme structure in a text (e.g., *Had I but world enough and time/ This coyness, Lady, was no crime!* etc.), while pattering of shape and sense of a text is very common and explicit in poetry, oratory, advertisement, etc.

(c) **Foregrounding[5]:** The notion of foregrounding comes originally from visual arts and refers to those elements of a work of art that stand out in some way. In linguistics it refers to the use of devices of language in such a way that the usage itself appears to be uncommon and attracts close attention of readers to generate new perception. The purpose of art and literature is to defamiliarise the familiar ideas and objects and by way of defamiliarising, a work of art or a text we make stands out from the norm – and it becomes foregrounded. Foregrounding is seen as a method of explaining the difference between poetic and everyday language and it has become widely accepted as one of the important strategies of stylistics. In linguistics, the term *foregrounding* is first postulated by Mukarovsky when he (1970) says, "In poetic language, foregrounding achieves maximum intensity to the extent of pushing communication into the background as the objective of expression and of being used for its own sake; it is not used in the services of communication, but in order to place in the foreground the act of expression, the act of speech itself".

7.3.3 Dell Hymes

American anthropologist Dell Hymes (1962) argues that any speech event can be seen as comprising several components and the analysis of these become crucial in *ethnography of speaking*. There are seven different factors or components that can be discerned in most of the speech events: a **sender**, a **receiver**, a **message form**, a **channel**, a **code**, a **topic** and a **setting** (scene and situation). A set of seven factors is rudimentary in a framework of an act of communication. Based on the observations of Hymes, each of the factors may be defined in the following manners:

The sender (addresser) is the most important member in any kind of verbal interaction at a particular setting. He is the person who starts the act of communication triggered by some linguistic or non-linguistic factors and thereby, fabricates a network of relation with the receiver.

The receiver (addressee) is the person who receives the message made by the sender directly or indirectly. Once he receives the message and responds accordingly controlled by the situation, topic and setting, he strengthens the network of communication already started by the sender.

For any group, the basic indigenous categories may vary in number and in kind, while their instances and classes need to be empirically identified. For example, sender or addresser and receiver or addressee need not be the same. In general, the categories of these two factors may be investigated in terms of the role system of the group studied. Besides, based on the beliefs and practices, the categories of senders and receivers may vigorously overlap the membership of the human group.

The form of a message, or a class of messages, is a descriptive fact that becomes significant especially as an aesthetic and stylistic matter, whether in relation to the resources of a code, or to a particular context, or to a particular referential content.

The cross-cultural differences in channels are well known facts, not only in the presence of writing, but also in the elaboration of channels available in the form of instruments (e.g., The West African people using *Jabo* and the whistling tones among some of the Mazatecs of Mexico, etc.)

It is already observed that the code factor is a variable, which is focussed on the speech habits of a population. The range is from communities with different levels of a single dialect to communities in which many individuals command several different languages. The presence of *argots, jargons, forms of speech in disguise* and the like can enter here. It is clear that the status of a form of speech as a *dialect* or *language* cannot be determined from linguistic features alone. There is a sociocultural dimension and indigenous categories must be discovered, together with their defining attributes and the import of using one or the other in particular situations. Depending on the attitude, the presence of a very few features can stamp a form of speech as a different style or dialect.

The topic factor points to the study of lexical hierarchy of the languages spoken by a group, including idioms and the content of any conventionalised utterances, for evidence and knowledge of what can be said. To a large extent this means that semantic study is necessary to any study of speaking. The *ethnography of speaking* does also call for special attention to the indigenous categories for the topics. One needs to know the categories in terms of which people will answer the question *(what are they talking about?)*, as well as the attributes and patterns of occurrence for these categories.

The setting factor is fundamental and yet difficult. It underlies much of the rest and yet its constituency is not easily determined. We accept as meaningful such terms as *context of situation* and *definition of the situation* but seldom ask ethnographically what the criteria for being a *situation* might be, what kinds of situations there are, how many and the like. Native terms are good guides to determine behaviour settings and to segment the continuum of behaviour.

While Jakobson treats the last two factors (*context* and *referent*) together as one factor, Hymes defines *context* as a different factor, retaining *setting* with *scene* and *situation* as alternatives. As factors, Hymes distinguishes setting and *topic* because the same statement may have different import, as between, say, a rehearsal and a performance. In one sense, it is simply a question of what one has to his inventory in describing the speech economy of a group. *Settings* and *topics* seem to him to involve two obviously different lists and thus he lists on the same level as *addressers, addressees, channels,* etc.

Although Hymes cannot avoid using *context* with functions, he agrees with Jakobson that *referential function* involves *context*, but finds this of no difficulty if a function is defined in relation to more than one factor. He also agrees with Jakobson that all aspects of a speech event are aspects of *context* from one point of view, but he argues that all aspects may be viewed in terms of any one factor and the level at which all the aspects of *context* can merge. Since Hymes imports these factors with regard to the functions of speech in the context of identifying the *ethnography of speaking*, he considers that the native lexical categories are important resources in understanding the whole process of communication. Moreover, he also considers that the contrast within a frame is a basic technique for identifying both the instances and classes and for discovering their dimensions of contrast.

7.3.4 M.A.K. Halliday

Michael Halliday (1973) studies language from a different perspective known as **Systemic Functional Linguistics** (SFL), which is based on the notion of language function. It accounts for the syntactic structure of language and considers the function of language as the central point (what language does and how it does it) in preference to structural approaches, which place the elements of language and their combinations as central. This theory starts at social context and looks at how language both acts upon and is constrained by, the social context.

To establish his proposition, Halliday first describes the ways in which the earlier scholars from diverse disciplines classify language use according to the function of language. He not only demonstrates the similarities found among these categories but also lays down a blue print of the functional categories (Halliday 1973: 17). He summarises by arguing that language is, by its very nature, functional and that the organisation of language must be explained in terms of a functional theory of language[6]. Finally, he illustrates all his arguments by doing a linguistic (not literary) analysis of a simple line of text composed by Ben Jonson:

"Or leave a kiss within a cup and I'll not ask for wine".

Since Halliday argues for analysing a linguistic text in terms of functional theory within a network of functions, the network, according to Halliday, has three basic functions as the followings (Halliday 1973: 143):

(a)   **Ideational function:** In terms of ideational function, Halliday shows how the words in the line stated above are associated with the events of the world. The sentence stated above is about something that we all have probably experienced in some way or the other (*kiss, cup, wine*). It refers to the message about the real physical world and the imaginary world of the speaker. This function is however, same with the *cognitive* or *emotive* or *referential* function mentioned by earlier scholars.

(b) **Interpersonal function:** It refers to the interpersonal meaning. It is a social interaction between the two people ('I' and 'you'). The focus here is on the participants only. Also, there is a *logical meaning*. We have to infer that 'and' really implies, "If you leave a kiss within the cup, then I will not ask for wine". The interpersonal function is used to establish as well as maintain social relationships among the speakers of a language. This function is similar to *contact* function proposed by earlier scholars.

(c) **Textual function:** It refers to the textual meaning which is understood in the wider context of the poem. The text has some features that make this a poem—repetition, parallelism, rhythm, the intonational contours one will hear in the recitation and so on. The textual function is used to make the literary creation. This function is same with the *poetic function* proposed by earlier scholars.

These functions, are however, indirectly connected to the terms used in register, known as **Field, Tenor** and **Mode.** Halliday shows how *field* is expressed in *ideational function* of language—looking at words themselves and their relationship to the world; the fact that 'kiss' is used as a noun almost metaphorically, since it is an unusual noun—one which is derived from an action, a verb. Through further analysis, he shows that the field of this discourse is a love poem.

Tenor is expressed through the interpersonal function. The relationship between the lover and the beloved, as expressed through the pronouns 'I' and 'you' and through a command and a request: if you do this then I shall do this. The beloved has to be convinced.

Finally, *mode* is expressed through the textual function. It is a lyric poetry and it has a certain metrical patterns in which there is a phonological feature of tone groups. Moreover, it is strongly person-oriented in which 'I' and 'you' come first. There is a balance in the structures of the phrases.

Halliday also develops a framework that identifies functions or purposes for language use (Halliday 1975). This framework recognises the importance of language in the development of a child as a social being and serves as a guide to integrate language arts and social studies curricula. He tries to build on the theories and arguments of Malinowski (who argues that language is multi-functional and is a response to society's demand); Firth (who believes that there is a multiplicity of languages within a total language); and Whorf (who demonstrates a relationship between language and culture as well as the need for categories of language). Thus, Halliday identifies seven major functions of language for children in the early years of language acquisition.

(a)　**Instrumental function:** This is triggered when children use language to express their needs and requirements, e.g., *I want a ball.*

(b)　**Regulatory function:** This is triggered when they use language to tell others what to do and what not to do, e.g., *Go away, come here!*

(c)　**Interactional function:** Here children use language to make contacts with others and to form relationships, e.g., *I love you, mummy.*

(d)　**Personal function:** This is the use of language when children use it to express feelings, opinions and individual identity, e.g., *Me good girl.*

(e)　**Heuristic function:** This is when language is used by children to gather knowledge about the environment, e.g., *What is the cow doing?*

(f)　**Imaginative function:** Here language is used by children to tell stories and jokes and to create an imaginary environment, e.g., *I have made a big red car.*

(g)　**Representational function:** Here children use language to convey facts and information they experience in their life, e.g., *I went to the park with my daddy.*

Children are motivated to acquire language because language serves certain purposes or functions for them. The first four functions help the children to satisfy their physical, emotional and their social needs. Halliday calls them *instrumental, regulatory, interactional* and *personal functions.* The next three functions are *heuristic, imaginative* and *representational,* which help children to come to terms with the environment they live in. According to Halliday, as the child gradually roots into his or her mother tongue, these functions give way to the three metafunctions of a fully tri-stratal language. These metafunctions are *ideational, interpersonal* and *textual functions.*

By following Halliday's framework, language teachers can calculate how much class-time they need to devote to certain language functions in case of language teaching. For example, the lecture-oriented as well as the textbook-reading-based approach to the social studies teaching typically emphasises on regulatory language and informative language but does not emphasise on personal and imaginative language uses. A teacher's over reliance on the strategies that require an informative language capacity debilitates children because this language function is the last one they need to develop for attaining complete linguistic skill.

Furthermore, research into oral language learning suggests that sufficient knowledge of language function is as essential to communicative competence as understanding the grammatical structure of language. A child's learning of language functions evolves through an experiential process as give and take of conversations allows children to extend their own language system and in the process, practice new forms.

7.3.5 Other Observations

Eugene Nida (1975) identifies three functions of language: **(a) informative** or communicative function where communication of information is the central issue (e.g., *news paper, railway timetable, telephone directory*, etc.), **(b) expressive** function, which refers to referential aspects of language and **(c) imperative** function, when any information or expression directs or motivates the hearer to initiate some deeds or actions.

The names of the functions are different but their explanations are almost same with the functions mentioned by earlier scholars. All the functions of language result in certain *identificatory features* (also called *indexical features*), which will enable the listener or reader to identify respectably the speaker or writer and to a certain extent the context. These *identificatory features* play an important role in novels, short stories and plays in the art of characterisation to mark the speaker as a member of a social group or a class.

John Lyons (1972) mentions three functions of language: **(a) descriptive function**, which is used to receive information about the external world, **(b) expressive function**, which is used to express ideas and feelings of speakers and **(c) social function**, which is regularly used in different social contexts and situations. The functions mentioned by Lyons are more or less similar to those of Jakobson with limited deviations in the perspective of observations triggered by social needs.

7.4 Hallidayan Interface with Others

7.4.1 Halliday and Benveniste

The *ideational function* proposed in Halliday can be linked to the concept of **Subjectivity in Language** as defined by Benveniste (1966-1974). According to Benveniste, it is a speaking man whom we find in the world (a man speaking to another man) and language works to provide the very definition of a man. She also argues that it is 'in' and 'through' the language that man constitutes himself as subject, since language alone can establish the concept of 'ego', in its reality which is that 'of being'. The concept of *empty sign* of Benveniste implies that every time a reference is triggered, a sign points out to the contextual clues otherwise meaningless and, thus, the relation with the referents in the real world become essential. For example, when we say 'that' or 'there', there is an existential axis of 'here-now' from which other relations with the world are established. When Halliday defines the *ideational function*, he categorically argues that language serves for the *expression of content,* so that an individual can speak about his or her experiences of the real world as well as his or her inner thoughts. If any person can tell about something, it means that he or she has the capacity to establish himself or herself as subject in relation to others.

The *interpersonal function* of Halliday can be linked up with the concept of **Intersubjectivity** as visualized by Benveniste. It refers to the change of roles between the members of a speech act. In the views of Benveniste, man needs language to establish, fabricate and maintain social relations, without which man will fail to establish his or her existence with the real world. In the same tune Halliday states that language serves to establish and maintain the social relations and enables a person to interact with others. Also, language serves for expressing social roles, which include the communication roles created by the language itself. Besides, language helps in expression and development of personality of every individual. Communication cannot exist without the presence of speaker or writer and listener or reader, respectively. Whenever an individual poses himself as a speaker, the other person present before him becomes automatically a listener.

Finally, the *textual function* of Halliday can be linked to idea of the **Deixis** as proposed by Benveniste. The indicators of deixis, according to Benveniste, organise spatial and temporal relationships around the subject considered as the referent: *this, here* and *now*. The *textual function* is, according to Halliday, what enables the speaker or writer to construct texts or connected passages of discourse, what are situationally relevant and also what enable listener or reader to distinguish a text from a random set of utterances.

The concepts of *text* and *discourse* of Halliday are related to Benveniste's distinction between *story* and *discourse*, in which the first one takes the third person singular, is usually in the passive voice and is represented by the non-I and the second one takes the first person singular, active voice and is represented by the presence of 'I'. Both *story* and *discourse*, in the views of Benveniste, are two different ways of textual organisation.

7.4.2 Halliday and Jakobson

Comparing and contrasting the theories about the functions of language as presented by Jakobson and Halliday, **it can be assumed** that there are several differences and similarities. First of all, in his theory, Jakobson presents not only the language functions, but also its factor or constituents; while Halliday concentrates only on language functions, *per se*. When Halliday proposes the first function of language (i.e., *ideational function*), he describes that in serving this function, language also gives structure to our experience and helps us in determining our ways of looking at things. This function can easily be made parallel with what Jakobson indicates in the *referential function*, also referred to as *denotative* or *cognitive function*, i.e., how we perceive reality.

The *interpersonal function* of Halliday can be linked with *conative*, *phatic* and *emotive functions* of Jakobson. Halliday defines *interpersonal function* by saying that language serves to establish and maintain the social relations and through this function, social groups are delimited and the individuals are identified and reinforced. Jakobson's *conative function* has orientation towards the addressee. It finds its purest grammatical expression in the vocative and imperative. One clear example for this would be an utterance like, *"Close the door"*. By this example one can state that there is an *addresser* who utters an expression and an *addressee* who responds in a certain context. But beyond that one may also like to infer what kind of relationship they maintain, as it is not the same to say *"Close the door"* and *"Could you please close the door?"*

In the *phatic function* there are messages primarily serving to establish, to prolong, to discontinue communication and to check whether the channel works perfectly. This sets for the contact, which may be displayed by profuse exchange of ritualised formulae. This function serves, as Halliday explains, to establish and maintain social relations. Finally, the *emotive function* focusses on the addresser and aims at the direct expression of attitude of the speaker towards what he is speaking about.

In case of the *textual function* Halliday argues that language makes links with itself and with features of the situation in which it is used. That means one of the vital aspects of the *textual function* is the establishment of cohesive relations from one sentence to another in a discourse. We can argue that this particular function relates to the *poetic function* of Jakobson as he discusses in his theory that when dealing with the *poetic function*, linguists cannot delimit themselves to the field of poetry, but rather focus on the message as such.

7.4.3 Halliday and Voloshinov

The *ideational function* of Halliday can be also related to the **Ideological Sign** of Voloshinov (1973), as according to Voloshinov, to understand ideologies we often need to make some intellectual effort to go beyond language and see other values that words denote. Halliday's argument in this regard is that in serving the *ideational function*, language also gives structure to experience and helps to determine our way of looking at things. Therefore, we require some intellectual effort to see things in any other way than that which language suggests to us.

This observation of Halliday implies that the *ideational function* can easily be related to *ideological sign* of Voloshinov on a few grounds. First, there exist ideological signs, which possess semiotic values, i.e., they reflect and refract reality. Second, Voloshinov states that ideology is a fact of consciousness; the understanding of a sign is an act of reference between the sign apprehended and the other, already known signs. If language shapes our way of looking at things and if it requires some intellectual effort to see them in any other way, it means that we know what we want to say because it is agreed upon among the members of a community. Since some signs are filled in with ideological content, at certain times, it becomes difficult to see them in any other way.

Also, the *interpersonal* and *textual function* of Halliday become related to the theory of Voloshinov when he says that signs emerge, after all, only in the process of interaction between one individual consciousness and with that of the other individual.

7.4.4 Halliday and Grice

The functions proposed by Halliday can also be related to Grice's theory, as there are some clear connections between Halliday's *ideational function* with what Grice proposes as **Pragmatics** (Grice 1991). While Grice observes that communication is a form of intentional behaviour and the understanding an utterance is a matter of recognising the intentions behind it; Halliday opines that language gives structure to experience and helps to determine our way of looking at things, so that it requires some intellectual effort to see them in any other way than which our language suggests to us.

Moreover, while Grice argues that humans are genetically predisposed to recognising the underlying intentions of an utterance; Halliday states that in order to interpret something other than what language suggests speakers and hearers surely require some intellectual efforts. In the argument of Halliday, understanding an utterance actually involves many other things than merely knowing the meaning of a sentence uttered. The speaker has to make himself understood to the listener and avoid producing 'a random set of utterances'. Similarly, a writer has to establish cohesive relations within a text so as to make his message come across successfully.

The *textual function* proposed by Halliday can also fabricate a fine line of connection between what Grice suggests as **Cooperative Principle**. While Grice argues that a communication is a cooperative activity and that each conversation has an accepted purpose or direction, which participants work towards; Halliday opines that the *textual function* enables a speaker or a writer to construct texts and it enables the hearer or reader to distinguish a text from a random set of sentences.

7.4.5 Halliday and Austin

An insightful investigation may link up Halliday's concept of *interpersonal function* with Austin's **Speech Act** theory, particularly to *locution, illocution, perlocution* and the *roles of the addressee*, the *ratified participant*, the *bystanders* and the *eavesdropper*, as well (Austin 1962).

Austin argues that a speech act is created when speaker or writer makes an utterance to hearer or reader in a context. These speech acts are actually parts of social interactive behaviours taking place between the people of a community. The idea of the subjective marks left by the speakers becomes related to, what Halliday says, the *communication roles created by language itself*.

7.5 Some Indian Observations

7.5.1 Tolkappiyam

Ancient Dravidian linguist Tolkappiyam (300 AD - 1,000 AD)[7] treats language from the perspective of communication, which according to him, is a highly complex linguistic phenomenon that can be achieved not just by using the language in any manner, but by combining language with many other issues related to an event of communication. The success of any kind of linguistic communication depends on several external factors like the flora and fauna, the seasons of the year, the time of the day, natural objects and forces like the sun, the moon and the wind, cultural aspects and conventions, emotional and psychological status of the communicators, the status of the individuals and the linguistic appropriateness required in a particular context. Language is destined to fail in evoking expected results if all or some of these issues are ignored in an act of communication. Thus, Tolkappiyam shows that the use and function of language is not related to linguistics only; it is also related to many other areas of human existence and experience such as ethnography, ecology, sociology, demography and psychology.

The parallelism drawn by Tolkappiyam can be referred to the playing of Indian classical music, in which some ragas are sung only in the morning, some only at night and some others during certain seasons (since the mood of a given raga can be communicated only at specific time). Similarly, the use and function of language should be in harmony with the landscape of the heart of the speaker as well as with the landscape outside the heart of the speaker to make language functionally penetrative as well as the process of communication maximally effective[8].

7.5.2 Rabindranath Tagore

Some Bengali scholars of the 20th century have made observations about the functions of language from a different angle. These are mostly different from the observations made by Locke, but are aligned toward the views expressed by Wittgenstein.

Among Bengali scholars, Rabindranath Tagore, the Nobel Laureate, has observed in *Bangla Bhasa Parichay*, the functions of language in the following way:

> "mānuṣ ẏeman jānābār jiniṣ bhāṣā diye jānāy, temani tāke jānāte hay sukh-dukhṣa bhālalāgā-mandalāgā ... mānuṣ nirmāṇ kare prayoẏane, sṛṣṭi kare ānande. tāi bhāṣār kāje mānuṣer duṭo bibhāg āche ... ekṭā tār garajer ār ekṭā tār khuśir, tār kheẏāler ... mānuṣer buddhisādhanār bhāṣā āpan pūrṇatā dekhiyeche darśaṇe, bijñāne. hṛdaybṛttir cūṛānta prakāś kābye".

[Translation (by me)]: Human beings convey message—what to be conveyed—through language. He also uses language to express his joy and sorrow, likings and dislikings. Man constructs to fulfil his needs, but creates out of pleasure. So language has two functions—one is for his urgency and another is for his joy and emotions. The language of mind culminates in the works of philosophy and science, while the language of heart is fully manifested in poetry.

7.5.3 Buddhadeb Basu

Almost in the similar fashion, noted Bengali scholar Buddhadeb Basu in his *Kālidāser Meghadut* has observed:

> "ājker dine sakalei svīkār karen ẏe bhāṣā dui bhābe kāj kare. ek dike se khabar dey, anya dike se jāgiye tole. tathya bā jñāner jagate āmrā cāi spaṣṭa o susaṅlagna bhāṣā, ẏār āyatan tār sambāder saṅge khāpe-khāpe mile ẏābe. kintu kabitār bhāṣāy āmrā khūji prabhāb, ẏā tār byākaraṇ nirdiṣṭa arthake atikram kare bahudūre chaṛiye paṛe, ẏār bege āmāder maner anek svapna, smṛti, cintā o anusaṅger ẏena ghum bheṅge ẏāy, dhvani theke pratidhvani anabarata prahata hate thāke"

[Translation (by me)]: In today's world everybody admits that language works in two ways. In one way it informs, in other way it awakens. In the world of information we want clear and cohesive language whose form and content should have a perfect synchrony. But in the language of poetry we search for impact which will spread beyond the realms of meaning defined by grammar and due to this many of our dreams, memories, ideas and thoughts are awakened—where the echo of sound buzzes on and on into our mind.

7.6 Recent Observations

7.6.1 Stephen Pinker and Peter Bloom

Recently, Pinker and Bloom (1990) try to analyse what is the function (if any) of language purely from the point of view of **Natural Selection**. They want to consider only the expressive part of language taking into consideration the functional roles of the linguistic properties used in a natural language. They present their arguments in the following manner[9]:

"Human knowledge and reasoning is couched in a 'language of thought' that is distinct from external languages such as English or Japanese. The propositions in this representational medium are relational structures whose symbols pertain to people, objects and events, the categories they belong to, their distribution in space and time and their causal relations to one another. The causal relations governing the behaviour of other people are understood as involving their beliefs and desires, which can be considered as relations between an individual and the proposition that represents the content of that belief or desire. This makes the following kinds of content as worthy of communication among humans" (Pinker and Bloom 1990).

In their proposition Pinker and Bloom also want to refer to individuals and classes, to distinguish among the basic ontological categories (such as *things, events, places, times, manners* and so on), to talk about the events and states, distinguishing the participants in the event or state according to the roles (i.e., *agents, patients, goals*) and to talk about the intentional states of the participants and others. Also, they want ability to express distinctions of truth-value, modality (i.e., *necessity, possibility, probability, factivity*, etc.), to comment on the time of an event or state including both its distribution over time (i.e., *continuous, iterative, punctuate*, etc.) and its overall time of occurrence.

Moreover, they argue that one might demand the ability to encode an unlimited number of predicates, arguments and propositions. Further, it would be useful to be able to use the same propositional content within different speech acts; for instance, as a question, a statement, or a command. Superimposed on all of this they might ask for an ability to focus on or to put into the background different parts of a proposition, so as to tie the speech act into its context of previously conveyed information and patterns of knowledge of the listener.

According to Pinker and Bloom, the vocal-auditory channel of language has some desirable features as a medium of communication. It has a high bandwidth, its intensity can be modulated to conceal the speaker or to cover large distances and it does not require light, proximity and a face-to-face orientation, or tying up the hands. However it is essentially a serial interface, lacking full two-dimensionality needed to convey graph or tree structures and typographical devices such as fonts, subscripts and brackets. The basic tools of a coding scheme that employ it are inventory of distinguishable symbols and their concatenation. Thus, grammars for spoken language map with propositional structures onto a serial channel, minimising ambiguity in context, under the further constraints that the encoding and decoding is done rapidly, by creatures with limited short-term memories, according to a code that is shared by entire community of potential communicants.

They clearly mention that language is a highly complex system made of many parts, each one of which is tailored to mapping a characteristic kind of semantic or pragmatic function to a characteristic kind of symbol sequence. This function is, however, so obvious in all kinds of linguistic practices that it is usually not seen as worth mentioning. Therefore, they want to list some uncontroversial facts about substantive universals, the building blocks of grammars that all theories of universal grammar posit, either as an explicit inventory or as a consequence of somewhat more abstract mechanisms involved in language acquisition and generation.

For them, grammars, either explicit or implicit, of a natural language are built around the symbols for major lexical categories such as nouns, verbs, adjectives and preposition, etc. that can enter into rules specifying surface distributions. For instance, it is the verbs, not nouns that generally can take unmarked direct objects, inflections and lists of lexical items. Thus, together with the minor categories that characteristically co-occur with the major ones (e.g., articles with nouns), different categories are provided with the means of being distinguished in speech strings. These distinctions are exploited to distinguish the basic ontological categories such as things, events, states and qualities.

The major phrasal categories (such as, *noun phrases, verb phrases,* etc.), according to them, start off with a major lexical item—the head— and allow it to be combined with specific kinds of affixes and phrases. The resulting conglomerate is then used to refer to the entities in the mental models of the world. Thus a noun like *dog,* which does not describe itself anything, can be combined with articles and other parts-of-speech to make noun phrases, such as *those dogs, my dog* and *the dog that bit me* and it is these noun phrases that are used to describe things of the external world. Similarly, a verb like *hit* is made into a verb phrase by marking it for tense and aspect and adding an object, thus enabling it to describe an event or an action. In general, words encode abstract general categories and only by contributing to the structure of major phrasal categories they can describe particular things, events, states, locations and properties. This mechanism enables the language users to refer to an unlimited range of specific entities of internal and external world while possessing only a finite number of lexical items.

The phrase structure rules, (e.g., *X-bar theory* or *immediate dominance rules*) according to Piker and Bloom, force concatenation in the string to correspond to the semantic connectedness in underlying propositions. Phrase structure rules, thus, provide linear clues of the underlying structure to distinguish closely similar syntactic forms like *Large trees grow dark berries* and *Dark trees grow large berries.*

In their view, the rules of linear order (such as, *directional parameters* for ordering heads, complements and specifiers, or *linear precedence rules*) allow the order of the words within these concatenations to distinguish among the argument positions that an entity assumes with respect to a predicate to distinguish forms like *Man bites dog* and *Dog bites man.*

The case affixes used with nouns and adjectives can take over all these functions, marking nouns according to argument role and linking noun with predicate even when the order is scrambled. This redundancy procedure frees up the device of linear order and allows it to be exploited to convey the relations of prominence and focus, which can thus mesh with the necessarily temporal flow of attention and knowledge acquisition in the listener.

Language and Linguistics

The verb affixes, on the other hand, signal the temporal distribution of an event that a verb refers to (known as *aspect*) and the time of the event (known as *tense*). When separate aspect and tense affixes co-occur in a construction, they are in a universally preferred order as the aspect affixes generally come closer to the verb. Given that man-made time-keeping devices play no role in species-typical human thought, some other kind of temporal coordinates need to be used. Languages employ an ingenious system that can convey the time of an event relative to the time of the speech act itself and relative to a third, an arbitrary reference time. Thus we can distinguish between *John has arrived, John had arrived (when Mary was speaking), John will have arrived (before Mary speaks)* and so on. Verb affixes also typically agree with the subject and other arguments and thus provide another redundant mechanism that can convey predicate-argument relations by itself. For instance, several Native American languages such as Cherokee and Navajo eliminate ambiguity left open by other mechanisms to distinguish between the sentences like *I know the boy and the girl who like chocolate* and *I know the boy and the girl who likes chocolate.*

The auxiliary affixes, which often occur either as affixes of a verb (where these are distinguished from the tense and aspect affixes by proximity to the verb itself) or in one of three sentence-peripheral positions (e.g., first, second, last), convey relations that have logical scope over the entire proposition (i.e., mirroring their peripheral position) such as truth-value, modality and the illocutionary force.

All languages also contain a small inventory of phonetically reducible morphemes, which are identified as pronouns and other anaphoric elements. These elements, that by virtue of encoding a small set of semantic features such as gender and humanness and being restricted in their distribution, can convey patterns of co-reference among the different participants in complex relations without the necessity of repeating the lengthy definite descriptions, such as, *A boy showed a dog to a girl and then he/she/it touched him/her/it/ himself herself/itself.*

The mechanism of complementation and control governs the expression of propositions that are arguments of other propositions. It employs specific complementiser morphemes to signal periphery of embedded propositions, indicates its relation to the embedding one and licenses omission of repeated phrases referring to participants playing certain combinations of roles. This allows the expression of a rich set of propositional attitudes within the belief-desire folk psychology, e.g., *John tried to come, John thinks that Bill will come, John hopes for Bill to come, John convinced Bill to come* and so on.

In case of wh-movement (as in *wh-questions* and *relative clauses*), there is a tightly constrained co-occurrence pattern between an empty element (a *trace* or *gap*) and a sentence-peripheral quantifier (e.g., wh-words). The quantifier-word can be specific as to illocutionary force (e.g., *question vs modification*), ontological type (e.g., *time, place, purpose*), feature (i.e., *animate/inanimate*) and role (i.e., *subject/object*) and the gap can occur only in the highly constrained phrase structure configurations. The semantics of such constructions allow the speaker to fix the reference of, or request information about, an entity by specifying its role within any proposition. One can refer not just to *any dog* but *to the dog that Mary sold to a student last year*; one can ask not only for the names of just any old interesting person but specifically *Who was that woman I saw you with ___?*

This is only a partial list, which focuses on sheer expressive power of language. One can add to it many other syntactic constraints and devices whose structure enables them to minimise memory load and the likelihood of pursuing local garden paths in speech comprehension, or to ease the task of analysis for the child learning the language. On top of that there are the rules of segmental phonology that smooth out arbitrary concatenations of morphemes into a consistent sound pattern that juggles demands of ease of articulation and perceptual distinctness. Moreover, there are prosodic rules that disambiguate sentences and communicate pragmatic and illocutionary information. Also there are several articulatory programmes that achieve rapid transmissions through parallel encoding of adjacent consonants and vowels. In sum, language appears to be a fine example of "that perfection of structure and co-adaptation which justly excites our admiration" (Darwin 1859: 26).

7.7 Concluding Remarks

The functions of language introduced and propagated by different scholars at different points in time, are criticised on several grounds from theoretical standpoints. In most cases, attempts are made to suggest a few novel ways of exploiting the potential of language in various dimensions of existence of human life. When one tries to analyse the functions of language for a given unit (e.g., *a word, a text or an image*), one tries to specify to which class or type it belongs (e.g., *a textual or pictorial genre*), which functions are present or absent and the characteristics of the functions, including the hierarchical relations and any other relations that may operate between them.

Within a scheme of proper analysis, one starts by determining whether each of the functions of language is present or absent. In theory, each factor is necessary in a communication. This does not, however, imply that each of the functions is always present. One will assume that while one or more (or even all) of the functions of language may be absent in short units (e.g., isolated words), lengthy units can activate all of them. Where more than one function is present, one can try to establish either the simple hierarchy, by identifying the dominant function and not ranking the other functions, or the complex hierarchy by specifying the degree of presence of some or all of the functions.

It is considered that various criteria may be used to establish functional hierarchy of language. For example, one can use an intention-based criterion where the dominant function is the one that answers a question. However, one needs to distinguish the intention associated with each fragment from the overall intention, which is a sentence or series of sentences that corresponds to an intention. The most striking thing is that since intention can be hidden, the function that is dominant in terms of overt degree of presence may not be dominant in terms of intention.

Moreover, one can distinguish between direct and indirect manifestations of intention, which correlate to the opposition between the actual and overt functions of language. The appellative (i.e., *conative*) function is manifested directly in a sentence like *"Go, answer the door"* and indirectly in *"The doorbell rings"* (which is somewhat equivalent to *"Go, answer the door"*), where the overt function is a referential (or informative) function. In addition, one also needs to distinguish between cause and effect functions, as well as ends and means functions (the ends being the effect that is sought). For example, when the *phatic function* (cause) is over-activated, it can trigger the *poetic function* (effect); over-activation can be also used for aesthetic ends and in this case the *poetic function* is an end and the *phatic function* is a means.

When one studies relations between the functions to establish hierarchy, one traces two kinds of correlation that exist between the functions. The first one is converse or direct correlation when the intensification of one function is accompanied by the intensification of the other. On the other hand, a decline in one function may cause a decline in the other. This correlation is said to be inverse if an intensification of one function is accompanied by a decline in the other and vice versa. However, some functions are generally paired in more definite inverse relation, where the most obvious pairings are the *expressive* and *conative functions* and the *referential* and *poetic functions*.

Therefore, it is difficult to draw the line between interaction and merging of functions. For instance, the *referential function* changes the knowledge stock of a receiver, which is the *conative function*. Also, the information leads to the change of behaviour as its final result. It still remains to be determined how different functions are merged together in achieving goals of various kinds of the participants engaged in linguistic communication.

Notes and Comments

[1] The difference between functions of language can be realised by recognising the fact that correct evaluation of any text requires knowledge about the functions relevant to the situational context. Other things being equal, a text of physics or biology is predominately informative, that of a novel or story is predominately expressive, while that of logic or mathematics is normally directive.

[2] Karl Bühler (1879-1963) was not well-known in the English-speaking world, as his master work was not published in English until 1990 although it was first published in 1934. This famous book entitled *Sprach Theorie* (1934) is translated by Donald Fraser Goodwin in 1990 as *The Theory of Language: The Representational Function of Language*.

[3] Within Anglo-American tradition, the arguments presented by Wittgenstein are considered as the most important philosophical insights of the 20th century and these continue to influence contemporary philosophers, especially those studying mind and language.

[4] After the presentation of the model by Jakobson, several competing names have been proposed for the 'same' factors and functions, although different name may indicate, insist on, reveal, hide, or even result in important conceptual differences. Some other names for the factors are (referring to the table): referent (*context*), sender or enunciator (*addresser*), receiver or enunciate (*addressee*), channel (*contact*). Similarly, the other names for the

functions are: denotative, cognitive, representative and informative (*referential*), expressive (*emotive*), appellative, imperative, directive (*conative*), relational or contact (*phatic*), metasemiotic [in order to extend the function to any semiotic act, such as an image] (*metalingual*) and aesthetic or rhetorical (*poetic*).

[5] The English term *foregrounding* has come to mean several things at once. First, it is used to indicate the psycholinguistic processes by which, in an act of reading, something is given special prominence. Second, it refers to specific devices (as produced by author) located in the text itself. Third, it is employed to indicate the specific poetic effect on the reader. Fourth, it is used as an analytic category in order to evaluate literary texts, situate them historically and to explain their importance and cultural significance. Finally, it is used to differentiate literary texts from other varieties of language use, such as everyday conversations and scientific reports. Thus the term covers a wide area of meaning. This may have its advantages, but may also be problematic: which of the above meanings is intended is deduced from the context in which the term is used.

[6] This is in direct contradiction to the Chomskyan approach which is a theory of form. Halliday's work represents a competing viewpoint to the structuralist approach of Chomsky. Halliday is concerned with what he claims to be 'naturally occurring language in actual contexts of use' in a large typological range of languages whereas Chomsky is concerned only with the formal properties of English, which he thinks are indicative of the nature of what he calls *Universal Grammar*.

[7] There is not much information about who Tolkappiyam was and when he lived (Takahashi 1995: 18). It was thought that there could have been only one author but given the fairly long time span it seems to have taken for the final redaction of the book to become available, it is reasonable to ascribe the work to multiple authors. Zvelebil (1973) argues that the final redaction may even have been the work of a systematised school of grammar than the work of any individual (Zvelebil 1973: 26).

[8] Interestingly, a notable function of language, according to some ancient Indian sages lies in its healing effect on human body and mind. It had been observed that recitation of some mantras of the *Vedas* and other ancient Indian scriptures could cure various ailments, bring mental harmony and peace, as well as could

control blood pressure. Some such Indian concepts may question the notion that 'language is arbitrary'.

[9]   The discussion presented in this Section (Section 7.6) is mostly developed in the own words of the authors. No effort is made to paraphrase the actual content of their proposition with a belief that it may distort the actual arguments of the authors furnished in the article.

Chapter 8
Non-Verbal Human Communication

8.1 Introduction

Non-verbal communication, like that of verbal communication, is one of the intriguing areas of human communication system. In general, it refers to the exchange of messages primarily through non-linguistic means that includes *paralanguage* (i.e., vocal but non-linguistic cues like pitch, stress, intonation, etc.), *body movement, kinesis, facial expression, eye contact, tactile communication* (i.e., communication through touch), *personal space and territory, environment, smell, silence* and *time*. It involves those physical means of communication, which we use consciously or unconsciously to transmit and receive wordless messages across space and time. In case of purely information exchange and sharing, it usually includes various physical forms and representations like *gestures, facial expressions, postures, body language, eye contact,* etc.; while in case of creative and aesthetic fields, it includes s*inging, painting, dancing, music* and *sculpturing,* etc.; and in case of **object communication,** it refers to body-decorating objects such as *clothing, hairstyles, tattoos, caps, shoes, wrist bands,* etc. All these means of non-verbal communication are collectively called as **behavioural communication.**

Within the broader frame of communication non-linguistics symbols and sign language are also included in non-verbal communication as well as the body language. Body posture and physical contact convey a large amount of information as body posture matters a lot when an individual communicates verbally to someone. For instance, folded arms and crossed legs are some of the signals, which are conveyed by body posture. Similarly, physical contacts like *shaking hands, pushing, patting, hugging* and *touching,* etc. expresses feeling of intimacy or closeness between the communicators. Also, facial expressions, gestures and eye contact, etc. can equally be effective in communication if used intelligently and purposefully.

Written texts also exhibit some non-verbal elements such as the style of *handwriting, spatial arrangement of words*, or *the use of emoticons*[1]. Some other channels of communication such as telegraphic information transfer may also fall into this category, where the signals are made to travel from one person to another by deployment of an alternative non-human method. These signals are representatives of words and objects as well as the projectors of emotional states of the communicators.

Several experiments have been carried out for estimating the functional and communicative relevance of non-verbal communication over the years and most of these studies have shown that humans can communicate directly by non-verbal means without using speech or texts quite effectively (Warwick *et al.* 2004). In this chapter an attempt is initiated to discuss some of the basic strategies and means used in non-verbal communication by human beings. It has described all the major means of non-verbal communication in a situation where person-to-person communication is the central theme for information exchange and emotion sharing.

8.2 Features of Non-verbal Communication

The first scientific study on non-verbal communication may be credited to Charles Darwin. In his book entitled *The Expression of the Emotions in Man and Animals* (1872), Darwin had argued that all mammals exhibited emotion quite reliably in their faces, which may differ from mammal to mammal. Recent studies on human facial expressions have attested this observation and have shown that expression of anger, disgust, fear, joy, sadness and surprise, etc. are more or less universal in nature (Ekman 1972, Ekman 2003). Moreover, physical elements such as physique, height, weight, hair, skin colour, gender, odour and clothing, etc. have some amount of universality in transmitting non-verbal messages during a verbal interaction.

In the interplay of all these elements in communication, two important factors are found to work silently: **(a) time**, which refers to punctuality and willingness to wait, the speed of speech and how long a listener is willing to listen to a speaker; **(b) posture**, which determines the degree of attention or the depth of involvement of the participants[2].

The elements that are found to operate in non-verbal communication are divided into four broad categories in the following manners:

(a) **Physical elements:** In a situation of personal type of communication, the elements that become prominent include facial expressions, tone of voice, sense of touch, sense of smell and motions of body of the interactants.

(b) **Aesthetic cues:** The non-verbal communication that takes place through creative expressions includes elements like playing instrumental music, dancing, painting, drawing, writing, narrating, sculpturing, teaching and guiding, etc.

(c) **Sign elements:** The mechanical type of communication includes elements like the use of signal flags, gun salutes, lights, horns and sirens, etc.

(d) **Symbolic forms:** Special kinds of non-verbal communication make use of elements of religion, status, or ego-building symbols, etc.

Proper understanding about these elements of non-verbal communication becomes indispensable for the communicators in exchange of information at least for two reasons: (a) to interact effectively and successfully as a member of an interaction with the opponent members. In these situations, non-verbal cues, if interpreted correctly, can provide one a strategy to do so and (b) as a member of a team it is necessary for an individual to understand the attitudes and feelings of fellow members who may express through some non-verbal communication means.

Besides understanding mind and attitude of the members of opponent or peer groups, non-verbal means of communication are also used for achieving personal needs such as approval, growth, achievement and recognition. The extent to which these needs are addressed is closely related to how a person is perceptive to these means of non-verbal communication in him/herself and in fellow members of the team. If the team members show a true awareness to the non-verbal cues, the team will have a better chance to succeed, for it will be an open, honest and confronting unit.

Several features of non-verbal communication are identified by scholars in last few years (Bull 1987, Argyle 1988, Burgoon, Buller and Woodall 1996, Floyd and Guerrero 2006). These features are broadly divided into two types: **static** and **dynamic** features, which are further sub-divided into several types based on several factors mentioned below:

Language and Linguistics

(1) Static Features

(a) **Distance:** Distance existing between two communicators indirectly refers to their degree of closeness in their social relationship. An individual who stands close or at a distant place from another person frequently conveys poignant non-verbal message. In some cultures, distance indicates a sign of attraction, while in others, it reflects on the status or the intensity of the exchange.

b) **Orientation:** At the time of verbal communication people may present themselves in various manners: face-to-face, side-to-side, or even back-to-back. It is observed that while cooperating people are likely to sit side-by-side, competitors frequently sit or stand face-to-face to each other.

(c) **Posture:** In verbal communication, a communicator may lie down, seat, or stand while speaking to others. These are, however, not very impressive or poignant postures that can convey good messages. On the other hand, one can slouch or be erect, or can keep legs crossed, or arms folded at the time of verbal communication. Such postures can either convey a degree of formality or a degree of relaxation in the communication exchange.

(2) Dynamic Features

(a) **Physical Contact:** Shaking hands, touching, holding, embracing, hugging, kissing, pushing, pulling, patting on the back, spanking – all these actions convey messages in non-verbal communication. These may reflect on the elements of intimacy or feeling of (or lack of) attraction on the part of the interactants engaged in communication.

(b) **Facial Expressions:** A smile, a frown, a raised eyebrow, a yawn, a sneer or a drop of tear convey valuable information in non-verbal communication. It is noted that facial expressions change continually during an interaction and are monitored constantly by the informants.

(c) **Hand Movement:** One of the most frequently observed but least understood cues in non-verbal communication is hand movement. Most people use hand movements regularly when talking either in face-to-face or in telephonic conversation. While some types of hand movement (e.g., *clenched fist, waving, raising hands,* etc.) have universal meanings, most of the other hand movements are culture-specific and idiosyncratic. These need to be learned individually.

(d) Looking: An important element in face-to-face communication is looking, which has culture-specific significance. In some societies it is permitted to one and all in all types of verbal interaction, while in other societies, it is monitored by various sociolinguistic factors such as gender, age, status, race, etc. In general, looking conveys emotion, signals when to start and stop talking and when to avert an altercation. While high frequency of looking into each-other's eye may suggest interest, its low frequency may indicate boredom or lack of interest.

Both *static* and *dynamic features,* as non-verbal means, transmit important information from the sender to the receiver. The basic proposition is that an effective communication does not always depend on the use of verbal signals or speech only. It also depends on subtle use of non-verbal cues for creating required impact on the addressee.

8.3 The Interface of Verbal, Non-verbal and Setting

In a context of person-to-person communication, messages or information we want to transfer to the recipient is simultaneously sent through two broad levels, namely, **(a) verbal level** and **(b) non-verbal level**. These two levels are actually controlled by the **(c) Setting,** which indirectly monitors what kinds of verbal (speech) and non-verbal elements and cues are to be deployed to make a communication maximally successful. The interface of verbal, non-verbal and setting is represented below (Fig. 8.1) to show these actually synchronise on successful communication.

The most striking factor is that if the cues of the non-verbal level and the content of the verbal level (i.e., the spoken message) are incongruous, then the flow of communication is bound to be hindered with a high possibility for miscarriage. On the other hand, if non-verbal cues and verbal content are synchronised properly maintaining a harmony with setting, a communication is bound to yield expected results for which the communication is made. The recipient of information in communication, consciously or unconsciously, tends to correlate intentions of sender with non-verbal cues he receives along with verbal message. Thus, non-verbal cues, verbal content and the physical setting combine together to play a parametric role in communication—from interacting in family, to talking to friends, to discussing with colleagues, to romantic engagements, to quarrels, to wining the enemy's heart.

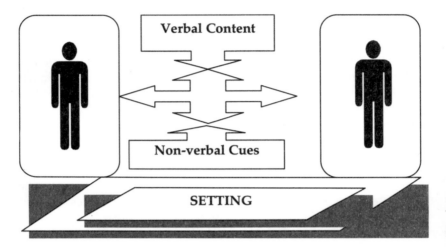

Fig. 8.1: Interface of verbal content, non-verbal cues and setting

Several studies on non-verbal communication have focussed on the cues and elements deployed in face-to-face communication. In general, the event of non-verbal communication is classified into three principal areas (Burgoon, Buller and Woodall 1996):

(a) Environment or setting where the communication takes place.
(b) Physical characteristics of verbal communication.
(c) Non-verbal cues the communicators use during an interaction.

Usually, whenever an individual speaks, his or her attention is focused on the words used in interaction rather than on his/her body language. But the basic reality is that our judgement related to the interaction includes both the elements. The non-verbal cues, which play crucial roles in communication, include *paralanguage, visual communication, tactile communication, environment, time, gestures, facial expressions, kinesis, proxemics, silence* and *eye contact*, etc. Some of these cues are briefly sketched in the following sections.

8.4 Paralanguage

The term paralanguage[3] refers to the non-verbal elements of communication used in speech to modify meaning and convey emotion. Normally a speech event contains many non-verbal elements, which include notable properties such as voice quality, emotion, speaking style and some prosodic features such as rhythm, intonation and stress. These may be expressed consciously or unconsciously. The term is also used in a restricted sense to refer to vocally produced sounds only.

Sometimes the content of a message is contradicted by the paralanguage with which it is communicated. An example is *"And Brutus was a noble man!"* Those who work on the nature of non-verbal communication identify that paralanguage, which is superimposed on the linguistic system, adds an extra dimension of meaning to utterances. Tone, pitch, quality of voice and rate of speed of speaking, etc. can convey emotions, which can be accurately judged regardless of the content of the message. The important thing to gain from this is that the voice is highly important, not just as the conveyor of the message, but as a complement to the message. As a communicator one should be sensitive to the influence of tone, pitch and quality of one's voice on the interpretation of one's message, since it is acknowledged that paralinguistic properties of speech play important roles in human verbal communication.

There is no utterance or speech signal that lacks paralinguistic properties, as speech of any kind requires the presence of a voice that can be modulated. This voice must have *some* properties and all properties of a voice, as such, are paralinguistic. One can identify the following aspects of speech signals and perceived utterances (Traunmüller 2005):

(a) Perspectival aspects: Speech signals that reach to listeners' ear have some acoustic properties that may allow listeners to localise the speaker with regard to distance and direction. Sound localisation operates in a similar fashion for non-speech sounds. The perspectival aspects of lip reading become more obvious and have more drastic effects when head-turning is involved into it.

(b) Organic aspects: Speech organs of different speakers differ in size also. As children grow up, their organs-of-speech become larger. However, there are differences between male and female adults. The differences concern not only size, but also proportions. They affect the pitch of the voice and the formant frequencies, which characterise different speech sounds. Organic quality of speech has a communicative function in a restricted manner, since it is merely informative about speakers. It will be expressed independently of the speaker's intention.

(c) Expressive aspects: The properties of the voice and the way of speaking are affected by emotions and attitudes. Typically, attitudes are expressed intentionally and emotions without intention, but attempts to fake or to hide emotions are not unusual in verbal interaction. Since expressive variation is central to paralanguage, it affects loudness, pitch, pitch range, speaking rate and to some extent, also the formant frequencies.

(d) Linguistic aspects: Ordinary phonetic transcriptions of utterances reflect only the linguistically informative quality. The problem of how listeners extract linguistically informative quality from speech signals is a topic of future research and exploration.

Some of the linguistic features of speech, in particular of its prosody, are paralinguistic or pre-linguistic in origin. The most fundamental as well as widespread phenomenon of this kind is known as **frequency code** (Ohala 1984). The code works even in communication across species. It has its origin in the fact that the acoustic frequencies in the voice of small vocalisers are high, while these are low in the voice of large vocalisers. This gives rise to the secondary meanings such as *harmless, submissive* and *unassertive*, which are naturally associated with smallness, while the meanings such as *dangerous, dominant* and *assertive* are associated with largeness.

In most languages, frequency code serves the purpose of distinguishing questions from statements. It is universally reflected in expressive variation and it is reasonable to assume that it has phylogenetically given rise to the sexual dimorphism that lies behind the large difference in pitch between the average female and male adults.

For some scholars, paralanguage does not only indicate the variations of pitch, stress, pause and intonation in speech, but also indicates the manner of speaking the communicators adopt to communicate particular meanings. For Robbins and Langton, "Paralanguage is communication that goes beyond the specific spoken words. It includes pitch, amplitude, rate and voice quality of speech. Paralanguage reminds us that people convey their feelings not only in *what* they say, but also in *how* they say it" (Robbins and Langton 2001: 21).

Paralanguage is composed of various scales. It is assumed that in normal verbal communication, utterances will fall near the centre point of each scale. However, in special types of verbal communication, where emotions and feeling are attached, speakers may move up or down of a particular scale or scales, as mentioned below:

(a) Loudness-to-softness Scale: Most of the utterances we produce usually do not draw any attention to themselves on this scale, since utterances are mostly produced with right intensity of sound considered well received and apprehended appropriately by listeners. But in some situations, some utterances may strike us as 'loud' or 'very loud', whereas in some other situations, it may appear 'soft' or 'very soft'. For instance, while speech in loud voice is very common in political slogan or in deliberation at mass rally, soft speech is normal at the side of death-bed or in the conversation of young lovers.

(b) Pitch Scale: It determines how high or low a voice is pitched in speaking. Every normal speaker is endowed with a considerable range of variation in pitch, which he/she uses in his/her speech to communicate the same message in various sub-ranges of pitch. We also learn to associate certain ranges of pitch with certain speakers. When a person speaks in different pitch, we assume that something unusual or extraordinary might have happened. Sometimes these different ranges are, however, considered quite appropriate in some situations, as it becomes rational for a teacher to use her speech in high pitch to control the unruly students in the class. Whereas extra high pitch is often regarded as manifestation of excitement and jubilation, extra low pitch is linked with pathos, grief, monotony, displeasure, disappointments and exhaustion.

(c) Rasping-to-openness Scale: Rasping indicates the presence of unusual amount of friction in an utterance or speech, as in *Ouch! Another Client!* On the other hand, openness is associated with certain types of speakers, particularly with political leaders and religious preachers, who speak to huge crowds in large and often unenclosed spaces during rituals. These speakers often give their speech as kind of 'resounding' character by way of using high sounding and impressionistic terms and phrases. They also make use of various rhetoric devices like *metaphors, similes, alliterations, bathos* and *hyperboles,* etc. to captivate target audience.

(d) Drawling to clipping Scale: Drawling refers to the act of pulling length of vowel sounds in syllables in speech to indicate insolence or reservation. For instance, a speaker may utter words in an elongated form as in *w-e-l-l, b-u-t,* or *y-e-s,* etc. to indicate reservation on an issue. On the other hand, clipping refers to the act of speaking in short and clipped utterances for indicating sharpness, irritation or displeasure, e.g., *Oh! No! Yes! Certainly! That's it!* Drawling and clipping are used in verbal interactions to change literal meaning of utterances as well as to invoke a diametrically opposite implication, e.g. *And Caesar was a noble man!*

(e) Tempo Scale: Tempo in an utterance can vary due to various factors and these variations provide important cues about the speaker or the speech event. Regular observations show that while young people and children usually speak in high tempo, old and aged people tend to speak in low tempo or speed. Such variation in tempo scale becomes quite significant in understanding a speech event as well as the speaker in the context of normal and exceptional utterances.

The number and variety of paralinguistic cues are used differently based on the choice of type of communication. Face-to-face communication employs the highest number of paralinguistic cues and these are gradually reduced in number in telephonic conversations and dictations. Since paralinguistic cues are essential elements for dissolving ambiguities in speech, they play crucial role in bridging the emotional gaps existing between the people engaged in verbal communication.

Paralinguistic cues are not only applied to speech. These are also used to writing and sign language as well, as these are not bound to any sensory modality. Even vocal language has some paralinguistic cues and linguistic properties that can be seen (e.g., *lip reading*) and felt. In literary texts also, it is possible to convey the full gamut of emotions in the text although it may ask for long time and talent on the part of the text composer. The paralinguistic cues, which are normally used in written text, include **explicit marks** such as *emoticons, cartoons, underlines, call-out descriptions;* **style** which is related to *font, colour, typography, layout, location,* etc.; and **implicit marks** such as *flex, rhetoric, rhythm, sound, vocabulary,* etc. In case of personal communication through written texts (e.g., *letters, emails, instant messaging,* etc.), people also use paralinguistic cues, which are often displayed by *emoticons, font and colour choices, capitalisation and the use of non-alphabetic or abstract characters,* etc. Nonetheless, the use of paralinguistic cues in written text is more or less limited in comparison with face-to-face conversations and dialogues.

Recently scholars (Rutter 1987, Sproull and Kiesler 1988) have argued that due to impoverishment of text and audio communications compared to face-to-face communication, the absence of paralinguistic cues may depersonalise the communication and increase antigonisation. This can be a major cause of **flame wars**[4], which is why it becomes imperative for the communicators to **assume-good-faith**[5] in all verbal and textual communication.

8.5 Visual Communication

Visual communication is a kind of non-verbal communication, which is performed through visual forms and aids. It is the conveyance of information and ideas in visual forms that can be read or looked upon. It is associated with two types of representation:

(a) **Non-electronic representation:** Signs, symbols, illustrations, graphic designs, drawing, follow charts, colours, typography, tables, etc.

(b) **Electronic representation:** All the above forms in digital form— either in static or in animated form. These solely rely upon vision as these are the forms of communication with visual effect.

A visual image attached with a piece of written text carries an extra load of information, which has greater power to inform, educate, or persuade a person or an audience. The importance of a visual image in communication is measured on the comprehension scale of the audience, not on the aesthetic or artistic value of the visual images. There are variety of ways for presenting information visually—painting, photography, video, television, gesture, body language, etc.

In an event of communication, the focus is on the presentation of texts, pictures, diagrams, photos, images and tables, etc., which are integrated with written or printed texts made for display. In fact, translation of ideas, stories and concepts that are largely textual and/ or word based into a visual format demands for utilisation of an interface of complex processes the goal of which is to provide suitable representation of information for proper understanding of ideas and concepts intended in communication. As visual communication is used as a process of presentation of information, scientists in this field have focused on designing graphically informative images, which can address the needs of visual communication completely.

The primary tool by which the mankind has succeeded to visualise ideas and information through generations is writing. It is the visual manifestation of a spoken word with which people have succeeded to communicate across the scale of time and space. It is, therefore, not an overstatement if we say that writing is the essence of all kinds of visual communication; and the present scenario of visual communication is an extension of visual communication made by writing. Writing is simply the single most important element that we put on a page, as it inherently carries the essence of communication.

The graphic or multimedia communication, which is extensively used in the present world of information exchange and display, is a distant progeny of visualisation of spoken words in written form. Therefore, it will not be wrong if we argue that the origin and development of script or orthography carries tremendous importance in the history and development of non-verbal communication. The pictorial elements used in textual communication, such as *font, shape, design, colour, illustration, illumination, photography,* etc., although carry vital information, are of secondary importance; and primary importance lies with letters and other orthographic symbols used in a piece of writing.

8.6 Gesture

Gesture is a form of non-verbal communication in which the visible bodily actions are used in parallel with speech to communicate messages across the communicators at a particular time and place (Kendon 2004: 32). This non-vocal bodily movement is intended primarily for expressing those messages, which cannot be expressed by speech alone. Gestures, in general, include different movements of limbs, i.e., the movement of hands, arms, legs, body, head, face and eyes, which manifest various bodily actions such as raising, shaking, winking, nodding and rolling of eyes, etc. Moreover, various tactile strategies, which are normally used in intimate personal communication, are included within gesture as these play crucial roles in communication. These include bodily actions such as hand shakes, holding hands, scratching head, pressing hands, kissing (e.g., cheek, lips, hand, etc.), back slapping, high fives, a pat on shoulder and brushing an arm, etc. These bodily movements are normally identified as **emblematic gestures**, which are broadly classified into different types based on the mode of using hands, hand and other body parts and body and facial gestures. In a broad scale, gestures are classified into three different types:

(a) **Single hand gestures:** O-kay, *abhaya mudra,* benediction and blessing, beckoning sign, clenched fist, crossed fingers, finger gun, hand shake, high five, patience sign, pointing index finger, poking, raised fist, salute, telephone sign, thumb-up, V-sign, *vardan mudra,* wanker[6], waving, etc.

(b) **Two hand gestures:** Air quotes, *anjali mudra,* applause, hand rubbing, jazz hands, time-out, victory clasp, whatever sign (made with the thumb and forefinger of both hands, to form the letter "W"), etc.

(c) **Gestures made with other body-parts:** Air kiss, bowing, *dhyan mudra,* cheek kissing, choking, curtsey, drinking sign, elbow bump, eye rolling, face-palm, hand kissing, hand-over-heart, nod, shrug, shush for silence, sign of cross, cut-throat, nose thumbing, cheek twisting, etc.

Another broad type of gesture includes those actions, which are generated spontaneously when people are engaged in speech. These gestures are called **beat gestures** as these are closely coordinated with speech and these are used in conjunction with speech to keep rhythm of speech or to emphasise certain words and phrases. These types of gestures are integrally connected to speech and thought processes (McNeill 1992: 107). Beat gestures—when used by the people engaged in a speech event—become far more contentful to elaborate the meaning of co-occurring speech. For example, a gesture that depicts the act of throwing may be synchronous with the utterance, *He threw the ball right into the window.*

Gesture is characteristically different from some other physical non-verbal means of communication (e.g., *expressive displays, proxemics, displays of joint attention*[7], etc.) in the sense that whereas these systems fail to communicate specific messages, gesture allows individuals to communicate a variety of feelings, emotions and thoughts such as liking,

199

interest, approval, affection, contempt, disliking, hostility, etc. All these feelings and emotions become poignant in expression when these are coupled together with body language and words, at that time when people are engaged in speech (Kendon 2004).

As a powerful strategy of non-verbal communication, gestures have been studied for centuries from different points of view (Kendon 1982). Quintillian made some observations on how gesture might be fruitfully used in rhetorical discourse, while Bulwer (1644) analysed dozens of gestures to provide a guideline about how to use gestures to increase eloquence and clarity for public speaking. De Jorio (1832) presented an extensive account of gestural expression people tend to use in verbal and non-verbal interactions, while Kendon (2004) has investigated many aspects of gestures, including their role in communication, conventionalisation of gesture, integration of gesture and speech and the evolution of language. Susan (2003) has carried an intensive investigation to identify the role of gestures in problem solving in case of children, while McNeill (1992, 2005) has developed a broad theory about how gesture and speech are parts of a single thought process.

Investigations have revealed that gesture processing takes place at the left inferior frontal gyrus of the **Broca's Area**; and the posterior middle temporal gyrus, posterior superior temporal sulcus and superior temporal gyrus of the **Wernicke's Area** (Xu *et al.* 2009). These parts of the brain originally support the pairing of gesture and meaning, which are adapted in human evolution for comparable pairing of sound and meaning, since voluntary control over the vocal apparatus was established as the spoken language evolved. Their common neurological basis also supports the idea that symbolic gesture and spoken language are two vital parts of a single fundamental semiotic system that underlies human discourse (McNeill 1992: 157).

Although the study of gesture is still in its infancy, some broad categories of gestures have been identified by researchers. The most familiar forms are the so-called emblems or quotable gestures, which are used as replacements for words, such as the hand-waves used to mean *hello* and *goodbye*. Due to their conventionality and culture-specificity, a single emblematic gesture can have different significance based on different cultural contexts, ranging from complimentary to highly offensive ones (Morris *et al.* 1979). Moreover, gestures play a central role in religious or spiritual rituals[8].

In ANICOMS, gestures are used as effective strategy for initiating mating rituals. This may include elaborate dances and other bodily movements. In essence, gestures play a major role in many spheres of human life as visual communication without gesture is insipid and less penetrative. Gesture is a universal phenomenon of human society, since there has been no report of a speech community that does not possess gesture. Gesture is a crucial part of everyday conversation such as chatting, describing a route, negotiating prices in market, gossiping with friends, criticising someone, mimicking others and establishing some points of arguments.

8.7 Kinesis

Alongside the paralinguistic systems of voice modulation and gestures there exists another system known as **kinesis**, which in principle, may be defined as movement or activity of a cell or an organism in response to a stimulus. Unlike taxis[9], the response to the stimulus made in kinesis is non-directional. The two main types of kinesis include:

(a) **Orthokinesis:** Where the speed of reaction of an individual is dependent upon the intensity of the stimulus. Consider, for example, the immediate reply or response made by an individual in a quarrel.

(b) **Klinokinesis:** In which the frequency or rate of response is proportional to the intensity of the stimulus. Consider, for example, the rising of voice of the interlocutors in heated arguments.

In non-verbal human communication, both kinds of kinesis result from the aggregations of stimulus. However, it should be noted that it is not the stimulus but the body language that actually does attract or repel individuals (Kendeigh 1961). While explaining the role of kinesis in understanding the impact of a verbal text in any given situation it is argued that the best way to access a person's potential is not to listen to what he says, but to observe what he does when he is saying it (Lamb 1965).

Within the broader scheme of behavioural science kinesis is recognised as **movement analysis**, where movements and gestures are analysed together in the following ways:

(a) **Forward and backward movements** which respectively indicate positive and negative energy of individuals.

(b) **Vertical movements** which denote potentiality of an individual in making oneself a good presenter in dialogic interaction.

(c) **Side-to-side movements** which reflect on good informing and listening quality of an individual in an interaction.

There exists a close relationship between the position of the body and the movements of limbs and facial expressions of an individual engaged in verbal communication as there is an inherent harmony between the two. On the other hand, if certain gestures are carefully rehearsed, such as those made to impress others belonging to different statuses, genders, or social classes, there is a tendency to separate posture from movements and in such situations, the internal harmony existing between the two parts disappears. Effective and fruitful communication is possible only when there is a high degree of body flexibility in interactions (Lamb and Watson 1979). If a person begins a kinesis with considerable force and then decelerates, the person is called the **gentle-touch**. On the other hand, if a person performs the same act with equal force from the beginning to the end, the person is identified as the **pressuriser**[10].

One can also investigate how different parts of human body are used as manifestation of kinesis in interactive situations. For instance, one can use his or her feet and legs in different manners in different kinds of sitting, standing and walking while speaking to others. There are appropriate occasions when one needs to keep his or her feet and legs straight and in other occasions he or she can keep these turned and twisted. Similarly, one can tap his or her toes on certain occasions for various reasons in face-to-face verbal interactions. We can also observe how legs are crossed and uncrossed at the time of sitting and how these are used in different styles at the time standing, walking and running. For instance, depending on demands of various situations, an army officer may stand on guard on duty, a bride may walk slowly to the altar, or a child may run fast from school and in all these situations, these people will use their legs very differently. From the perspective of kinesis, the variations of this kind are **learned behaviours**, which communicate something about the person who manifests these.

8.8 Facial Expressions

In non-verbal communication, facial expressions of different kinds usually convey or communicate emotions. These expressions not only reflect on the attitudes of the communicators, but also act as non-verbal cues to trigger and monitor the behaviours of the opponents involved in communication. It has been observed that certain areas of our face reveal our emotional state better than others. For example, eyes are highly expressive in revealing happiness, sadness and surprise; the lower face can reveal happiness or surprise; smile can communicate friendliness and cooperation; and lower face, brows and forehead can reveal anger and anxiety (Mehrabian 1981).

Recent studies have also claimed that in case of communication, while verbal expressions provide seven per cent (7%) of meaning of a message, vocal cues or paralanguage provides thirty-eight per cent (38%) of the same, while facial expressions supply fifty-five per cent (55%) of information (Mehrabian 1972). This signifies that, as a receiver of a message, a person needs to rely heavily on the facial expressions of the sender of a message because his/her expressions are better indicators of the meaning behind the message than his/her words.

Facial movements and expressions differ between the sexes, particularly the movements of eyes and eye-lashes. For instance, the amount of closure of eyes and the occasions of such closures as well as the frequency to flutter of the eye-lashes differ depending on gender of the communicators. In general, female members have a greater tendency for eye-closure as well as higher frequency in fluttering of eye-lashes than their male counterparts.

Similarly, the style of shoulder-shrugging and head-tossing, maintaining appropriate distances between the feet when standing, positioning of pelvis and the characteristic curvature of the wrist, are different between the sexes engaged in conversation. Also, the preening behaviour of the sexes varies in the same manner. For instance, touching up lipstick is a characteristic feature of females while straightening tie is a characteristic feature of males. All these behaviours are learned to the point of becoming habitual for an individual and often go unrecognised for what they are in an act of communication.

Other parts of human face may be studied in the same way to recognise their functional utilities in non-verbal communication. For instance, the lips can be studied to understand how it changes its shape and form in greeting, pointing and eating and on pleasurable and distasteful occasions.

8.9 Eye Contact

Eye contact[11] is the meeting of eyes between two individuals either engaged or not in verbal communication. It is considered as one of the direct and most powerful forms of non-verbal communication, as it has lasting influence on the social behaviour of the communicators. Along with facial expressions, eye contact provides important socio-cultural as well as some emotional cues and information, since the speakers, perhaps without consciously doing so, probe each other's eyes and faces for positive or negative mood signs.

Recognised as an important strategy of non-verbal communication in the early 1960s, eye contact has been defined as a meaningful and important sign of confidence in social communication. It is used as an indispensable element in flirting, where it serves to measure, gauge and establish interest in others in some situations. In some other contexts, meeting of eyes may arouse strong emotions or likings as mutual eye contact signals attraction, which initially begins as a brief glance and progresses into a long and repeated volleying of eye contact. It also reveals the depth of personal involvement and creates an intimate relational bond as mutual eye contacts or gazes narrow the physical gap between the communicators. Downward glances are generally associated with modesty, while eyes rolled upward are associated with fatigue.

Since the customs and significance of eye contact vary based on cultures, the meaning it denotes is greatly altered with religious and social differences. For instance, in some parts of the world, particularly in Asian countries, eye contact can provoke misunderstandings between the people belonging to different nationalities. Also, keeping direct eye contact with a senior or elderly people may lead one to assume that the person who keeps straight eye contact is aggressive and rude.

Almost opposite reactions are recorded in western societies. For instance, the superior in an organisation generally maintains direct eye contact longer than the subordinates, since direct stare of the sender of the message conveys candour and openness and elicits a feeling of trust.

8.10 Tactile Communication

Human beings communicate a great deal of information, feeling and emotion through tactile communication with others. In general, tactile communication refers to the physical contact or touching each other in various ways through which one can communicate many non-verbal messages and information. Touch is regarded as one of the most basic forms of communication, because it is the primal means through which things are communicated to the infants before they learn anything about other modes of communication. Also, it is used as one of the most convenient means of communication by the visually challenged people.

Communication through touch is obviously a powerful non-verbal means of message transfer and is highly effective in those situations, where verbal means of communication may not succeed to yield expected results. If used properly, it can create more direct impact on the part of the recipients, which hundreds of words cannot create. On the other hand, if used inappropriately, it can build barriers and cause mistrust among the communicators.

Touch is a central theme in many realms of social life, from parent-child attachments to cooperation amongst the peers and aliens. Recent researches on tactile communication suggest that touch not only promotes functioning of group members during competition by enhancing cooperation (Hertenstein 2002), it also generates trust and cooperation among the members for better performance (Watsen and Ecken 2003), inspires for greater commitment and strengthens bonds between the lovers (Simpson 1990). In addition, touch is associated with elevated status and suggests that certain forms of touch help individuals to ascend status hierarchies within a team setting (Wieselquist *et al.* 1999).

Touch is one of the most powerful means by which one can easily invade the space of others—both private and public. If it is used reciprocally, it may indicate solidarity; if not used reciprocally, it tends to indicate differences in status. Tactile communication not only facilitates the sending of the message, but the emotional impact of the message as well. It tends to convey aspects of emotional and attitudinal states as touch can convey anger, love, affection, warmth, coldness, hostility, etc. It promotes cooperation between the people, communicates distinct emotions, soothes in times of stress and is used to make inferences of warmth and trust. Based on this observation, one assumes that within a peer-group, physical touch may increase both individual

205

and group relations. In addition to soothing and communicating emotions, touch can enhance group performance through building cooperation. Even, absence of touch in certain contexts communicates many things relating to coldness or distance of social relations among people.

Although tactile communication is a basic instinct of humans, it does not mean that culture and context do not have any role to play in the equation of meaning. While, in general, people tend to respond to touch regardless of any culture, it varies considerably depending on culture, society, life experience and similar socio-cultural factors. For instance, holding hands by two adult male members in Indian society denotes closeness or friendship, but indicates gay-relationship in most of the western societies. Thus, defining the nature of tactile communication becomes difficult, if one explains it without reference to the socio-cultural factors involved into it. Indeed, there is hardly anything called 'universal' in tactile communication.

8.11 Proxemics (Personal Space)

Proxemics refers to the event of handling space elegantly between the people engaged in communication, as spatial changes have a role on speech. Noted anthropologist Edward T. Hall first introduced the term *proxemics* in 1966 to refer to the study of set measurable distances between the people when they interact. Hall has summarised the effects of proxemics in the following loose rule: "Like gravity, the influence of two bodies on each other is inversely proportional not only to the square of their distance but possibly even the cube of the distance between them" (Hall 1966: 36).

According to Hall, body spacing and posture are unintentional reactions to sensory fluctuations or shifts, such as subtle changes in the sound and pitch of a person's voice. Physical distance is an indirect manifestation of the social distance underlying between the people. Broadly, physical distance can be classified into four types, as the followings:

(a) Intimate distance: It is often used for embracing, touching, or whispering among the people who are linked by blood or have long relational bonds between themselves for various reasons.

(b) Personal distance: It is usually activated for interactions among the close friends or family members. It is linked with personal space, which refers to the region surrounding people, which they regard as psychologically theirs. Invasion of personal space often leads to discomfort, anger, or anxiety on the part of the victim.

(c) Social distance: It is used for making verbal communications among the acquaintances. It also describes the distance between different groups of society. The notion also includes all the differences such as social class, race, ethnicity or sexuality, as well as the fact that the different groups do not mix[12].

(d) Public distance: It is used for speaking to the public in public places as normally done by political leaders and orators. These people use a public space, which is open and accessible to all, regardless of gender, age, race, sex, ethnicity and socio-economic status and communicate with the mass mostly one-directionally.

In general, the term *proxemics* is used to define the three different types of space (Littlejohn and Foss 2005):

(a) **Fixed-feature space :** This comprises things that are immobile, such as walls and territorial boundaries. However, some territorial boundaries can vary and are thus classified as semi fixed-features.

(b) **Semi-fixed-feature space :** This comprises movable objects, like mobile furniture, while fixed-furniture is a fixed-feature.

(c) **Informal space:** This comprises the individual space around the body, travels around with it, determining the personal distance among people.

The definitions of each of the above may vary from culture to culture. In non-verbal communication, such cultural variations amongst what comprises semi-fixed-features and what comprises fixed-features can lead to confusion, discomfort and misunderstanding. Investigations have shown how people use furniture such as chairs for guests to sit in as being fixed or semi-fixed and how the use of chairs by guests can create different impacts on the people (Low and Lawrence-Zúñiga 2003).

Proxemics also defines the eight factors of non-verbal communication or proxemic behaviour that are applied by the people engaged in conversation (Joseph 1986):

(a) **Posture-sex identifiers:** This relates to the postures of the participants and their sexes. Six primary sub-categories are defined in it: man prone, man sitting or squatting, man standing, woman prone, woman sitting or squatting and woman standing.

(b) **Sociopetal-sociofugal axis:** It denotes relationship between the positions of shoulder of a person with that of another person. Five orientations are defined: face-to-face, 45°, 90°, 135° and back-to-back. The effects of the orientations are either to encourage or discourage communication.

(c) **Kinesthetic factors:** This deals with how closely the participants are for touching; from being completely outside of the body-contact distance to being in physical contact; which parts of the body are in contact; and the positioning of the body parts.

(d) **Touching code:** This is concerned how the participants are touching one another, such as embracing, caressing, holding, prolonged holding, spot touching, pressing against, accidental brushing, or not touching at all.

(e) **Visual code:** This denotes frequency and duration of eye contact between the participants. Four types are defined: accidental eye-contact, short eye-contact, prolonged eye-contact and no eye-contact.

(f) **Thermal code:** This refers to amount of body heat that each participant perceives from another. Four sub-categories are defined here: conducted heat detected, radiant heat detected, heat probably detected and no heat detection.

(g) **Olfactory code:** It deals with the kind and degree of body odour detected by each participant from the other.

(h) **Voice loudness:** It deals with volume of speech used in communication. Seven sub-categories are defined: silent, very soft, soft, normal, normal+, loud and very loud.

It has been noted that people belonging to different cultures and societies maintain different standards of personal space. For instance, in Latin cultures, those relative distances are smaller and people tend to be more comfortable standing close to each other. On the other hand, in Nordic culture, relative distances are bigger and people do not feel comfortable to stand close to each other. The realisation and recognition of cultural differences will improve the cross-cultural understanding as well as will help eliminate discomfort people may feel if interpersonal distance is too large or too small. Also, comfortable personal distance depends much on several other social factors like culture, customs, social situations, gender, rituals and on individual preferences.

8.12 Environment

The impact of use of space in a communication process is related directly to the environment in which the space is maintained. How do we arrange the objects in our environment (e.g., desks, chairs, tables, boards and bookcases, etc.) is directly linked with this. The design of an office and the arrangement of furniture within the office can greatly affect the communications within it. For instance, some companies may divide their office space into personal and impersonal areas. This can improve the communication process if the areas are used for the purposes intended. The pecking-order in the organisation is frequently determined by such things as the size of desk, square feet in office, number of windows in the office, quality of the carpet and type of paintings (originals or copies) on the wall.

Personal space and environment affect the level of comfort and status and as a result of this environment can facilitate or hinder communication process of the people concerned.

8.13 Silence

Silence can also communicate as there is communication in silence. One must know when to say nothing since flashes of silence make communication more eloquent, effective and delightful. Poets and thinkers have celebrated silence because there is a time for speaking and a time for being silent. Carlyle has said, *"Silence is the element in which great things fashion themselves"*.

Silence can have positive or negative influence in communication process. It can provide a link between the messages or can terminate relationships. It can create tension and uneasiness or can create peaceful situations. Moreover, it can be judgmental by indicating disfavour or favour and disagreement or agreement. In personal communication short silence can strengthen personal relational bonds, while prolonged silence can ring the death-bell of relational closeness and warmth.

8.14 Time

Sometimes time can also be used effectively as an indicator of social relations in non-verbal communication. The amount of time one spends with others in communication in general and with a particular person, separately, can refer to the degree of intimacy they enjoy among themselves. In such a situation, the time scale becomes an indicator of social relationship.

Similarly, in a team or group, the leader may not spend equal amount of time in communication with each member. It varies from person to person which, in the reverse way, shows how an individual allots time for a person who is superior, junior, peer or subordinate.

Furthermore, the allotment of time may vary depending on the nature of social and personal relational bonds the communicators maintain among themselves when they participate in verbal or non-verbal communication.

8.15 Concluding Remarks

Regardless to various factors operating in an event of communication, it is important and necessary to develop some sensitivity to non-verbal messages implicitly tagged with verbal communication. It is observed that mutual faith, understanding and cooperation gradually improve when the communicators are successful to recognise and respond appropriately to the non-verbal cues, as it is understood that fifty per cent of impact of communication is actually determined by the body language (e.g., *postures, gestures* and *eye contact*, etc.), thirty-eight per cent is determined by the tone of voice and seven per cent is expressed by the content or the words used in a communication.

Although exact percentage of influence may differ based on the variables such as the listener and the speaker, non-verbal communication along with verbal communication as a whole strives for the same goal and thus, in some cases, is universal. Various modes of signal, such as voice, intonation, pitch, gesture, voice modulation and kinesis, facial expression, eye-contact, etc. communicate not only information but also thoughts and feelings of people who want to exchange and share at the time of speaking to others.

Notes and Comments

[1]   *Emoticon* is a portmanteau word made of English words *emotion* (or *emote*) and *icon*. An *emoticon* is a symbol or a combination of many symbols, which are deployed to convey emotional content in written texts or in written messages, as often found in SMS sent through mobiles.

[2]   Studies investigating the impact of posture on the basic nature of interpersonal relationships suggest about a phenomenon called the *mirror-image congruent postures*, where the left side of a speaker becomes parallel to the right side of a hearer and this often leads to a favourable perception of the communicators and positive speech output. Moreover, a person who displays a forward lean or a decrease in a backwards lean implies positive sentiment during a course of verbal communication.

[3]   The study of *paralanguage* is called *paralinguistics*. The term *paralanguage* is sometimes used as a cover term for body language, which is not necessarily tied to speech and paralinguistic phenomena of speech. The latter are the phenomena that can be observed in speech but that do not belong to the arbitrary conventional code of language.

[4]   Flame war: a flame war is a heated argument *ad hominem*. It primarily consists of personal insults, the rational arguments are secondary. Flame wars usually develop out of a normal discussion in six ways: (a) someone offends people through arrogant behaviour, (b) a thread of discussion touches upon a land mine, (c) the rules or values of the community are questioned, (d) *ad hominem* argument results when a poorly qualified contributor posts questions, (e) a participant tries to communicate with a chronic flamer (e.g., *it is difficult to stay cool and polite*) and (f) a vested contributor tries to pull rank.

[5]   Assume-good-faith: In most situations, we can encounter people who really do not want to get into a conflict. If they share a

superordinate goal, disagreements are over direction, not malice and thus these are not taken personally. Heated conflicts arise only when people do not have the freedom or opportunity to carry out their own plans. People may also not share a superordinate goal with others. If they have other goals in mind that do not interfere with one, then most people will avoid conflict because it is a waste of energy to engage in conflicts that will not contribute to their own advancement.

[6] *Wanker* gesture is made by curling the fingers into a loose fist and moving the hand up and down as though masturbating. The gesture has the same meaning as the English slang insult, 'wanker', or might indicate a failure or waste.

[7] *Joint attention* is a strategy by which one alerts another to a stimulus through non-verbal means, such as gazing or pointing. For example, one may gaze at another person and then point to an object and then return their gaze back to the other person. In this case, the pointing person is 'initiating joint attention' by trying to get the other to look at the object. The person who looks to the referenced object is 'responding to joint attention'. Joint attention is referred to as a *triadic skill*, meaning that it involves two people and an object or event outside of the duo (Leavens and Racine 2009).

[8] In Hinduism and Buddhism, a *mudra* (posture) is a symbolic gesture made with the hand or fingers. Each *mudra* has a specific meaning, playing a central role in Hindu and Buddhist iconography. An example is the *Vitarka Mudra*, the gesture of discussion and transmission of Buddhist teaching. It is done by way of joining the tips of the thumb and the index together, while keeping the other fingers straight.

[9] A *taxis* is an innate behavioural response by an organism to a directional stimulus or gradient of stimulus intensity. A taxis differs from *tropism* (turning response, often growth towards or away from a stimulus) in that the organism has motility and demonstrates guided movement towards or away from the stimulus source. It is sometimes distinguished from a kinesis, a non-directional change in activity in response to a stimulus.

[10] The accuracy of Lamb's analyses is not fully known or verified. However, it is important to know that multinational companies are becoming so sensitive to the importance of non-verbal messages that they are hiring consultants and experts to analyse

non-verbal communicational activities of their workers in their organisations.

[11] The study of eye contact is known as *oculesics*. In case of animals it is seen that animals of many species, including dogs, often perceive eye contact as a threat. Many programmes to prevent dog bites recommend avoiding direct eye contact with unknown dogs. Young children are more likely to fall victim to dog attacks because they maintain eye contact out of curiosity or belief that eye contact will subdue the animal. Visitors are advised to avoid direct eye contact if a black bear stands on its hind legs. Chimpanzees also can use eye contact to signal aggression in hostile encounters and staring at them in a zoo can induce agitated behaviour.

[12] The term *social distance* is often applied in cities, but its use is not limited to that. In sociology, the idea of social distance is conceptualized in several ways: *(a) affective social distance*, which is associated with affective distance, i.e., how much or little sympathy the members of a group feel for another group, *(b) normative social distance*, which refers to the widely accepted norms about who should be considered as an 'insider' and who as an 'outsider/foreigner' (such norms specify the distinctions between 'us' and 'them') and, *(c) interactive social distance*, which focuses on the frequency and intensity of interactions between the two groups. The more the members of two groups interact, the closer they are socially.

Chapter 9
Animal Communication System

9.1 Introduction

The animal communication system (ANICOMS) refers to the methods and systems animals use to communicate with each other belonging to the same species or to transmit signals to animals belonging to other species or to humans. It has been known that animals, like human beings, also use a communication system of their own for their basic biological needs, which is different from the language of human beings. ANICOMS is a kind of behaviour of animals that has an effect on the current or future behaviour of animals belonging to the same species. The study of ANICOMS is known as **Zoosemiotics**, which plays an important part in *ethology, sociobiology* and *linguistics*, as well as in the study of animal cognition. In fact, understanding the animal world as well as their communication systems in general are intriguing fields, which have been directly related to diverse fields such as linguistics, use of personal symbolic names, animal emotions, animal culture and learning and even the sexual conduct of animals, etc. The questions that generally arise when we try to explore this enigmatic world are the following:

(a) Do animals have the same communication system like human beings?
(b) Is it possible to establish proper communication between human beings and animals?
(c) Do animals have only one communication system for all or it differs from species to species?
(d) Can animals acquire human language through deliberate training during the process of rearing?

(e) What are the characteristic features of animal communication system?
(f) What are the functions of animal communication system?
(g) Which animals have highly developed communication system?
(h) Is animal communication syste quantitatively different from human language?

There are many other questions of similar types, for which we want to have answers. These are not just simple queries about the animal communication system, but are linked with the enigma of understanding the nature of human language. In this chapter I have made an attempt to present answers to some of the questions based on the information obtained from various studies and observations so far made by the ethologists, sociobiologists and linguists.

From cognitive perspective ethologists, sociobiologists and linguists have analysed ANICOMS of different types to identify the characteristic features in terms of more or less automatic responses to stimuli, without raising question of whether animals concerned understand the meaning of the signals they emit and receive. That has become now a key question in the study of animal cognition. There are some signalling systems of animals that seem to demand a more advanced understanding. A much discussed example is the use of alarm calls by the *vervet monkeys*. Seyfarth and Cheney (1997, 2003) have studied elaborately the signalling system of *vervet monkeys* to show how these animals can emit different alarm calls in the presence of different predators like leopards, eagles and snakes, etc. and how members of the group that receive the calls can respond differently and appropriately. However, according to the observations of the scientists, this particular ability of the *vervet monkeys* develops over time and takes into account experience of individuals emitting calls.

A sophisticated cognitive process is, however, required for understanding metacommunication[1]. It is a communication about the communication itself. According to Bateson (1972) there are many times when communication that is going on, is not deliberately conveyed as information. Examples of that are when we crack a joke, the metacommunication implies that *it is a joke*, which is sometimes understood and sometimes not. A metacommunication, in its primary form, is an act of communication between the two agents that can communicate something about the communication itself, or about the relationship between the two agents, or both (Watzlawick 1978).

In communication, information is transmitted between the sender and the receiver. Both the members interpret the information they receive and control the information they give. Much information in communication is usually implicit and not expressed in words. It is embedded within a situation, in which the communication takes place. For instance, *'put it there!'* may be a perfectly intelligible statement in a face-to-face meeting, although to an outsider it is completely indefinable. In communication it is, therefore, important to make it clear at all times *what kind of situation* (what kind of context) one is in. If we say (first) *this is play*, we can (afterwards) allow ourselves to do and say things that might otherwise be offensive (Bateson 1955). Such communication about the situation in which interaction takes place, is called as metacommunication in communication theory.

In recent studies (Jainik, Sayigh and Wells 2006) it has been shown that the *bottlenose dolphins* are able to recognise the identity information from the whistles given by their trainers even when they are not trained with other characteristics of the trainer. This capability makes *bottlenose dolphins* the only animals, other than human, which are capable of transmitting identity information independent of caller's voice or location. It is also observed that *signature whistle shape*[2] of *bottlenose dolphins* carries identity information independent of the caller's voice features. Similar to the use of names in case of humans, it opens up a possibility for using signature whistles as referential signals, either addressing individuals or referring to them. The cognitive abilities of the *bottlenose dolphins*, their vocal learning, copying skills and their ability for splitting their social structure open an intriguing scheme that asks for further investigation in ANICOMS.

9.2. Forms of Animal Communication

The best known forms of ANICOMS involve the display of four and / or five different strategies as mentioned below:

(a) Display of distinctive body parts.
(b) Display of distinctive bodily movements.
(c) Production of distinctive calls.
(d) Spray of body smells.
(e) Electro-communication.

Each strategy can occur in isolation or in combination of others. It has been observed that a distinctive bodily movement directly acts to reveal or to emphasise a distinctive body part. An explicit example was the presentation of parent *herring gull* of its bill to its chick in the nest (Tinbergen 1953). Like many gulls, the *herring gull* has a brightly coloured bill, yellow with a red spot on the lower mandible near the tip. When it returns to the nest with food, the parent stands over its chick and taps the bill on the ground in front of it. This elicits a begging response from a hungry chick (pecking at the red spot), which stimulates the parent to regurgitate food in front of it.

The complete signal thus involves a distinctive morphological feature (i.e., body part = the red-spotted bill), as well as a distinctive movement (i.e., tapping towards the ground), which makes the red spot highly visible to the chick. Investigations by Tinbergen (1953) showed that the red colour of the bill and its high contrast are crucial for eliciting the appropriate response from the chick although it still remains unresolved whether this actually is an inborn behaviour in all its complexity or simply a combination of generalised curiosity on the part of the chick and generalised parental feeding instincts acting together to produce a simple learning process via reward. Herring gull chicks peck at everything that is brightly coloured, mainly red, yellow, white, or shining, high-contrast objects, but the parent's bill is the only such object that will constantly yield food as a reward when pecked at[3].

Another important form of animal communication is the production of distinctive call such as the song of birds, which is usually performed mainly by the male members, although in some species, the female members can also sing in alternation (known as **duetting**). Bird song is considered as the best known case of **vocal communication,** while other instances include warning cries of monkeys, territorial calls of gibbons, community calls of jackals and mating calls of many species of frog.

The less obvious form of ANICOMS is the spray of body smells, which is known as **olfactory communication**. Many mammals, in particular, tigers, elephants, leopards, cats, etc. have special glands that excrete distinctive and long-lasting smells and have corresponding behaviours that leave smells in places where they have been. Often the scented substance is introduced into urine or faeces. Sometimes it is distributed through sweat, although this does not leave a semi-permanent mark as scents deposited on the ground do. Some animals have glands on their bodies whose sole function appears is to deposit scent marks. For example, the *Mongolian gerbils* have a scent gland on their stomachs and a characteristic ventral rubbing action excretes scent from it. The *golden hamsters* and the *cats* have scent glands on their flanks and they deposit scent by rubbing their sides against objects. Cats also have scent glands on their foreheads. Honey-bees carry with them a pouch of material from the hive which they release as they re-enter, the smell of which indicates whether they are the parts of the hive and grants their safe entry.

A rare form of animal communication is observed in case of **electro-communication**, which is primarily used by aquatic animals, although some mammals, such as *platypus* and *echidnas* are also capable of *electroreception* and thus theoretically capable of electro-communication.

9.3 Functions of Animal Communication

There are several forms of animal communication, which are actually the representation of several types of social behaviour of animals. These forms can perform a number of biological functions as has been observed in various studies (Noë, Hammerstein and Hooff 2001). In general ANICOMS includes the following functions.

9.3.1 Agonistic Interactions

This refers to general trend of animal life where everything has to be done with contests and aggression between the individuals. Many species have distinctive threat displays that are made during the competition over food, selection of mates, or occupying the territories. Much of bird songs functions in this direction. Often there is a matched submission display, which the threatened individual will make if it is acknowledging the social dominance of the threatener. This has an effect of terminating the aggressive episode and allowing the dominant animal unrestricted access to the resources in dispute. Some animal species also have displays of approval, which are expressed to indicate that a dominant animal can accept the presence of another.

9.3.2 Courtship Rituals

In animal world signals are often made by the members of one sex to attract or to maintain the attention of the potential mates, or to cement a **pair bond**. These signals frequently involve the display of body parts as noted in case of some monkeys and baboons; display of body postures

219

as observed in case gazelles, which assume characteristic poses as a signal to initiate mating; the emission of body scents, as noted in case of tigers, elephants, horses, dogs and cats; and making of unique mating calls as noted in case of dogs, ducks, cuckoos, etc. These courtship rituals are unique to the species, because these allow individuals to avoid mating with the members of other species which will be infertile. The animals that form *pair bonds* often display symmetrical rituals which they make to each other in unique manner. Famous examples are the mutual presentation of reeds by *Great Crested Crebes*, the *triumph displays* shown by many species of *geese* and penguins on their nest sites and the spectacular courtship displays by the *Birds of Paradise*, *Bastards* and the *Manakins*.

9.3.3 Food-related Signals

Many animals can make *food calls* that can attract a mate, or offspring, or the members of a social group generally to a food source. When the parents are feeding offspring, offspring often have begging responses (particularly when there are many offspring in a clutch or litter as it is found in case of the hens and some birds).

The most elaborated food-related signal is the *dance language* and the orientation of *honey-bees* (Frisch 1950). Frisch, while studying the habits of bees in their natural settings, observed that an altogether different kind of dance is performed by a foraging bee on its return to the hive to report about the source of pollen to other bees. It is observed that the returning bee used a type of dance, which involved different speed of movement and direction in relation to the sun to specify the distance and direction of the source of pollen with regard to position of the hive. The jointly shared dance system allowed the other bees to share the information with other members to specify that the source of pollen is not more than four miles away to the north of their hive. According to Frisch, all bees can use the system, as it shows only occasional minor deviations among different colonies of bees[4].

9.3.4 Alarm Calls

Signals are made by animals about the presence of a threat from a predator that allows all the members of a social group (and often members of other species) to run for cover, become immobile, or gather into a group to reduce the risk of attack. This is often observed in case of crows, monkeys and dogs, as they make specific signals to make other members of their group and others aware about the presence of a threat that can cause damage to their existence.

9.3.5 Metacommunication

In case of communication of animals we observe a different kind of use of the metacommunication where it refers to the signals that eventually modify the meaning of the subsequent signals. The best known example is the **play face** events among the dogs, which signals that subsequent aggressive signals are the parts of a play fight rather than a serious aggressive episode.

9.3.6 Ownership or Territorial Signals

Animal world is always full of fights and quarrels as the parts of showing supremacy or ownership. Animals often make clear signals to claim or to defend a particular territory, food, or a mate. This is clearly noticed in case of lions, elephants, tigers and dogs and even in case of some birds like ducks and swans who leave marks at their territories to make others aware about their dominance at that particular territory as well as to threaten their peers or competitors for keeping safe distance away from their protected zones and possessed partners.

9.4 Evolution of Animal Communication

The importance of communication in the animal world is clear from the fact that animals have evolved elaborate body parts to facilitate it. They include some of the most striking structures and designs in the animal kingdom, such as the peacock's tail. Bird song appears to have their brain structures entirely devoted to its production. Even the red spot on a herring gull's bill and the modest but characteristic bowing behaviour that displays it also require evolutionary explanation. Also there are two important evolutionary aspects of animal communication that require investigation:

(a) Identifying a route by which an animal, that lacked the relevant feature or behaviour could acquire it.
(b) Identifying the selective pressure that makes it adaptive for animals to develop structures that facilitate communication, emit communications, as well as respond to them.

Significant contributions to the first problem are made by Konrad Lorenz (1979). By comparing related species within the groups, he had shown that movements and body parts in primitive forms had no communicative function that could be 'captured' within a context where communication would be functional for one or both partners and could evolve into a more elaborate, specialised form. For instance, Desmond Morris (1961) has recorded in a study on *grass finches* that a beak-wiping response occurred in a range of species, serving a preening function, but that in some species, this had been elaborated into a courtship signal.

The second problem has been far more controversial. Early ethologists had assumed that communication occurred for the good of the species as a whole, but this would require a process of **group selection** which, however, was believed to be mathematically impossible in case of evolution of sexually reproducing animals. Altruism towards an unrelated group is not accepted in scientific community, but rather it can be considered as a sort of reciprocal altruism, expecting the same behaviour from others—the benefit of living within a group. Sociobilogists argued that behaviours that benefited a whole group of animals might emerge as a result of selection pressures acting solely on individuals. A **gene-centred view of evolution** proposed that behaviours that enabled a gene to become widely established within a population would become positively selected for even if their effect on the individuals or the species as a whole was to some extent detrimental. In case of ANICOMS, an important observation was made by Krebs and Dawkins (1978) who proposed to establish the hypotheses for evolution of apparently altruistic or mutualistic communications as the alarm calls and the courtship signals to emerge under individual selection. This has led to realise that communication might not always be an honest event. Indeed, there are several obvious examples where it is not, as observed in mimicry.

The possibility of evolutionarily stable and dishonest communication has been the subject of severe criticism. Amotz Zahavi (1975), in particular, has categorically argued that it cannot exist in the long term. Sociobiologists have also been concerned with the evolution of apparently excessive signalling structures such as the peacock's tail which is widely thought that these can only emerge as a result of the *sexual selection*, which can create a *positive feedback* process that leads to the rapid exaggeration of a characteristic that confers an advantage in a competitive mate-selection situation.

The theory that tries to explain the evolution of traits like a peacock's tail is known as **runaway selection**. This requires two traits: a trait that exists like the bright tail and a pre-existing bias in the female to select for that trait. Peahens prefer more elaborate tails and thus those males which have brighter tails, are able to mate successfully. Exploiting the psychology of the female, a positive feedback loop is enacted and the tail becomes bigger and brighter. Eventually, the evolution will level off because the survival costs to the male do not allow for the trait to be elaborated any further.

There are two hypotheses to explain the theory of runaway selection. The first one is the **good gene hypothesis**, which states that an elaborate display is an honest signal of fitness and truly is a better mate. The second one is the **handicap hypothesis**, which explains that the peacock's tail is a handicap, as it requires energy to keep and make it more visible to predators. Regardless to other factors, individuals are able to survive, even though their genes are not as good *per se*.

8.5 Interpretation of Animal Communication

Whilst many gestures and actions observed in ANICOMS have common and stereotypical meanings; researchers have found that animal communication is often far more complex and subtle than previously believed; and that same gestures or actions may have multiple distinct meanings based on the context and other behaviours. So generalisations such as 'X means Y' are *often*, but not *always* accurate. For example, even simple tail wagging of domestic dogs may be interpreted in different ways to convey different meanings including excitement, anticipation, relaxation, playfulness, contentment, enjoyment, anxiety, questioning another animal or human as to intentions, tentative role assessment on meeting with another animal, reassurance (e.g., *I am hoping to be friendly, are you?*), brief acknowledgement (e.g., *I hear you* or *I am aware and responsive if you want my attention*), statement of interest (e.g., *I want that food/toy/activity, if you will*), uncertainty, apprehension and submissive placation (if worried by a more dominant animal).

Combined with other representations of body movements, in a specific context, many gestures of animals such as yawns, direction of vision and so on can convey different meanings. Thus the statements that a particular action 'means' something should always be interpreted as to mean 'often means' something rather than a particular thing or sense. As with human beings, one may smile, hug or stand in a particular manner for multiple reasons; many animals reuse their gestures in the same manner.

For anyone who owns a pet, communication with the pet is a confirmed event. However, the issue of whether animals really do communicate with each other and with human beings—from a scientific viewpoint—is still an open question. In scientific terms, communication of animals is historically defined as the transfer of information from the sender (or communicator) to the recipient (or the receiver). There have been many different viewpoints regarding how and why this information transfer occurs and four principal schools of thought have been referred to so far.

Edward Osborne Wilson (1975), a supporter of the **1st School** has argued that communication must (a) change the behaviour of the receiver in some way, (b) be adaptive (or useful) to one or both the participants, and (c) must involve intent on the part of the communicators. Therefore, the only clue with regard to answering the question, 'do animals communicate?' is by way of direct observation of the overt behaviour exhibited by the animals concerned, especially the behaviour of the recipient(s).

William Homan Thrope (1979), a member of the **2nd School**, has argued that a communication event in case of animals should be a deliberate act (thus implying the conscious intentions of the communicator) or be adaptive to the sender (i.e., the behaviour of the communicator must be goal-directed). His ideas, therefore, concurred with those of Wilson.

Daniel Otte (1974), a member of the **3rd School**, has suggested that we should only apply the term 'communication' to the systems that have been under pressure from natural selection to provide information. The key term for Otte is *evolution*, where an animal scans its environment with its sensory preceptors and to him only a limited number of signals, which are capable of transmitting information, are available (those which have specifically evolved through generations). These signals can have behavioural, physiological and morphological characteristics, which are evolved and maintained via natural selection due to their ability to convey information to other animals. Otte has suggested that researchers should focus on observing behaviours of the signal emitter (communicator) and not on those of the receiver, thus his viewpoints are direct opposites to that of Wilson. Otte has also introduced the concept of **legitimate receiver** (i.e., animal to whom a communicator attempts to signal to). It is advantageous for the signaller to communicate with the legitimate receiver; otherwise, it will spend energy signalling to bystanders. Finally, he has stated that there are six types of signal that animals produce: attention, identification, spatial, response, temporal and event information[5].

William J. Smith, (1977), a member of the **4th School**, has argued that the researchers of ANICOMS should focus on the three basic levels:

(a) **Syntactic level:** It is related to the formal characteristics of signals, e.g., vision, hearing and scent markings, etc. Within this frame, all animal signals should be split into two structural categories: discrete category and graded category. Since most of the animal signals are graded, they allow for more information to be carried.

(b) **Semantic level:** It relates to the meaning and informational content of the signals. There are two types of such information: behavioural and non-behavioural. Behavioural information includes 'what messages', which have been selected evolutionarily (e.g., attack, run, escape, etc); and 'how messages' which are supplementary messages including probability, intensity, direction, etc. Non-behavioural signals include 'who messages' which identify the communicator (e.g., species and sex, etc.) and 'where messages' which carry information about the location of the sender.

(c) **Pragmatic level:** It is related to specific functions of signals—to warn, to threat, to copulate, etc. All three levels must be taken into account in a combined way to understand the animal communication system.

By the beginning of 1980s researchers became more interested to explore what benefit communication signals serve to those animals that use them. Krebs and Dawkins (1978) suggest that animals tend to manipulate events in their environment for their own benefit and that communication is basically the interplay between the two roles—the sender is 'manipulator', while the receiver is 'mind reader', the latter constantly trying to figure out what the communicator is actually going to transmit.

Getting back to the question 'do animals communicate?' the resounding answer has been 'yes!' Indeed there are evidences of many different kinds of communication in the animal kingdom. Some examples are cited below:

Konrad Lorenz (1952) in his study on animal communication has noted that jackdaws have a small repertoire to distinguishable calls.

One is a mating or courtship call which is made by male jackdaws; and two other calls are related to flying—one indicating the flight away from home and the other flight towards home. Besides these, the birds also sometimes make a kind of rattling sound to signal their anger at the sight of a threatening object. The jackdaws living in all parts of the globe are able to make these sounds, even the birds, which are brought up and reared in captivity or in isolation, are also able to make these calls.

The *black-backed gulls* are extremely territorial. They can communicate 'threat' to intruders via extending neck, pointing beak downward and pushing forewings forward. They also use communication signals in mating, where the birds pair for life. It is the female bird who circles in the air looking for a mate, while the earth-bound male bird 'calls' to her. The female then uses a courtship routine whereby she attempts to pacify the male (she is encroaching on his territory)—where she bows her head and faces away from the male. If the male bird does not attack, she will peck at the bottom of his beak and receive a free meal for her trouble! Copulation begins with the female bird singing throughout!

Afterwards the birds will go in search for a nesting site together, assist each other in constructing the 'home' and when the eggs are laid they will take it in turn to incubate them. The newly hatched young are born with an innate communication system that they use to indicate to their parents that they are hungry (they peck on the red spot on either parents beak). The black-backed gulls' chicks can recognise the 'voice' of their parents from a very young age.

Karl von Frisch (1953) was the first researcher to unravel the behaviour of the *honey-bees*. He discovered that honey-bees had a 'language', whereby they inform each other where the food was located by performing elaborate dance routines. Kenneth Norris (1991) has observed that *humpback whales* can use complex songs to communicate their location and other information to the rest of the school. *Dolphins* can combine symbols and sounds in many different ways as their social life mostly depends on sounds (Norris 1991). Even *parrots* have also complex linguistic abilities for communication among themselves.

A recent interesting discovery is the 'use of syntax' in animal language and the ability to produce 'sentences', which were considered to be the sole property of human beings. The first good evidence of syntax among animals is reported in *The New York Times* (May 18, 2006 p. 3) from the *greater putty-nosed monkey* of Nigeria. This is the first evidence that some animals can take discrete units of communication and build them up into a sequence, which carries a different meaning from the individual 'words'. The *putty-nosed monkeys* have two sets of alarm sounds. The first set of sounds warns against a lurking leopard (onomatopoeically, *pyow*), while the second sets of sound resembles to coughing sound (onomatopoeically, *hack*), which is used when an eagle is hovering nearby. Both observationally and experimentally it has been observed that a sequence of up to three *pyows* followed by up to four *hacks* serves to elicit group movement. The *pyow-hack* sequence means something like "let's move!" (a command that tells other members to move). The discovery implies that primates are able to ignore the usual relationship between an individual alarm call and the meaning it might convey under certain circumstances. To our knowledge this is, perhaps, the first evidence of a syntax-like natural communication system in non-human species.

9.6 Interspecies Communication

Several forms of *intraspecies communication* among the animals can also be used effectively for *interspecies communication*. The sender and receiver of a communication may belong to same species or different species. Normally, the majority of animal communication is *intraspecies* (i.e., between two or more individuals of the same species) that occurs within a single species and this is the context in which it has been most intensively studied. Most of the forms and functions of animal communication described above are relevant to *intraspecies* communication.

There are, however, some instances of *interspecies* communication where communication takes place between the members of different species. The possibility of *interspecies* communication and the form it takes, has become important test of some theoretical models of animal communication. The *interspecies* communication that takes place between the members belonging to different species is mostly of two types:

(a) Prey-to-predator pattern.
(b) Predator-to-prey pattern.

In case of *prey-to-predator pattern*, if a prey animal moves or makes a noise in such a way that a predator can easily detect and capture it that fits the definition of communication given above. This type of communication is often referred to as **interceptive eavesdropping**, where a predator intercepts the message being conveyed to co-specifics.

There are, however, some actions of the prey species that are invariably communications to actual or potential predators. A good example is **warning colouration** in which species such as wasps, which are capable of harming potential predators, are mostly endowed with brightly coloured body and this modifies the behaviour of the predator, who either instinctively or as the result of experience will avoid attacking such an animal. Also, some forms of mimicry fall in this category. For example *hoverflies* are coloured in the same way as wasps and although they are unable to sting, the avoidance of wasps by predators gives hoverflies some kind of protection.

There are also behavioural changes that act in a similar way to warning colouration. For example, canines such as *wolves* and *coyotes* may adopt an aggressive posture, such as growling with their teeth bared to indicate that they are ready to fight if it is necessary. Similarly, *rattle snakes* use their well known rattle to warn potential predators of their poisonous bite. Sometimes, a behavioural change and warning colouration will be combined, as in certain species of amphibians which have a brightly coloured belly, but on which the rest part of their body is coloured to blend in with their surroundings. When confronted with a potential threat, they show their belly, indicating that they are poisonous in some way.

Another example of prey-to-predator communication is called **pursuit-deterrent signal**. It occurs when the prey indicates to a predator that pursuit will not be profitable because the signaller (or the pray) is prepared to escape. Pursuit-deterrent signals provide a benefit to both signaller and receiver; they prevent the sender from wasting time and energy, as well as they prevent the receiver from investing in a costly pursuit that is unlikely to result in capture. Such signals advertise a prey's ability to escape in two ways. It reflects on the **phenotypic condition** (i.e., quality advertisement) as well as implies that the prey has already detected the predator (i.e., perception advertisement).

Pursuit-deterrent signals have been reported for a wide variety of fish (Godin and Davis 1995), lizards (Cooper *et al.* 2004), ungulates (Caro 1995), rabbits (Holley 1993), primates (Zuberbuhler *et al.* 1997), rodents (Shelley and Blumstein 2005, Clark 2005) and birds (Alvarez 1993, Murphy 2006, 2007). A familiar example of quality advertisement of pursuit-deterrent signal is *stotting*, where a pronounced combination of running while simultaneously hopping is shown by some antelopes such as *Thomson's gazalle* in the presence of a predator. Several hypotheses for stotting have been proposed so far. A leading theory is that it alerts predators that the element of surprise has been lost. It has been observed that predators like cheetahs, which rely on surprise attacks, hardly chase when *gazalles* stot. They do not waste energy on a chase that will likely be unsuccessful (i.e., *optimal foraging behaviour*).

In case of *predator-to-prey pattern*, some predators communicate to prey in ways that change their behaviour and make them easier to catch, in effect, deceiving them. A well-known example is the *angler fish*, which has a fleshy growth protruding from its forehead and dangling in front of its jaws to lure smaller fish. Smaller fish try to grab the lure and in trying to do so, become perfectly placed for the *angler fish* to eat them.

Interspecies communication can take place in various kinds of symbiosis and mutualism. For example, the **grouper-system** of the cleaner fish, where the group members signal their availability for cleaning each other by way of adopting a particular posture at a cleaning station.

9.7 Human-Animal Communication

Human-animal communication is easily observed in our day-to-day life. The various ways in which humans interpret the behaviour of domestic animals, or give commands to them, fit the definition of inter-species communication, in general. The interactions between pets and their owners, for example, reflect a form of spoken, while not necessarily verbal, dialogue. A dog being scolded does not need to understand every word of its admonishment, but is able to grasp the message by interpreting cues such as the owner's stance, tone of voice and body language. This communication is two-way as the owners can learn to discern the subtle differences between barks and meows (one hardly has to be a professional animal trainer to tell difference between the bark of an angry dog defending its home and the happy bark of the same animal while playing). Human-animal communication (often non-verbal) is also significant in equestrian activities such as dressage (or horse training). Based on contexts, these activities might be considered to be predator-to-prey communication or to reflect on the forms of **commensalisms**[6].

Although human-animal communication has always been a topic of great public comments and attention, for a period in history, it has surpassed this and became the sensational and popular entertainment.

Language and Linguistics

From the late 1700s through the mid 19th century, a succession of pigs and various other animals were displayed to the public in for-profit performances, boasting about their ability to communicate with their owners (often in more than one language), write, solve math problems and the like. One poster dated 1817 showed a group of 'Java sparrows' who were advertised as knowing *seven languages,* including Chinese and Russian. One pig of that era was so famous that it performed for royalty and an obituary upon its death claimed that it made more money than any actor or actress of that time. In Germany, in the middle of 19th century, it was reported that a horse (named Clever Hans) had been trained by its master to understand everything that was said to it. It could stamp out the replies to all kinds of questions asked to it. Close examination, however, revealed that the horse was 'clever', but much of its cleverness was actually dependent on someone whom the horse watched minutely to reply to the questions it was asked. The horse actually depended on the visual cues for giving answers, not on his linguistic skills (Hans was never asked to speak out for replying the question!).

By the end of the last century it has been clearly understood that the feats of animals like using cards to spell out words or tapping hooves to solve the equations and the likes were actually products of training rather than proper communication[7]. Even then, several experiments on animal language have been carried out to understand the nature of human-animal communication and notable breakthrough has been achieved in this direction, as the following reports can show.

Although *word-repetition skill* is observed in case of many birds (such as parrots, cockatoo, etc.) it should not be mistaken as linguistic communication. This event has nonetheless influenced fictional portrayals of human-animal communication as sentient talking parrots and similar other birds are common in fiction of children[8]. This implies that achieving a deeper level of communication between animals and humans has long been a goal of science. Perhaps the most famous example of recent decades has been *Koho,* a gorilla who was supposedly able to communicate with humans using a system based on *American Sign Language,* with a 'vocabulary' of over 1,000 words.

The earliest experiment which attempted to teach human language to the chimpanzees may be credited to Winthrop and Luella Kellogg (1933) who, alongside their son Donald, raised Gua, a chimpanzee with an intention to teach the animal to speak human language. In tests Gua often tested ahead of Donald in reading and understanding. Slight differences in their placement included people recognition. Gua recognised people from their clothes and their smell while Donald could recognise them by their faces. However, the striking differences came with language. Donald was about sixteen months and Gua was a little over a year old when they had language testing. Gua could not speak, but Donald could form words. When Donald began to copy Gua's sounds the experiment ended. Their effort for teaching human speech to chimpanzee was not successful because chimpanzees do have neither the articulatory nor the cognitive ability to speak human language. Gua learned three or four words which she could speak very badly. However, she learned to respond to human speech to a considerable extent.

Karl and Catherine Hayes raised a chimpanzee Viki by name in the same manner as a human infant to see if she could learn human words. She was given speech therapy, which involved the trainer to manipulate her lower jaw. Eventually, she was able to voice four words: *mama, papa, up* and *cup*. This extremely limited success was at first interpreted as evidence that apes were not capable of using human language. However, further experiments in which chimpanzees were instructed in the use of *American Sign Language* indicated that Viki's achievements had been significantly hampered by physiological limitations—chimpanzees are not able to produce the sounds that make up human speech (Hayes and Hayes 1952).

In 1967, Allen and Beatrix Gardner started a project to teach Washoe, the chimpanzee, *American Sign Language* at the University of Nevada, Reno. At that time, previous attempts to teach chimpanzees to imitate human speech (Gua and Viki projects) had failed. They believed that these projects were flawed because chimps are physically unable to produce the voiced sounds required for spoken language. Their solution was to utilise the chimpanzee's ability to create diverse body gestures, which is how they communicate in the wild. After the first couple of years of the language project, it was observed that Washoe had developed an ability to communicate with human beings by using *American Sign Language*. It could pick up the gestures without operant conditioning methods by observing humans around her that were signing amongst themselves. Washoe was able to exchange conversation, rather than mere repetition of individual signs and displayed the ability to combine signs in novel and meaningful ways. For example, she referred to her toilet as 'dirty good' and refrigerator as 'open food drink', even though the scientists around her always called them 'potty chair' and 'cold box'. It is reported that Washoe was able to use about 250 signs and

Language and Linguistics

could communicate information under conditions in which the only source of information available to a human observer was the signing of the chimpanzee (Gardner, Gardner and Cantfort 1989).

Another important experiment along this line may be reported here. In the 1960s, John Lilly (1961) began an experiment in the *Virgin Islands* aiming at establishing meaningful communication between the humans and bottlenose dolphins. The team financed, mostly personally, a human-dolphin co-habitat, a house on the ocean's shore that contained an area that was partially flooded and allowed a human and dolphin to live together in the same space, sharing meals, play, language lessons and even sleep. The first experiment was more of a test to check psychological and other strains on the human and cetacean participants, determining the extent of the need for other human contact, dry clothing and so on. Despite tensions after several weeks, the experimenter agreed to a two-and-a-half month experiment, living isolated with 'Peter', the dolphin.

The basic outline of Peter's linguistic progress is as follows: early lessons involved mostly noise and interruptions from Peter during English lessons and a food reward of fish was necessary for him to 'attend the classes'. After several weeks, a concerted effort by Peter to imitate the instructor's speech was evident and human-like sounds were apparent and were recorded. More interesting was the dolphin's immediate grasp of basic semantics, such as the different aural indicators for *ball* and *doll* and other toys present in the aquarium. Peter was able to perform some tasks such as retrieval on aurally indicated object without fail.

Later in the project Peter's ability to process linguistic syntax was made apparent, in that Peter could distinguish between commands (e.g., *bring the ball to the doll* and *bring the doll to the ball*). This not only demonstrates the *bottlenose dolphin's* grasp of basic grammar, but also implies that dolphins' own language must include some such syntactical rules. The correlation between length and syllables (bursts of dolphin's sound) with the instructor's speech also went from essentially zero at the beginning of the session to almost a perfect correlation by its completion (a sentence spoken by the instructor involving 35 syllables and lasting 8 seconds would be met with an 8-second burst of sound from Peter dolphin involving 35 easily-discernible 'syllables' or bursts of sound).

Much later, experiments by many others (Herman, Richards and Wolz 1984; Pack and Herman 1995, Herman 2002; Pack and Herman

232

2004) have demonstrated cross-modal perceptual ability of dolphins. Dolphins typically perceive their environment through sound waves generated in the melon of their skulls, through a process known as **echolocation** (similar to that seen in bats, though the mechanism of production is different). Dolphin's eyesight however is fairly good, even by human standards and Herman's research found that any object, even of complex and arbitrary shape, identified either by sight or sound by the dolphin, could later be correctly identified by the dolphin with the alternate sense modality with almost 100 per cent accuracy, in what is classically known in psychology and behaviourism as a **match-to-sample test**.

The only errors noted were presumed to have been a misunderstanding of the task during the first few trials and not an inability of dolphin's perceptual apparatus. This capacity is a strong evidence for abstract and conceptual thought in the dolphin's brain, wherein an idea of the object is stored and understood not merely by its sensory properties; such abstraction may be argued to be of same kind as complex language, mathematics and art and implies a potentially very great intelligence and conceptual understanding within the brains of dolphins and many other cetaceans.

9.8 Human vs Animal Communication

The above experiments and the results obtained thereof have established the truth that language is primarily human as the human beings alone do possess language and use it for communication. Language is, in that sense *species-specific* as it is specific to only one set of species. Also, all the human beings uniformly possess language. It is only a few deaf and dumb persons who cannot speak. Thus language becomes species-uniform to its full extent.

Animals have their own system of communication but communication between them is extremely limited to a small number of messages. However, the controversial issue is the extent to which humans have behaviours that resemble animal communication, or whether all such communications have disappeared as a result of our linguistic capacity. Some of human bodily features such as eyebrows, beards and moustaches, deep adult male voices and female breasts, etc., strongly resemble adaptations to producing signals. Ethologists have argued that facial gestures such as smiling and grimacing, etc.

and *eye-brow flashes* on greetings are universal human communicative signals that can be related to corresponding signals in other primates.

Accepting the argument that spoken language has emerged at much later stage of human evolution, it is likely that human body language did include some more or less involuntary physical responses that had similar origin to communication we see in animals. Humans also often seek to mimic animals' communicative signals in order to interact with animals. For example, cats have a mild **affiliative response** involving closing their eyes; humans often close their eyes towards a pet cat to establish a tolerant relationship. Stroking, petting and rubbing pet animals are all actions that probably work through their natural patterns of inter-species communication. Dogs also have shown an ability to understand communication from species other than their own. They are able in using human communicative gestures such as pointing and looking to find hidden food and toys.

Even then, the difference between animal and human communication is obvious. Humans use a complex system (including syntax, semantics and pragmatics—as animals also use but in a different fashion), involving highly developed cerebral cortices and sophisticated voice boxes. Some researchers believed that language was species-specific, implying that only human beings have the *proper language* (Lenneberg 1967), while other scientists suggested that human language evolved from the animal communication. The greatest possibility for language training existed among great apes, which also possess highly developed cerebral cortices. The researches carried out by Kelloggs (1933), Hayes (1951) and Gardners (1989) revealed that chimpanzees could develop some kinds of linguistic comprehension to understand phonetic content of human speech but could not 'produce' the human speech.

Since there was limited success, apes have been taught to communicate using plastic symbols (Premack and Premack 1983) as well as the computer key-boards specially developed for animal use (e.g., Rumbaugh 1977). The over-riding findings however were that although apes could be trained to comprehend language and use it to some degree, they cannot achieve the sophistication of language observed in human children. It was concluded that apes may learn language via imitation, reduction, expansion, or using novel or new symbols; and that the majority used imitation – it was possible that the human trainers were 'cueing' the animals.

Animals definitely communicate when we consider that the definition of communication involves information transfer from a sender to a receiver. No animal has, however, evolved and achieved sophistication found in human language communication system, although animals can convey their needs, desires and reactions, etc. to others through some sophisticated signalling systems of their own. For linguists, interest in ANICOMS lies because of its similarities to and differences from that of human language. The differences between human language and animal communication system are primarily due to the fact that human brain is different from that of animals. The human brain has an innate capacity for learning linguistic creativity. In essence, ANICOMS differs from human language in the following points:

(a) **Duality of Patterning:** Human language is characterised with having a feature called **double articulation**. It signifies that the complex linguistic expressions can be broken into some meaningful elements (e.g., *syllables, morphemes, words*, etc.), which are made of smallest phonetic elements that affect meaning (i.e., *phonemes*). Since human language is made up of sounds (i.e., patterns of sound) and of smaller formal units called morphemes and words, a stretch of speech in any human language can be analysed into smaller units and several meanings can be expressed by means of a limited number of signals. Animal signals, however, cannot and do not exhibit dual structure as animal communication consists of meaningful cries which cannot be analysed into words.

(b) **Displacement:** In general, animal utterances are responses to external stimuli and these do not refer to the matters removed in time and space. Matters of relevance at a distance, such as distant food sources, tend to be indicated to individuals by body language. For example, the activities of wolf before their hunt or the information conveyed in honey-bee dance language. It is therefore unclear to what extent utterances are automatic responses and to what extent deliberate intent plays a part. Human language is context-free. Human beings can talk about experiences without actually living them and of the objects and events not physically present at the time and place of speaking. Since human language is not directly controlled by stimulus, human beings alone are able to convey precise information to their fellows through speech. Only they can ask for the particular kind of food they want. In contrast to human language, signals of animal communication are mostly context-bound. No animal is able to express conceptual generalisations because, in case of animals, there is a direct relationship between stimulus and response and they can respond to their immediate environment. Only *cetaceans* and some primates may be considered as notable exceptions.

(c) **Creativity:** Human language can combine elements to produce many new messages. One factor in this is that much human language growth is based upon conceptual ideas and hypothetical structures, both being far greater capabilities in humans than animals. Using a few basic principles of construction, human beings create a large number of constructions. It allows a human to produce speeches that have never been said or heard before. In case of animal they have no ability to produce and send message that has never been sent before. Animal calls lack creativity or productivity as they draw all their calls from a fixed repertoire, which is highly limited and which does not allow any possibility for novelty. On the other hand, human language is open and creative in the sense that one can form new utterances by putting together the familiar old utterances and assembling them in new patterns of arrangement which are also familiar in old utterances.

(d) **Recursiveness:** Human language is recursive by nature. It has the ability of forming sentences inside other sentences as there is no limit to the length of any sentence. This appears far less common in ANICOMS, although current research into animal culture is still an ongoing process with many new discoveries. In ANICOMS, there is very little creativity or recursiveness. The number of discrete signals used in ANICOMS is highly limited. The approximate numbers of basic vocal signals made by different species are as follows: jackdaws (4), cow (8), dog (10), chicken (20), monkey (10-32), dolphin (7-19), pig (23), fox (36), ape (10-37) and human (20-90).

(e) **Arbitrariness:** There is no inherent connection between sounds and symbols, or between symbols and their referents. Since the relation between word and meaning is quite arbitrary, it becomes just a matter of convention. Language may be called a system of conventional symbols, where each symbol represents a stretch of sounds with which a meaning is associated. Animal signalling system, on the contrary, is normally iconic, as no signal can be broken into parts where each part has separate sense or meaning. No animal has ever succeeded in producing a combination of words on its own to meet the needs of new situations. Animals are not capable to define that a particular sound is to denote a particular meaning. Animals cannot make the choice of foods but most of them can only indicate that they are hungry.

(f) **Redundancy:** Human language manifests a large amount of redundancy. That means, it can convey many things through implication and non-specification. As observed in human languages, **ellipses** has been a very recurrent process where many implied things are not uttered by speaker but appropriately understood by hearer. For instance, in case of dialogic interactions, in question answering sessions and even in case of writing general texts, we often make certain things redundant, which we assume, can be understood by listeners or readers with reference to texts. Perhaps, 'yes-no' type of statements are the most suitable and valid examples for questions. It is done by two ways: using 'yes' or 'no' to reply without replying in full forms, or rising the tone with which the question is asked. In the world of ANICOMS, there is no such facility to make redundant some of the elements of a signal or message.

(g) **Culture Preservation:** Human language is learned through culture, not by genetic inheritance. That means learning a language is a culturally controlled affair. On the contrary, the ANICOMS is learned largely by instinct or genetically controlled factors. Moreover, human language is culture-preserving as well as culture-transmitting. For this reason, Rene Descartes said, "Thanks to language, man became man". Although there are several other forms of preservation of culture such as *architecture, sculpture, painting, music, dance,* etc., it is the language that is found to be the most dynamic in form and function in which cultures are preserved and transmitted through generations.

(h) **Dynamicity:** Human language is dynamic in nature. It keeps on changing at all levels: at level of sounds, words, meanings, idioms and sentences. Each generation of language users modifies and changes its language in its own ways to adapt to the changing needs and demands of the people who use it. In contrast, the feature of dynamicity is ruefully absent in ANICOMS, as signals animals use are transmitted through generations in an iconic manner without change or modifications of any kind.

However, experts have observed that there are some features common to both human languages and ANICOMS. These include **reciprocity** (senders are also receivers of signals and information under normal situations and circumstances), **specialisation** (linguistic signals do not serve other purpose rather than communicating something), **rapid fading** (all signals vanish very quickly. This is, of course, not true for written texts or body scents produced by animals to mark their maturity or territory), **directionality** (anyone close enough to hear can pick up message) and **vocal-auditory channel** (majority of the communicating signals are made via vocal tract and are perceived by ears).

9.9 Concluding Remarks

If a language is about communicating with signals, voice, sounds, gesture and with written symbols, then is it fair to consider ANICOMS as language? Animals do not have a written form of a language, but they tend to use a 'language' of their own to communicate with one another belonging within their own species. In that sense, ANICOMS can be considered **delanguage** (i.e., different language) having its own distinctive set of features and which is complete and sufficient in its form and content for the purposes for which it is inherited and deployed.

Notes and Comments

[1]   Metacommunication constitutes signals that are open to modify the meaning of subsequent signals. The best example is the *play faces* of dogs, which they often carry out with other members of the same group. In this process they generate signals which are parts of a play fight and a source of their bonding with peers rather than a serious aggressive event.

[2]   Bottlenose dolphins develop individually distinctive signature whistles that they use to maintain group cohesion. Unlike the development of identification signals in most other species, signature whistle development is strongly influenced by vocal learning. This learning ability is maintained throughout life and

dolphins frequently copy each other's whistles in the wild. It has been hypothesised that signature whistles can be used as referential signals among conspecifics, because captive bottlenose dolphins can be trained to use novel, learned signals to label objects. For this labelling to occur, signature whistles would have to convey identity information independent of the caller's voice features. Several studies demonstrated that bottlenose dolphins extract identity information from signature whistles even after all voice features have been removed from the signal. Thus, bottlenose dolphins are the only animals other than human beings that have been shown to transmit identity information independent of the caller's voice or location.

[3] Accidental swallowing of pieces of brightly coloured plastic or glass is a very common cause of mortality amongst the *Herring Gull's* chicks.

[4] Recent studies (Michelsen 1993, Dreller and Kirchner 1993), however, have claimed that the bees communicate either through the smell of pollen, which the returning bee carries or through the sounds made during the conduct of the dance. Whatever be the exact means of communication, it is agreed that the bee-dance does result in messages being passed from one bee to others.

[5] The viewpoints proposed by Daniel Otte (1974) became most widely accepted model by the animal researchers in the 1970s and 1980s.

[6] In ecology, *commensalism* is a kind of relationship between two animals where one animal benefits but the other is unaffected. There are three other types of association: *mutualism* (where both animals benefit), *competition* (where both animals are harmed) and *parasitism* (one animal benefits and the other one is harmed). An example of commensalism: cattle egrets foraging in fields among cattle or other livestock. As cattle, horses and other livestock graze on the field, they cause movements that stir up various insects. As the insects are stirred up, the cattle egrets following the livestock catch and feed upon them. The egrets benefit from this relationship because the livestock have helped them find their meals, while the livestock are typically unaffected by it.

[7] A good example of one-way human-animal communication is *BowLingual*—a Japanese device which was made to translate barking of dogs into words. The system was based on *Animal*

Emotion Analysis System proposed by Matsumi Suzuki. The device could translate two hundred phrases (grouped into six different moods) supposedly reflecting 'meaning' of barking. The device was apparently successful enough in Japan and was even named one of 2002's best inventions by *Time Magazine*. However, reports on the accuracy of the device have been to a low 1.5 stars average in popular product rating in USA.

[8] The book entitled *Parrot Culture: Our 2500-Years Long Fascination with the World's Most Talkative Bird* by Bruce Thomas Boehner (2004) has explored this issue quite thoroughly.

Bibliography

Aitchison, J. (1978) *Linguistics*. London: Hodder and Stroughton.

Aitchison, J. (2000) *The Seeds of Speech: Language Origin and Evolution*. Cambridge: Cambridge University Press.

Alvarez, F. (1993) "*Alertness signaling in two rail species*". *Animal Behaviour*. 46(4): 1229–1231.

Argyle, M. (1988) *Bodily Communication*. 2nd Edition. Madison: International Universities Press.

Argyle, M., V. Salter, H. Nicholson, M. Williams, and P. Burgess (1970) "The communication of inferior and superior attitudes by verbal and non-verbal signals". *British Journal of Social and Clinical Psychology*. 9(2): 222-231.

Austin, J.L. (1962) *How to Do Things with Words*. Cambridge. MA: Harvard University Press.

Bang, J.C. and J. Door (2007) "Language, ecology and society: a dialectical approach". In, Steffensen, S.V. and J. Nash (Eds.) *Language, Ecology and Society: An Introduction to Dialectical Linguistics*. London: Continuum. Pp. 3-31.

Bastardas-Boada, A. (2002) "The ecological perspective: benefits and risks for sociolinguistics and language policy and planning". In, Fill, A., H. Penz, and W. Trampe (Eds.) *Colourful Green Ideas*. Berna: Peter Lang. Pp. 77–88.

Bateson, G. (1955) "A theory of play and fantasy". *Psychiatric Research Reports*. 2: 39-51.

Bateson, G. (1972) *Steps to an Ecology of Mind*. New York: Balantine Books.

Bell, R.T. (1976) *Sociolinguistics: Goals, Approaches and Problems*. London: Batsford Books.

Benveniste, E. (1966-1974) *Problems in General Linguistics*, translated by Mary Elizabeth Meek), 2 Volumes. Coral Gables, Florida: University of Miami Press.

241

Bloch, B. and G.L. Trager (1942) *Outline of Linguistic Analysis.* Maryland: Linguistic Society of America.

Bloomfield, L. (1926) "A set of postulates for the science of language". *Language.* 2(1): 153-164.

Bloomfield, L. (1933) *Language.* New York: Holt, Rinehart and Winston.

Boas, F. (1940) *Race, Language and Culture.* New York: Macmillan.

Boehner, B.T. (2004) *Parrot Culture: Our 2500 Year Long Fascination with the World's Most Talkative Bird.* Philadelphia: University of Pennsylvania Press.

Bréal, M. (1897) *Semantics: Studies in the Science of Meaning.* Paris: Hachette.

Brown K. (Ed.) (2005) *Encyclopaedia of Language and Linguistics.* Second Edition. Oxford: Elsevier Sciences.

Brown, C.M. and P. Hagoort (1999) "The cognitive neuroscience of language." In, Brown, C.M. and P. Hagoort (Eds.) *The Neurocognition of Language.* New York: Oxford University Press. Pp. 3-15.

Brown, G. and G. Yule (1983) *Discourse Analysis.* Cambridge: Cambridge University Press.

Brown, P. and S. Levinson (1987) *Politeness: Some Universals in Language Usage.* Cambridge: Cambridge University Press.

Brown, R. (1973) *A First Language: The Early Stages.* Cambridge, MA: Harvard University Press.

Brumfit, C. (1997) "How applied linguistics is the same as any other science". *International Journal of Applied Linguistics.* 7(1): 86-94.

Bühler, K. (1934) *Theory of Language: The Representational Function of Language.* (translated by Goodwin, D.F. and published in 1990). Amsterdam and Philadelphia: John Benjamins.

Bull, P.E. (1987) *Posture and Gesture.* Vol. 16. Oxford: Pergamon Press.

Bulwer, J. (1644) *Chirologia: Or the Natural Language of the Hand.* Longman: London.

Burgoon, J., D. Buller and W. Woodall (1996) *Non-verbal Communication: The Unspoken Dialogue.* Second Edition. New York: McGraw-Hill.

Caplan, D. (1987) *Neurolinguistics and Linguistic Aphasiology: An Introduction.* Cambridge: Cambridge University Press.

Caro, T.M. (1995) "Short-term costs and correlates of play in Cheetahs". *Animal Behavior.* 49(2): 333-345.

Chafe, W. (1980) *The Pear Stories: Cognitive, Cultural, and Linguistic Aspects of Narrative Production.* Norwood, NJ: Ablex.

Cheney, D. and R. Seyfarth (1990) *How Monkeys See the World: Inside the Mind of Another Species*. Chicago: University of Chicago Press.

Cheney, D. and R. Seyfarth (2007) *Baboon Metaphysics: The Evolution of a Social Mind*. Chicago: University of Chicago Press.

Cherry, C. (1956) "Roman Jakobson: distinctive features as the normal coordinates of a language". In, Halle, M. (Ed.) *For Roman Jakobson*. The Hague: Mouton.

Cherry, C., M. Halle, and R. Jakobson (1953) "Toward the logical description of languages in their phonemic aspect". *Language*. 29(1): 34-46.

Chomsky, A. N. and M. Halle (1968) *The Sound Pattern of English*. New York: Harper & Row

Chomsky, A.N. (1956) "Three models for the description of language". *IRE Transactions on Information Theory*. IT-26

Chomsky, A.N. (1957) *Syntactic Structures*. New York: Harper Collins.

Chomsky, A.N. (1959) "A Review of B.F. Skinner's *Verbal Behavior*". *Language*. 35(1): 26-58.

Chomsky, A.N. (1959) "On certain formal properties of grammars". *Information and Control*. 2: 137-167.

Chomsky, A.N. (1965) *Aspects of the Theory of Syntax*. Cambridge, Mass.: MIT Press.

Chomsky, A.N. (1968) *Language and Mind*. New York: Harcourt Brace.

Chomsky, A.N. (1972) *Studies in Generative Grammar*. The Hague: Mouton.

Clark, R.W. (2005) "Pursuit-deterrent communication between prey animals and timber rattlesnakes (Crotalus horridus): the response of snakes to harassment displays". Behaviral Ecolology and Sociobiology. 1(1): 1-4.

Cooper, W.E. and V.P. Mellado (2004) "Tradeoffs between escape behavior and foraging opportunity by the Balearic lizard (*Podarcis lilfordi*)". *Herpetologica*. 60(1): 321-324.

Cooper, W.E., V. P. Mellado and L.J. Vitt (2004) "Ease and effectiveness of costly autotomy vary with predation intensity among lizard populations". *Journal of Zoology*. 262(2): 243-256.

Cooper, W.E., V.P. Mellado, T.A. Baird, J.P. Caldwell and L.J. Vitt (2004) "Pursuit deterrent signalling by the Bonaire whiptail lizard: *Cnemidophorus murinus*". *Behaviour*. 141(2): 297-311.

Coulthard, M., and A. Johnson (2007) *An introduction to Forensic Linguistics: Language in Evidence*. Oxford: Routledge.

Croft, W.A. (2001) *Radical Construction Grammar: Syntactic Theory in Typological Perspective*. Oxford: Oxford University Press.

Crystal, D. (1980) *Dictionary of Linguistics and Phonetics*. Boulder, Colorado: Westview Press

Crystal, D. (1995) *A First Dictionary of Linguistics and Phonetics*. Boulder, Colorado: Westview Press.

Crystal, D. (1995) *The Cambridge Encyclopaedia of the English Language*. Cambridge: Cambridge University Press.

Crystal, D. (1997) *A Dictionary of Linguistics and Phonetics*. 4th Edition. Oxford: Blackwell.

Crystal, D. (2005) *How Language Works*. London: Penguin.

Crystal, D. and D. Davy (1969) *Investigating English Style*. London: Longman.

Darwin, C.R. (1859) *On the Origin of Species by Means of Natural Selection, or the Preservation of Favoured Races in the Struggle for Life*. First Edition. London: John Murray.

Dash, N.S. (2007) *Language Corpora and Applied Linguistics*. Kolkata: Sahitya Samsad.

Dash, N.S. (2008) *Corpus Linguistics: An Introduction*. New Delhi: Pearson Education-Longman.

Dash, N.S. (In Press) *Modern Bengali Words: A Structural Study*.

Davis, W., I. Mackenzie, and S. Kennedy (1995) *Nomads of the Dawn: The Penan of the Borneo Rainforest*. Vancouver: Pomegranate Art books.

deJorio, A. (1832) *Gesture in Naples and Gesture in Classical Antiquity*. Bloomington: Indiana University Press.

Derbyshire, A.E. (1967) *A Description of English*. London: Edward Arnold.

Dreller, C. and W.H. Kirchner (1993) "How honey-bees perceive the information of the dance language". *Naturwissenschaften*. 80(2): 319-321.

Eilenberg, S. (1974) *Automata, Languages, and Machines*. New York: Academic Press

Ekman, P. (1972) *Emotion in the Human Face: Guide-Lines for Research and an Integration of Findings*. Boston: Twayne Publishers.

Ekman, P. (2003) Emotions Revealed: Recognizing Faces and Feelings to Improve Communication and Emotional Life. New York: Times Books.

Embick, D., A. Marantz, Y. Miyashita, W. O'Neil, K.L. Sakai (2000) "A syntactic specialization for Broca's Area". *Proceedings of the National Academy of Sciences*. 97(11): 6150–6154.

Encyclopaedia Britannica 1996.

Fab, P. (1993) *Word Play: What Happens When People Talk*. London: Vintage Books.

Fill, A. (1996) "Ökologie der Linguistik - Linguistik der Ökologie". In, Fill, A. (Ed.) *Sprachökologie und Ökolinguistik*. Tübingen: Stauffenburg Linguistik. Pp. 3-16.

Fill, A. (2000) "Language and Ecology: Ecolinguistic perspectives for 2000 and beyond." *In the Proceedings of AILA-1999*, Tokyo.

Fill, A., H. Penz, and W. Trampe (2002) (Eds.) *Colourful Green Ideas*. Berna: Peter Lang.

Fillmore, C.J. (1968) "The case for case". In, Bach, E. and R.T Harms (Eds.) *Universals in Linguistic Theory*. New York: Holt, Rinehart and Winston. Pp. 1-88.

Fillmore, C.J. (1976) "Frame semantics and the nature of language". In, *Annals of the New York Academy of Sciences: Conference on the Origin and Development of Language and Speech*. Volume 280. Pp. 20-32.

Fillmore, C.J. (1982) "Frame semantics". In, *Linguistics in the Morning Calm*. Seoul: Hanshin Publishing Co. Pp. 111-137.

Fillmore, C.J. (1997) *Lectures on Deixis*. Stanford: CSLI Publications.

Fillmore, C.J. and S. Atkins (1994) "Starting where the dictionaries stop: the challenge for computational lexicography". In, Atkins, B.T.S. and A. Zampolli (Eds.) *Computational Approaches to the Lexicon*. Oxford: Oxford University Press. Pp. 349-393.

Floyd, K. and L. Guerrero (2006) *Non-verbal Communication in Close Relationships*. New Jersey: Lawrence Erlbaum Associates.

Francis, W.N. (1982) "Problems of assembling and computerizing large corpora". In, Johansson, S. (Ed.) *Computer Corpora in English Language Research*. Bergen: Norwegian Computing Centre for the Humanities. Pp. 7-24.

Francis, W.N. (1992) "Language corpora BC". In, Svartvik, J. (Ed.) *Directions in Corpus Linguistics: Proceedings of Nobel Symposium 82*. Berlin: Mouton de Gruyter. Pp. 17-32.

Friederici, A.D. (2002) "Towards a neural basis of auditory sentence processing". *Trends in Cognitive Sciences*. 6(2): 78–84.

Frisch, K.V. (1950) *Bees, Their Vision, Chemical Senses and Language*. Great Seal Books: Cornell University Press.

Frisch, K.V. (1953) *The Dancing Bees*. New York: Harvest Books.

Frisch, K.V. (1967) *The Dance Language and Orientation of Bees*. Cambridge, Mass.: Harvard University Press.

245

Fromkin, V. and R. Rodman (1993) *An Introduction to Language*. Third Edition. New York: Holt, Rinehart and Winston.

Gardiner, A.H. (1932) *The Theory of Speech and Language*. Oxford: Clarendon Press.

Gardner, R.A., B.T. Gardner, and T.E.V. Cantfort (Eds.) (1989) *Teaching Sign Language to Chimpanzees*. New York: State University of New York Press.

Gazdar, G., E. Klein, G.K. Pullum, and I.A. Sag (1985) *Generalized Phrase Structure Grammar*. Oxford: Blackwell.

Geeraerts, D. (1995) "Cognitive linguistics". In, Verschueren, J., J.O. Östman, and J. Blommaert (Eds.) *Handbook of Pragmatics*. Amsterdam: John Benjamins. Pp. 111-116.

Gera, D.L. (2003) *Ancient Greek Ideas on Speech, Language, and Civilization*. Oxford: Oxford University Press.

Gibbons, J. and M.T. Turell (2008) (Eds.) *Dimensions of Forensic Linguistics*. Amsterdam: John Benjamins.

Goatly, A. (1996) "Green grammar and grammatical metaphor, or language and the myth of power, or metaphors we die by". *Journal of Pragmatics*. 25(4): 537-560.

Goatly, A. (1997) "A response to 'schleppegrell': what makes a grammar green?". *Journal of Pragmatics*. 28(3): 249-251.

Goatly, A. (2000) *Critical Reading and Writing: An Introductory Course Book*. London: Routledge.

Godin, J.G. and S.A. Davis (1995) "Boldness and predator deterrence: a reply to Milinski and Boltshauser". In the *Proceedings of the Royal Society of London, Biological Sciences*. 262(1363): 107-112.

Godley, A., J. Sweetland and R. Wheeler (2006) "Preparing teachers for dialectally diverse classrooms." *Educational Researcher*. 35(8): 30-37.

Goffman, E. (1967) "On facework: an analysis of ritual elements in social interaction". In, Jaworski, A. and N. Coupland (Eds.) *The Discourse Reader*. London, Routledge. Pp. 306-321.

Goldin-Meadow, S. (2003) "The resilience of language". In, Beachley, B., A. Brown, and F. Colin (Eds). *Proceedings of the 27th Annual Boston University Conference on Language Development*. Somerville, MA: Cascadilla Press. Pp. 1-25.

Goldin-Meadow, S. (2003) *Hearing Gesture: How our Hands help us Think*. Cambridge, MA: Harvard University Press.

Graffi, G. (2001) *200 Years of Syntax: A Critical Survey*. Amsterdam: John Benjamins.

Greenberg, J. (1963) *Universals of Languages*. Cambridge, Mass.: MIT Press.
Greenberg, J. (1993) "Observations concerning Ringe's 'Calculating the factor of change in language comparison". *Proceedings of the American Philosophical Society*. 137(1): 79-90.
Greene, D. and F. Walker (2004) "Recommendations to public speaking instructors for negotiation of code-switching practices among Black English-speaking African American students." *The Journal of Negro Education*. 73(4): 431-438.
Gregory, M. and S. Carroll (1978) *Language and Situation*. London: Routledge and Keegan Paul.
Grice, P. (1991) *Studies in the Way of Words*, Cambridge, MA: Harvard University Press.
Grzega, J. (2003) "Borrowing as a word-finding process in cognitive historical onomasiology". *Onomasiology Online*. 4(1): 22-42.
Gurney, C. (2001) *The Language of Animals: 7 Steps to Communicating with Animals*. New York: Random House Inc.
Hall, E. (1963) "A system for the notation of proxemic behaviour". *American Anthropologist*. 65: 1003-1026.
Hall, E. (1966) *The Hidden Dimension*. London: Anchor Books.
Hall, R. (1968) *An Essay on Language*. New York: Chilton Books.
Halliday, M.A.K. (1973) *Explorations in the Functions of Language*. London: Edward Arnold.
Halliday, M.A.K. (1975) *Learning How to Mean*. London: Edward Arnold.
Halliday, M.A.K. (1978) *Language as Social Semiotic: the Social Interpretation of Language and Meaning*. London: Edward Arnold.
Halliday, M.A.K. (1990) "New ways of meaning: the challenge to applied linguistics". *Journal of Applied Linguistics*. 6(1): 7-36.
Halliday, M.A.K. and C.M.I.M. Matthiessen (2004) *An Introduction to Functional Grammar*. Third Edition. London: Edward Arnold.
Halliday, M.A.K. and R. Hasan (1980) "Text and context: aspects of language in a social-semiotic perspective". *Sophia Linguistica*. No. 6. Tokyo: Sophia University.
Hare, B., J. Call and M. Tomasello (1998) "Communication of food location between human and dog (canis familiaris)". *Evolution of Communication*. 2(1): 137-159.
Harré, R., J. Brockmeier and P. Mühlhäusler (1999) *Greenspeak: a Study of Environmental Discourse*. London: Sage.
Harris, Z. (1952) "Discourse analysis". *Language*. 28(1): 1-30.
Haugen E. (1972) *The Ecology of Language*. Stanford: Stanford University Press.

Hayes, C. (1951) *The Ape in Our House*. New York: Harper.

Hayes, K.J. and C. Hayes (1952) "Imitation in a home-raised chimpanzee". *Journal of Comparative and Physiological Psychology*. 45: 450-459.

Hayes, K.J. and C.H. Nissen (1971) "Higher mental functions of a home-raised chimpanzee". In, Schrier, A.M. and F. Stollnitz (Eds.) *Behaviour of Non-human Primates*. New York: Academic Press. Pp. 50-115.

Heart, S. (1996) *The Language of Animals*. New York: Henry Holt.

Heine, S.J., and D.R. Lehman (1997) "Culture, dissonance, and self-affirmation". *Personality and Social Psychology Bulletin*. 23: 389-400.

Heine, S.J., and D.R. Lehman (1997) "The cultural construction of self-enhancement: an investigation of group-serving biases". *Journal of Personality and Social Psychology*. 72:1268-1283.

Heredia, R. (1997) "Bilingual memory and hierarchical models: a case for language dominance." *Current Directions in Psychological Science* 10.

Herman, L. (2002) "Vocal, social, and self-imitation by bottlenosed dolphins." In, Nehaniv, C. and K. Dautenhahn (Eds.) *Imitation in Animals and Artifacts*. Cambridge, MA.: MIT Press. Pp. 63-108.

Herman, L., D. Richards, and J. Wolz (1984) "Comprehension of sentences by bottlenosed dolphins". *Cognition*. 16(2): 129-219.

Hertenstein, M.J. (2002) "Touch: its communicative functions in infancy". *Human Development*. 45(1): 70-94.

Hickock, G. and D. Poeppel (2007) "Opinion: the cortical organization of speech processing". *Nature Reviews Neuroscience*. 8(5): 393-402.

Hitchings, H. (2008) *The Secret Life of Words: How English Became English*. London: John Murray.

Hockett, C.F. (1958) *A Course in Modern Linguistics*. New York: Macmillan. (Indian edition New Delhi, Calcutta: Oxford and IBH).

Hockett, C.F. (1960) "The origin of speech". *Scientific American*. 203: 89-97.

Holley, A.J. (1993) "Do brown hares signal to foxes?" *Ethology*. 94(1): 21-30.

Humboldt, W.V. (1988) *On Language*. Cambridge: Cambridge University Press.

Hunston, S. (2002) *Corpora in Applied Linguistics*. Cambridge: Cambridge University Press.

Hymes, D. (1962) "The ethnography of speaking", In, Gladwin, T. and W.C. Sturtevant (Eds.) *Anthropology and Human Behavior*, Washington: The Anthropology Society of Washington. Pp. 13–53.

Jackendoff, R. (1983) *Semantics and Cognition*. Cambridge, Mass.: MIT Press.

Jackendoff, R. (1990) *Semantic Structures*. Cambridge, Mass.: MIT Press.

Jainik, V.M., L.S. Sayigh, and R.S. Wells (2006) "Signature whistle shape conveys identity information to bottlenose dolphins." In, *Proceedings of the National Academy of Sciences*. 103(21): 35-40.

Jakobson, R. (1960) "Closing statement: linguistics and poetics". In, Sebeok, T. (Ed.) *Style in Language*. Cambridge, Mass.: MIT Press. Pp. 350-377.

Jakobson, R. (1976) "What is poetry?". In, Matejka, L. and I.R. Titunik (Eds.) *Semiotics of Art: Prague School Contributions*, Cambridge, Mass.: MIT Press. Pp. 167-175.

Jespersen, O. (1921) *Language: Its Nature, Development and Origin*. London: George Allen and Unwin.

Jones, K. (1935) "This English: By Sir Richard Paget". *International Journal of Psycho-Analysis*. 16(4): 385.

Joseph, A.D. (1986) *The Communication Handbook: A Dictionary*. Harper & Row

Kellogg, W.N. and L.A. Kellogg (1933) *The Ape and The Child: A Comparative Study of the Environmental Influence Upon Early Behavior*. New York: Hafner Publishing Co.

Kendeigh, C. (1961) *Animal Ecology*. Englewood Cliffs, N.J.: Prentice-Hall, Inc.

Kendon, A. (1982) "The study of gesture: some observations on its history". *Semiotic Inquiry*. 2(1): 25-62.

Kendon, A. (1997) "Gesture". *Annual Review of Anthropology*. 26(1): 109-128.

Kendon, A. (2000) *Gesture in Naples and Gesture in Classical Antiquity*. An English translation, with an Introductory Essay and Notes of *La mimica degli antichi investigata nel gestire Napoletano* (Gestural expression of the ancients in the light of Neapolitan gesturing) by Andrea de Jorio (1832). Bloomington, Indiana: Indian University Press.

Kendon, A. (2004) *Gesture: Visible Action as Utterance*. Cambridge: Cambridge University Press

Kendon, A. (Ed.) (1981) *Nonverbal Communication, Interaction and Gesture: Selections from Semiotica. Vol. 41. Approaches to Semiotics*. The Hague: Mouton and Co.

Kenneally, C. (2007) *The First Word: The Search for the Origins of Language*. New York: Viking.

Kennedy, G. (1998) *An Introduction to Corpus Linguistics*. London: Addison Wesley Longman Inc.

Krebs, J. and R. Dawkins (1978) "Animal signals: information or manipulation?" In, Krebs, J. and N. Davies (Eds.) *Behavioural Ecology: An Evolutionary Approach*. First Edition. Oxford: Blackwell. Pp. 282-309.

Labov, W. (1966) *The Social Stratification of English in New York City*. Washington, DC: Center for Applied Linguistics.

Labov, W. (1972) *Sociolinguistic Patterns*. Philadelphia: University of Pennsylvania Press.

Lakoff, G. (1987) *Women, Fire and Dangerous Things. What Categories Reveal about the Mind*. Chicago: University of Chicago Press.

Lakoff, G. and M. Johnson (1980) *Metaphors We Live by*. Chicago: University of Chicago Press.

Lakoff, G. and M. Johnson (1998) *Philosophy in the Flesh. The Embodied Mind and its Challenge to Western Thought*. New York: Basic Books.

Lamb, S.M. (1971) The crooked path of progress in cognitive linguistics. *Georgetown University Monograph Series on Languages and Linguistics*. 24: 99-123.

Lamb, S.M. (1999) *Pathways of the Brain. The Neurocognitive Basis of Language*. Amsterdam: John Benjamins.

Lamb, W. (1965) *Posture and Gesture*. London: Brechin Books.

Lamb, W. and E. Watson (1979) *Body Code: The Meaning in Movement*. London: Routledge.

Landau, S.I. (2001) *Dictionaries: The Art and Craft of Lexicography*. 2nd Edition. Cambridge: Cambridge University Press.

Langacker, R.W. (1967) *Language and Its Structure*. New York: Harcourt Brace

Langacker, R.W. (1987) *Foundations of Cognitive Grammar. Vol. I: Theoretical Prerequisites*. Stanford: Stanford University Press.

Langacker, R.W. (1991) *Concept, Image, and Symbol: The Cognitive Basis of Grammar*. Berlin Mouton de Gruyter.

Langacker, R.W. (1991) *Foundations of Cognitive Grammar. Vol. II: Descriptive Application*. Stanford: Stanford University Press.

Leavens, D.A. and T.P. Racine (2009) "Joint attention in apes and humans: are humans unique?" *Journal of Consciousness Studies*. 16: 240-267.

Lenneberg, E.H. (1964) "The capacity for language acquisition." In, Fodor, J.A. and J.J. Katz. (Eds.) *The Structure of Language*. New Jersey: Prentice-Hall. Pp. 35-47.

Lenneberg, E.H. (1967) *Biological Foundations of Language*. New York: John Wiley and Sons, Inc.

Lily, J.C. (1961) *Man and Dolphin*. New York: Doubleday.

Lily, J.C. (1967) *The Mind of the Dolphin*. New York: Doubleday.

Littlejohn, S.W. and K.A. Foss (2005) *Theories of Human Communication*. Belmont, CA: Wadsworth.

Locke, J. (1997) *An Essay Concerning Human Understanding*. Edited by Woolhouse, Roger. New York: Penguin Books. P. 307.

Lorenz, K. (1952) *King Solomon's Ring: New Light on Animal Ways*. London: Methuen.

Lorenz, K. (1979) *The Year of the Greylag Goose*. New York: Harcourt Brace Jovanovich.

Low, S.M. and D.L. Zúñiga (2003) *The Anthropology of Space and Place: Locating Culture*. London: Blackwell Publishing.

Lyons, J. (1968) *Introduction to Theoretical Linguistics*. Cambridge: Cambridge University Press.

Lyons, J. (1977) *Semantics. Vol. I and Vol. II*. Cambridge: Cambridge University Press.

Lyons, J. (1981) *Language and Linguistics: An Introduction*. Cambridge: Cambridge University Press.

Lyons, J. (Ed.) (1972) *New Horizons in Linguistics*, London: Pelican.

Mackay, D. (2003) *Information Theory, Inference, and Learning Algorithms*. Cambridge: Cambridge University Press.

Makkai, A. (1993) *Ecolinguistics: Toward a New Paradigm for the Science of Language*. London: Printer Publishers.

Malinowsky, B. (1923) "The problem of meaning in primitive languages". In Supplement to C.K. Ogden and I. A. Richards (1923) *The Meaning of Meaning*. 9th Edition 1946. London: Keegan and Paul. Pp. 52-65.

Matthew, M., M. Davis, and P. Fanning (1983) *Messages: The Communication Skills Book*. Second Edition. New York: New Harbinger Publications.

251

Matthews, P.H. (2002) *The Concise Oxford Dictionary of Linguistics.* Oxford: Oxford University Press.

McCarthy, M. (2001) *Issues in Applied Linguistics.* Cambridge: Cambridge University Press.

McEnery T. and A. Wilson (2001) *Corpus Linguistics.* Second Edition. Edinburgh: Edinburgh University Press.

McMenamin, G.R. (2002) *Forensic Linguistics: Advances in Forensic Stylistics.* New York: CRC Press LLC.

McNeill, D. (1992) *Hand and Mind. What Gestures Reveal about Thought.* Chicago: Chicago University Press.

McNeill, D. (2005) *Gesture and Thought.* Chicago: Chicago University Press

McPartland J, and A. Klin (2006) "Asperger's Syndrome". *Adolescent Medical Clinic.* 17(3): 771-788.

Mehrabian, A. (1972) *Non-verbal Communication.* Illinois: Aldine-Atherton.

Mehrabian, A. (1981) *Silent Messages: Implicit Communication of Emotions and Attitudes.* Second Edition. Belmont, CA: Wadsworth.

Mehrabian, A. and S.R. Ferris (1967) "Inference of attitude from non-verbal communication in two channels". *The Journal of Counseling Psychology.* 31: 248-252.

Merriam-Webster Online Dictionary (2003)

Mey, J.L. (1993) *Pragmatics: An Introduction.* Oxford: Blackwell.

Michelsen, A. (1993) "The transfer of information in the dance language of honey-bees: progress and problems". *Journal of Comparative Physiology.* 173: 135-141.

Milroy, L. (1987) *Language and Social Networks.* London: Basil Blackwell.

Morris, C.W. (1965) "On the unity of the pragmatic movement". *Rice University Studies.* 51(4): 109-119.

Morris, D. (1961) *Curious Creatures.* London: Spring Books.

Morris, D., P. Collett, P. Marsh, and M. O'Shaughnessy (1979) *Gestures: Their Origins and Distribution.* London. Cape Publications.

Morris, S. (1952) "Lexicostatistic dating of prehistoric ethnic contacts", *Proceedings American Philosophical Society.* 96(2): 452-463.

Morris, S. (1955) "Towards greater accuracy in lexicostatistic dating". *International Journal of American Linguistics.* 21(1): 121-137.

Mozeson, I.E. (2006) *The Origin of Speeches: Intelligent Design in Language.* Dallas, Texas: Lightcatcher Books.

Mukarovsky, J. (1964) "The Esthetics of language". In, Garvin, P.L. (Ed.) *A Prague School Reader on Esthetics, Literary Structure, and Style.* Washington, D.C.: Georgetown University Press. Pp. 31-69.

Mukarovsky, J. (1970) "Standard language and poetic language". In, Freeman, D.C. (Ed.) *Linguistics and Literary Style,* New York: Holt Rine Hart. Pp, 40-56.

Mukarovsky, J. (1970) *Aesthetic Function, Norm, and Value as Social Facts* (translated by M. E. Suino). Ann Arbor: University of Michigan Press.

Murphy, T.G (2006) "Predator-elicited visual signal: why the turquoise-browed motmot wag-displays its racketed tail". *Behavioral Ecology.* 17(4): 547-553.

Murphy, T.G. (2007) "Dishonest 'preemptive' pursuit-deterrent signal? Why the turquoise-browed motmot wags its tail before feeding nestlings". *Animal Behaviour.* 73: 965-970.

Murphy, T.G. (2007) "Lack of melanized keratin and barbs that fall off: How the racketed tail of the turquoise-browed motmot *Eumomota superciliosa* is formed". *Journal of Avian Biology.* 38: 139-143.

Murphy, T.G. (2007) "Racketed-tail of the male and female turquoise-browed motmot: male but not female tail length correlates with pairing success, performance, and reproductive success". *Behavioral Ecology and Sociobiology.* 61: 911-918.

Myers, A. (1997) *Communicating With Animals: The Spiritual Connection Between People and Animals.*

Nida, E.A (1975) *Componential Analysis of Meaning: An Introduction to Semantic Structures.* The Hague: Mouton.

Noë, R., P. Hammerstein, J.V. Hooff (Eds.) (2001) *Economic Models of Human and Animal Behaviour.* Cambridge: Cambridge University Press.

Norris, K.S. (1966) *Whales, Dolphins and Porpoises.* Berkeley: University of California Press.

Norris, K.S. (1991) *Dolphin Days: The Life and Times of the Spinner Dolphin.* California: W. W. Norton and Company.

Ogden C.K. and I.A. Richards (1952) *The Meaning of Meaning.* New York: Harcourt Brace Jovanovich.

Ohala, J. (1984) "An ethological perspective on common cross-language utilization of F0 of voice". *Phonetica.* 41(1): 1-16.

Olsson, J. (2004) *Forensic Linguistics: An Introduction to Language, Crime, and the Law.* London: Continuum.

Otte, D. (1974) "Effects and functions in the evolution of signalling systems". *Annual Review of Ecology and Systematics*. 5(2): 385-417.

Oxford Advanced Learner's Dictionary (1989)

Pack, A. and L. Herman (1995) "Sensory integration in the bottlenosed dolphin: immediate recognition of complex shapes across the senses of echolocation and vision". *Journal of the Acoustical Society of America*. 98(4): 722-733.

Pack, A. and L. Herman (2004) "Dolphins (Tursiops truncatus) comprehend the referent of both static and dynamic human gazing and pointing in an object choice task". *Journal of Comparative Psychology*. 118(1): 160-171.

Paget, R. (1930) *A New Approach to the Study of English Words*. London: Kegan Paul, Trench, Trubner & Co.

Pennycook, A. (2001) *Applied Linguistics: A Critical Introduction*. London: Lawrence Erlbaum Associates.

Phillips, C. and K.L. Sakai (2005) "Language and the brain". *Yearbook of Science and Technology*. McGraw-Hill Publishers. Pp. 166–169.

Pinker, S. (1995) *The Language Instinct: The New Science of Language and Mind*. Middlesex, England: Penguin Books Ltd.

Pinker, S. and P. Bloom (1990) "Natural language and natural selection". *Behavioural and Brain Sciences*. 13(4): 707-784.

Premack, D. and A.J. Premack (1983) *The Mind of an Ape*. First Edition. New York: Norton.

Rastier, F. (1997) *Meaning and Textuality* (translated by Frank Collins and Paul Perron). Toronto: University of Toronto Press.

Robbins, S. and N. Langton (2001) *Organizational Behaviour: Concepts, Controversies, Applications*. Second Canadian Edition. Upper Saddle River, NJ: Prentice-Hall.

Robins, R.H. (1964) *General Linguistics: An introductory Survey*. London: Longmans.

Romaine, S. (1994) *Language in Society: An Introduction to Sociolinguistics*. London: Blackwell.

Rumbaugh, D. (Ed.) (1977) *Language Learning by a Chimpanzee: The LANA Project*. New York: Academic Press.

Rutter, D.R. (1987) *Communicating by Telephone*. Oxford: Pergamon Press.

Sapir, E. (1921) *Language: An Introduction to the Study of Speech*. New York: Harcourt Brace & World.

Saussure, F.D. (1966) *Course in General Linguistics* (Edited by Charles Bally, Albert Sechehaye and Albert Riedlinger and translated by Wade Baskin). New York: McGraw-Hill Book Company.

Saussure, F.D. (1986) *Course in General Linguistics*. Third Edition. Tanslated by Roy Harris). Chicago: Open Court Publishing Company.

Schmitt, N. (2002) *An Introduction to Applied Linguistics*. London: Arnold.

Sebeok, T. (1990) *Essays in Zoosemiotics*. Toronto: Toronto Semiotic Circle.

Sereno, J.A. and Y. Wang (2007) "Behavioral and cortical effects of learning a second language: the acquisition of tone". In, Ocke-Schwen, B. and M.J. Munro (Eds.) *Language Experience in Second Language Speech Learning*. Philadelphia: John Benjamins. Pp. 79-76

Seyfarth, R. and D. Cheney (1997) "Behavioral mechanisms underlying vocal communication in nonhuman primates". *Animal Learning and Behavior*. 25(1): 249-267.

Seyfarth, R. and D. Cheney (2000) "Social self-awareness in monkeys". *American Zoologist*. 40(4): 902-909.

Seyfarth, R. and D. Cheney (2003) "Signalers and receivers in animal communication." *Annual Review of Psychology*. 54(1): 145-173.

Shelley, E.L and D.T. Blumstein (2005) "The evolution of vocal alarm communication in rodents." *Behavioural Ecology*. 16(1): 169-177.

Simpson, J.A. (1990) "Influence of attachment styles on romantic relationships". *Journal of Personality and Social Psychology*. 59(4): 971-980.

Sinclair, J. (1991) *Corpus, Concordance, Collocation*. Oxford: Oxford University Press.

Sinclair, J. (1996) "The empty lexicon". *International Journal of Corpus Linguistics*. 1(1): 99-120.

Skinner, B.F. (1953) *Science and Human Behavior*. New York: Mcmillon.

Skinner, B.F. (1968) *The Technology of Teaching*. New York: Appleton-Century Crofts Library of Congress.

Smith, W.J. (1977) *The Behavior of Communicating*. Cambridge, M.A.: Harvard University Press.

Sommer, R. (1967) "Sociofugal space". *The American Journal of Sociology*. 72(6): 654–660.

Sproull, L. and S. Kiesler (1988) "Reducing social context cues: electronic mail in organizational communication". In, *Computer Supported Cooperative Work: a Book of Readings*. San Mateo, CA: Morgan Kaufmann.

Stanforth, A.W. (2002) "Effects of language contact on the vocabulary: an overview". In, Cruse, D.A. *et al.* (Eds.) (2002) *Lexicology: An International Handbook on the Nature and Structure of Words and Vocabularies.* Berlin: Walter de Gruyter. Pp. 805-813.

Starnes, D.W.T. and G.E. Noyes (1946) *The English Dictionary from Cawdrey to Johnson.* Chapel Hill: University of North Carolina Press.

Stibbe, A. (2005) "Counter-discourses and harmonious relationships between humans and other animals". *Anthrozoos.* 18(1): 3-17.

Stibbe, A. (2005) "Environmental education across cultures: beyond the discourse of shallow environmentalism". *Language and Intercultural Communication.* 4(4): 242-260.

Sturtevant, E.H. (1947) *An Introduction to Linguistic Science.* New Haven, Connecticut: Yale University Press.

Summers, P. (1998) *Talking With the Animals.* Newburyport, MA: Hampton Roads Publishing Co.

Sweet, H. (1900) *The History of Language.* London: Thomason.

Sykes, B. (Ed.) (1999) *The Human Inheritance: Genes, Language, and Evolution.* Oxford: Oxford University Press.

Takahashi, T. (1995) *Tamil Love Poetry and Poetics.* Brill's Indological Library. Vol. 9. Leiden: E.J. Brill.

Talmy, L. (2000) *Toward a Cognitive Semantics. Volumes I and II.* Cambridge, Mass.: MIT Press.

The Dictionary of Linguistics (1997)

The Oxford English Dictionary (1989). Second Edition. Oxford: Oxford University Press .

Thomason, S.G. (1991) "Past tongues remembered?" In, Frazier, K. (Ed.) *The Hundredth Monkey and Other Paradigms of the Paranormal.* Buffalo, NY: Prometheus Books. Pp. 85-94.

Thrope, W.H. (1979) *The Origins and Rise of Ethology.* Santa Barbara: Praeger Publishers.

Tinbergen, N. (1951) *The Study of Instinct.* Oxford: Clarendon Press.

Tinbergen, N. (1953) *The Herring Gull's World.* London: Collins.

Trager, G.L. (1949) *The Field of Linguistics. Studies in Linguistics Occasional Papers. No. 1.* Cambridge: Cambridge University Press.

Traunmüller, H. (2005) "Paralinguistic phenomena". In, Ammon, U., N. Dittmar, K. Mattheier, and P. Trudgill (Eds.) *Sociolinguistics: An International Handbook of the Science of Language and Society.* 2nd Edition. Vol. 1. New York: Walter de Gruyter. Pp. 653-665.

Trudgill, P. (1974) *The Social Differentiation of English in Norwich.* Cambridge: Cambridge University Press.

Trudgill, P. (1975) *Sociolinguistics: an Introduction.* London: Penguin

Van Lieshout, P., A. Bose, P. Square, and C.M. Steele (2007) "Speech motor control in fluent and dysfluent speech production of an individual with apraxia of speech and Broca's aphasia". *Clinical Linguistics and Phonetics.* 21(3): 159-188.

Voloshinov, V. (1973) *Marxism and the Philosophy of Language.* Cambridge, MA: Harvard University Press.

Wang, Y., J.A. Sereno, A. Jongman, and J. Hirsch (2003) "fMRI evidence for cortical modification during learning of Mandarin lexical tone". *Journal of Cognitive Neuroscience.* 15(7): 1019–1027.

Wardhaugh, R. (1977) *Introduction to Linguistics.* Second Edition. New York: McGraw-Hill.

Warwick, K., M. Gasson, B. Hutt, I. Goodhew, P. Kyberd, H. Schulzrinne, and X. Wu (2004) "Thought communication and control: a first step using radiotelegraphy", *IEEE Proceedings on Communications.* 151(3): 185-189.

Watson, M., and L. Ecken (2003) *Learning to Trust.* Indianapolis, IN: Jossey-Bass.

Watzlawick, P. (1978) *The Language of Change.* New York: Basic Books.

Whatmough, J. (1957) *Language.* New York: New American Library.

Whorf, B. (1956) *Language, Thought, and Reality: Selected Writings of Benjamin Lee Whorf.* (Edited by John Carroll). Cambridge, Mass.: MIT Press.

Wieselquist, J., C.E. Rusbult, C.A. Foster, & C.R. Agnew (1999) "Commitment, pro-relationship behavior, and trust in close relationships". *Journal of Personality and Social Psychology.* 77(4): 942-966.

Wilson, E.O. (1975) *Sociobiology: The New Synthesis.* Cambridge, Mass.: Harvard University Press.

Wittgenstein, L. (1953/2001) *Philosophical Investigations.* London: Blackwell Publishing.

Witzany, G. (2006) "Plant communication from biosemiotic perspective". *Plant Signaling and Behavior.* 1(4): 169-178.

Witzany, G. (2007) "Applied biosemiotics: fungal communication". In, Witzany, G. (Ed.) *Biosemiotics in Transdisciplinary Contexts.* Helsinki: Umweb. Pp. 295-301.

Witzany, G. (2007) *The Logos of the Bios-2. Bio-Communication.* Helsinki: Umweb.

Witzany, G. (2008) "Bio-communication of bacteria and their evolutionary roots in natural genome editing competences of viruses". *Open Evolution Journal.* 2(1): 44-54.

Witzany, G. (2010) *Biocommunication and Natural Genome Editing.* Dordrecht: Springer.

Witzany, G. and P. Madl (2009) "Biocommunication of corals". *International Journal of Integrative Biology.* 5(1): 152-163.

Xu, J., P.J. Gannon, K. Emmorey, J.F. Smith, and A.R. Braun (2009) "Symbolic gestures and spoken language are processed by a common neural system". In the *Proceedings of the National Academy of Science,* USA. 106: 20664–20669.

Zahavi, A. (1975) "Mate selection—a selection for a handicap". *Journal of Theoretical Biology.* 53(2): 205-214.

Zuberbühler, K., R. Noë, and R.M. Seyfarth (1997) "Diana monkey long-distance calls: messages for conspecifics and predators". *Animal Behaviour.* 53(4): 589-604.

Zvelebil, K. (1973) *The Smile of Murugan on Tamil Literature of South India.* Leiden: Brill.

General Index

Language and Linguistics

261

Language and Linguistics

Language and Linguistics

Language and Linguistics

267

Language and Linguistics

Language and Linguistics

Sprach Theorie 183
Sproull, L. 197
Stage of compilation 138
Stage of planning 138
Stage of production 138
Starnes, D.W.T. 151
Static features 189, 190
Statistics 73
Stibbe, A. 134
Stickleback courtship 48
Stickleback 37, 38
Stoics 72
Stotting 228
Street-corner conversation 158
Structure-dependence 21
Strutevant, E.H. 20
Style 196
Stylistic factors 109
Stylistic meaning 89
Stylistics 149
Subjectivity in language 171
Suzuki, M. 240
Svartvik, J. 101
Swedish 55, 68
Sweet, H. 19
Symbolic forms 189
Symbolism 18, 48, 49
Symbols 17, 38
Synchronic linguistics 8, 111
Synonyms 83
Synonymy 89
Syntactic arrangements 46
Syntactic level 225
Syntactic rules 30
Syntax 88, 104, 119
Synthetic theory 62
System 77, 78
System of symbols 24
Systematic 26
Systematicity 18
Systemic functional linguistics 167

T

Tactical arrangements 46
Tactile communication 10, 187, 192, 205
Tagore, R. 176
Tagore's language 31

Takahashi, T. 184
Talk in interaction 146
Tamil 26, 40, 87, 90
Ta-Ta theory 61
Tattoos 187
Taxis 201, 212
Taxonomical device 89
Telugu 23
Tempo scale 196
Tenor 168
Territorial signals 221
Text 77, 78
Textbook preparation 105
Textual function 168, 169,172, 173, 174
Thematic meaning 89
Thematic roles 89
Theoretical computational linguistics 124
Theoretical linguistics 8, 104, 104, 108
Theoretical linguistics and applied
linguistics104
Theories about origin of language 51
Thermal code 208
Third language 13
Third level: syntax 81
Third school 224
Thomason, S.G. 68
Thomson's gazalle 229
Thrope, W.H. 224
Time 10, 187, 188, 192, 210
Time Magazine 240
Tinbergen, N. 218
Tolkappiyam 175
Topic 165
Topics of discourse 31
Touching 187
Touching code 208
Tower of Babel 55
Traditional grammar 88
Traditional linguistics 97, 98
Traditional views 156
Traffic lights 22
Trager, G. 16, 20, 109
Trampe, W. 134
Translation 2, 97, 106
Traunmuller, H. 193
Triumph displays 220
Tropism 212

270

271